Bigger Than The Beatles

By Bill Harry

"Bigger Than The Beatles" is published by:

Trinity Mirror NW²

Trinity Mirror North West & North Wales
PO Box 48
Old Hall Street
Liverpool L69 3EB

Business Development Director:
Mark Dickinson

Business Development Executive Editor:
Ken Rogers

Written by:
Bill Harry

Design/production:
Vicky Andrews, Zoë Egan, Peter Grant

Cover Design:
Lisa Critchley, Zoë Egan

Images courtesy of:
Daily Post and Echo archive, Bill Harry, Bob Bird

ISBN 9781906802042

Contents

Introduction
The Real Mersey Sound

THE Beatles are the biggest and most popular group of musicians of the 20th and early 21st Century.

Nearly forty years have passed since the group disbanded, yet their popularity seems as strong as ever. Records, feature films, television documentaries, stage shows and DVDs continue to flow and there is a new Beatles book issued every two weeks to add to the more than 3,000 already published.

In addition, the Beatles' music is also being kept alive by hundreds of tribute bands in almost every country in the world, from the Ukraine to the Urals from Peru to Patagonia, from Austria to Australia and every item of their lives has been detailed to an incredible degree on literally thousands of websites. If you wanted to look up Beatles on the internet, it would take you weeks to scroll through the information.

The Beatles were born and nurtured in Liverpool and their birthplace had a huge influence on their success. Yet, surprisingly, their popularity has tended to overshadow the remarkable musical crucible that Merseyside really is, a melting pot of incredible musical talent which has existed, in the popular music sense, since the beginning of the Fifties to the present day.

A 2008 poll placed Liverpool as Britain's premier music city, while the Guinness Book of Records proclaimed it 'The World Capital City of Music', an official, international stamp of achievement for a city which has seen more No. 1 records than any other city in the world.

Yet it is the entire area of Merseyside which was the Beatles stomping ground and when that is taken into consideration, a wealth of further No. 1 hits can be added. After all, Merseyside artists who have hit the No.1 spot in the charts include Southport's Marc Almond and Rick Astley from Newton le Willows, but because they come from the area, not the city, their recording success hasn't been acknowledged as such.

In this book, when I refer to Liverpool I will also be covering the entire Merseyside area where the most exciting musical revolution in popular music sprang up in the late Fifties.

It was no coincidence that in early 1960s John Lennon, Stuart Sutcliffe, Rod Murray and I, under the name the Dissenters, decided to use our particular talents to make Liverpool famous. We loved our city; we felt that it was a remarkable place, full of history, beautiful buildings, talented musicians, writers, comedians – and people with a unique sense of humour.

This was in contrast to the outer image which the British media had projected about the city, focusing on the crime, poverty, closing factories, decaying buildings, the squalor of the slums and the strikes by workers, albeit with their genuine grievances. Of course, such things existed in the city, whose population was shrinking with swathes of the population being relocated to new towns such as Kirkby and Skelmersdale.

But little was written about the humour of the people and their sheer grit in the face of hard times. The days of being a grand port were over, the ocean liners now sailed to Southampton, the dock-work had now moved to Rotterdam, and seeds of discord were growing which eventually exploded in the Toxteth riots of the Nineties.

It was no coincidence that when the Beatles started to achieve their amazing success throughout the country, the Daily Worker produced the headline: "The Mersey Sound is the voice of 80,000 crumbling houses and 30,000 people on the dole."

This was always apparent to me when dealing with the media. One television team I took to Penny Lane on a summer afternoon on a beautiful day when the sunshine was beaming down, didn't like the fact that it looked so nice and uplifting, they searched around until they found an alleyway littered with dustbins and then excitedly set their cameras up.

The same could be said of one of the early Mersey documentaries,

'Beat City.' Even though I was programme assistant to this Redifussion production, I didn't realise that the team had concentrated on filming in the slums, tenement buildings and empty debris, painting a very grim picture, while ignoring the beautiful areas of the city, the parks or the wonderful architecture of the buildings.

The fact that there were two versions of Liverpool which existed in people's minds is a particular point I wish to make. There was the Liverpool portrayed as a city of Scallys where your car would be stolen or set alight if you tried to park it, and the Liverpool which is a hotbed of talent with beautiful surroundings in the city centre and so many exquisite buildings that numerous films and television productions are set in the city.

Fortunately, the latter is now beginning to emerge with the Guinness Book of Records acknowledgement, the fact that Liverpool became the European City of Culture in 2008 and during the same year Liverpool was voted England's premier music city in an Arts Council poll.

All too often, books about the Beatles intimate that the group virtually created the Mersey scene, presuming that it was only in the wake of their success that groups in Liverpool began to emerge. Numerous writers have taken the line that it was only following the Beatles' national breakthrough that every youngster in Liverpool suddenly wanted to join a group.

In fact, the groups were already active in what was probably the most amazing nucleus of youth culture in the world between the years 1958 and 1964. Far from leading to an increase in the number of bands in Liverpool, the success of the Beatles possibly resulted in the local music scene diminishing.

At a time when the British music scene was firmly controlled from London, the Beatles forced a crack in the barrier through which groups from the provinces poured, until the powers that be in the capital closed it again. After 1964 groups from Liverpool, no matter how talented, were personae non gratae.

Talent in the city didn't dry up, as many presumed: it was simply condemned to isolation once more when London regained control of the music business. Yet whenever any enterprising recording manager or entrepreneur did take an interest in Liverpool, they discovered as much talent as they could handle. For example, in 1976 the British charts found themselves with a host of Liverpool bands in the Top 30.

They included Liverpool Express, Our Kid, The Real Thing, Supercharge, Buster – then a few years later there were Orchestral Manoeuvres In the Dark, Teardrop Explodes, Echo and the Bunnymen, China Crisis and Icicle Works.

On 28 January 1984, for instance, a combination of Liverpool artists old and new dominated the Top 20:

1. Frankie Goes To Hollywood – 'Relax'
2. Paul McCartney – 'Pipes of Peace
3. Joe Fagin – 'That's Livin Alright'
6. John Lennon – 'Nobody told me'
9. China Crisis – 'Wishful Thinking'
17. Echo & the Bunnymen – 'The Killing Moon'
19. Icicle Works – 'Love is a Wonderful Colour'

And it took Liverpool band Frankie Goes to Hollywood to repeat fellow Liverpudlians Gerry & the Pacemakers' record of a hat trick of No. 1 hits with their first three releases.

The Mersey scene was unique for its time, yet an acknowledgement of its real contribution to the forging of the Beatles has not really been apparent in the many books that have been written about them.

In fact, the Hamburg scene has been given more prominence in the birth of the Beatles' story. But there was no Hamburg scene when the Beatles arrived there in 1960. It wasn't a city like Liverpool, where thousands of youngsters were pouring into venues to listen to hundreds of bands. Rock 'n' roll hardly existed in Germany at the time and the only two British bands to precede the Beatles were the Jets and Derry & the Seniors.

It's true, as I've always pointed out, that the Beatles' initial months in Hamburg, from August to December 1960, were a real baptism of fire. It made them a better group than they'd been previously, but it was their battles with the other bands in Liverpool over the following two years that gave them their edge.

Basically, the Hamburg scene comprised of only three clubs, all within walking distance of each other: the Kaiserkeller, the Top Ten and the Star Club. As a rock venue the Kaiserkeller didn't last more than a year, leaving just two venues.

In contrast, Liverpool had far in excess of 300 venues where groups would play, including those like the Tower and Locarno Ballrooms that were large enough to accommodate thousands of youngsters.

However, these were not where the Mersey sound was originally forged.

In the late 1950s groups began to thrive in Liverpool in 'jive hives', the ballrooms and town halls booked by enterprising local promoters, who are among the unsung heroes of the Mersey scene. They promoted regularly at dozens of venues across the area.

The three music venues in Hamburg were situated in the notorious red-light district of St Pauli, where audiences were generally composed of punters seeking 'adult entertainment' in clubs, which actively encouraged their patrons to drink. In Liverpool it was the youth of Merseyside who crowded the venues, where, with a couple of exceptions, only soft drinks were available. They went because they loved the music. The kids attended the venues throughout the area in their thousands in what was arguably the first major youth movement in the British Isles.

Between 1958 and 1964 there were probably around 500 different bands in the Merseyside area. The figure at any one time probably stood at 350. When Bob Wooler and I originally compiled a list of groups that we knew personally in 1961, it ran to almost 300 names.

The most popular line-up was a quartet with three guitarists – lead, rhythm and bass – plus a drummer. The three guitarists up front would engage in vocal harmony. The Beatles were particularly adept at this as Paul McCartney, being left-handed, could use the same microphone as John Lennon, when they sang together – also producing a visual effect that many of the other groups couldn't imitate.

This basic line-up was the one generally referred to when people later talked of the 'Liverpool Sound' or the 'Mersey Sound', and it was most apparent with groups such as the Beatles, the Searchers, Faron's Flamingos and the Swinging Blue Jeans. However, this image tends to make people forget just how extensive the range of the music scene in Liverpool was: there were duos, trios, quintets, and groups with pianos and saxophones in their line-ups.

Comedy outfits such as the Fourmost were parodying other artists long before Duke D'Mond & the Barron Knights became famous for numbers such as 'Call Up The Groups.'

There were folk groups, country music bands, vocal groups, girl rock bands, Christian Music groups – even speciality bands such as the Mersey Monsters. I remember hearing that there was a Chinese rock 'n' roll group in Chinatown, but I was never able to track them down to interview them for Mersey Beat.

Liverpool had been called the 'Nashville of the North', because it had the largest Country music scene in Europe. There were approximately 40 C&W bands contemporary with the Beatles. They had their own clubs such as the Black Cat Club and Wells Fargo, their own Country Music Federation and they ran their 'Grand Ole Opry' annually at the Philharmonic Hall. Their attempt to revolutionise country music, just as the rock groups in Liverpool revolutionised rock 'n' roll, has never been properly acknowledged.

There were basically two forms of country bands in Liverpool – the purists, who played in the traditional manner, parroting the American records, and wearing Stetsons and cowboy clothes, such as Hank Walters & the Dusty Road Ramblers – and the new wave such as the Hillsiders, young bands with a fresh approach to the music, who did not dress in country style, but provided a new and exciting beat to country sounds.

Unfortunately, this movement tended to be overshadowed by the Beatles and the Mersey Sound, and the new revolution in country music didn't occur until the late 1980s, with young Nashville artists who gave the music a fresh image – but it was happening on the banks of the Mersey in the late 1950s!

There were also several all-girl rock 'n' roll groups in Liverpool, the most noted being the Liverbirds. The girls became so popular in Hamburg that they remained in Germany for several years, missing out on the Mersey boom. But the fact remains that there were girl rock bands in Liverpool a decade before American groups such as Fanny.

In the field of folk music, Liverpool gave rise to the Spinners, who remained Britain's premier folk outfit for 30 years, until their retirement.

There was also a black music scene on Merseyside.

Apart from artists such as Derry Wilkie and Steve Aldo, there were several vocal outfits in the Liverpool 8 district such as the Chants, the Valentinos, the Sobells, the Challengers and the Poppies.

Only the Chants were to have a limited degree of success. It seemed that when Britain eventually accepted black artists into the charts – with the Motown acts and soul music, the black hit artists were almost exclusively American. Few black British artists made it until the 1970s. Ironically enough, the group to make the breakthrough and hit the top of the charts was the Real Thing, formed by Eddie Amoo of the Chants – it had taken him more than a decade to achieve the success.

Coexisting with the rock, folk, country, Christian and black music scenes was the poetry scene. Local poets used to hold readings at clubs such as Streates. I also organised and promoted a poetry-to-jazz concert at the Crane Theatre – the first concert of its kind to be held in the north of England. Three of the Liverpool poets, Roger McGough, Adrian Henri and Brian Patten, established themselves as the leading British poets of the decade.

My newspaper Mersey Beat also reported on 'Clubland', the thriving entertainment scene for an older generation. Over 300 clubs were affiliated to the Merseyside Clubs Association. There were social clubs for unions, stores and factories that provided entertainment for their members – in addition to drinks at prices far below the normal prices in public houses.

It was on the Clubland scene that many local comics, such as Ken Dodd and Jimmy Tarbuck, developed. Liverpool has always had a reputation for providing more than its fair share of comedians, including Ted Ray, Arthur Askey, Tommy Handley and Norman Vaughan.

Liverpool had already provided chart acts from this background in the 1950s, with artists such as Frankie Vaughan, Lita Roza and Michael Holliday.

Although Clubland was the training ground for comedians, speciality acts and country bands, there was also work for numerous rock groups in the various clubs. Early gigs for groups with Gerry Marsden and Ringo Starr took place at Peel Street Labour Club, and a Quarry Men gig was on behalf of the Speke Bus Depot Social Club.

Imagine groups taking the stage at cinemas in intervals between the films; performing in coffee bars; strutting their acts at swimming baths; performing at ice rinks; learning their craft in almost every youth club, church hall, synagogue and village hall in the Merseyside area; blasting their music from the stages of town halls; lugging their gear into the bandrooms of the numerous ballrooms; performing before audiences of varying ages at social clubs; playing in the city centre cellar clubs and pulling in audiences by the thousand in the larger venues – no place in the world at that time had so many young groups performing virtually nightly in such a compact area.

In 1961 I dubbed Liverpool 'The Rocking City.'

Liverpool's maritime heritage had resulted in the city becoming a melting pot of cosmopolitan influences. As the main port during the days of the slave trade, its black population became established centuries ago. Ironically, the large mansions built by the slave traders became the abodes in the twentieth century of the black population, who mainly dwelt in the Liverpool 8, or Toxteth, district.

The city was also a main destination for the Irish fleeing the potato famine in the mid-Nineteenth Century and Liverpool boasts a huge Irish population – it's often jokingly referred to as the capital of Ireland. There is also a substantial Welsh intake and Liverpool had the first Chinatown in Europe.

Different cultural influences also led to the development of a wide range of musical tastes, and, from sea shanties to Irish folk songs, Liverpool danced to the music of the world for more than two centuries. Most specifically, pub sing-alongs were a standard form of Liverpool entertainment and the musical heritage was strong.

This is where the truth and myth part, for the maritime heritage had no direct influence on the development of the Mersey sound.

Writers in the 1970s began to suggest that the reason Liverpool groups were different from groups in other parts of the country was that 'Cunard Yanks' brought them records that couldn't be obtained elsewhere in Britain.

Cunard Yanks were the Liverpudlians who went to sea in the ocean liners and brought presents back to their families. The story is that they brought American records for their younger brothers and sons, and this is how the Liverpool bands built up their repertoire.

Sounds nice, but it's something of an exaggeration.

In the 1950s Liverpool was still a seaport and a number of Liverpool men still sailed the seas, but it was a feeble number compared to the pre-War days and the turn of the century.

One or two members of groups, such as John McNally of the Searchers, had brothers who went to sea and brought them records.

However, the most important records in the Searchers collection came from drummer Chris Curtis, who gathered them in his trips around the record stores. Some of the country bands, such as Hank Walters & His Dusty Road Ramblers were able to obtain rare country albums from merchant seamen, but the 'Cunard Yank' theory remains something of a myth. A study of the Beatles repertoire from the time, laying aside the original Lennon and McCartney numbers, proves that every song they played was available on record in Britain through the normal channels.

The first major musical influence in Liverpool was a British artist, Lonnie Donegan, who sparked off the skiffle boom.

When the boom began to wane, Liverpool groups turned to rock 'n' roll. Buddy Holly and the Crickets, Eddie Cochran, Elvis Presley, Chuck Berry, Little Richard, Ray Charles, the Everly Brothers, Gene Vincent, Carl Perkins, the Coasters, Arthur Alexander, Jerry Lee Lewis, the Olympics, Larry Williams, the Isley Brothers, Bobby Freeman, the Shirelles, Chan Romero, Lloyd Price, Bo Diddley, the Drifters and Fats Domino were their inspiration.

While rock 'n' roll bands were thriving in Liverpool, the music was encountering problems in America. Buddy Holly, the Big Bopper and Ritchie Valens were killed in an air crash 'the day the music died'; Little Richard got religion; Eddie Cochran died in a car crash, while Carl Perkins' career suffered following his road accident; Chuck Berry was in jail; Elvis had joined the army; Jerry Lee Lewis was in 'disgrace' for marrying an under-age cousin.

This was the opportunity American media moguls had been waiting for – the chance to kill this devil's music!

They titillated teenagers by saturating the airwaves with records by clean-cut handsome white youngsters who sanitized the sound – Pat Boone, Bobby Rydell, Fabian, Ricky Nelson (although he turned out to be more influential than first imagined), Dion, Tommy Roe, Tommy Sands, Frankie Avalon and Bobby Vinton.

Rock 'n' roll might literally have been safely caged in the States, but Liverpool bands began to adapt the music to their own style. What was also different about the Mersey groups was their age – they were actually teenagers, whereas the American rock 'n' roll giants were almost a decade older.

My own involvement with the scene began in 1958, while I was attending Liverpool College of Art. I was asked to contribute to a magazine produced by the local music store Frank Hessy. Mr Hesselberg, the owner, insisted on the rather uncommercial title 'Frank Comments,' but gave complete editorial freedom in all other respects. I designed the covers and produced interior illustrations, reviewed local events, wrote about jazz legends such as Bunk Johnson and even penned a science-fiction jazz serial.

In the meantime, Stuart Sutcliffe and John Lennon were amongst my closest friends and we used to spend a great deal of time together, mainly discussing the subjects young people discuss – what the future held, the latest books and films, art, academic life and so on.

John had a group and two of its members, Paul McCartney and George Harrison, were pupils of Liverpool Institute, which was situated next door to the college. They used to come to our canteen during lunch breaks and also rehearsed in the life rooms. Stu and I were members of the Students' Union Committee and put forward the proposal that we use students' funds to buy a PA system, which John's group could use when they appeared at our college dances.

I referred to them as the 'college band' at the time and they were booked regularly for our dances as support to headliners such as the Merseysippi Jazz Band.

Skiffle music had been popular for the last couple of years and I used to study the history of American folk music and railway songs at Picton Library, in addition to producing a duplicated magazine at the college, simply called Jazz.

With the experience of editing a number of fan magazines behind me, my involvement with Frank Comments, my association with their printers, James E. James and studies in typography, printing and newspaper design and layout at the college I had visions of producing a magazine called Storyville & 52nd Street.

One evening we all went along to Liverpool University to hear a poetry reading by Royston Ellis. Later, at the local art college drinking hole Ye Cracke, in a discussion with John, Stu and Rod Murray, I pointed out that Ellis, in common with a lot of other poets, was inspired by the American beat poets such as Lawrence Ferlinghetti, Allen Ginsberg and Gregory Corso.

My feeling was that people were more likely to stretch themselves creatively by expressing their own environment and experience rather than by copying someone else's. I suggested that we should use our creative talents to express what we were personally involved in, that we should take a vow to make Liverpool famous: John with his music, Stu and Rod with their painting and myself by writing about the city.

I even suggested that we call ourselves the Dissenters.

At one time Stu and I were going to produce a book about Liverpool. I would write about interesting and unusual facets of the city and its people and he would illustrate it. We never did the book, but the seeds of Mersey Beat were sown.

In addition to Ye Cracke, the college canteen and various students' flats, we would also hang around the Jacaranda coffee bar, run by a gregarious Liverpool-Welshman, Allan Williams.

It was here in May 1960 that I met Virginia. She was 16 years old, was wearing black barathea trousers and a green sweater and had flowing auburn hair.

The lads were playing downstairs in the 'coal hole', while their girl-friends held broom handles to which their mics were attached. In those days we were all skint, yet managed to get by, even when we didn't have the proverbial 'two halfpennies to rattle together.'

Virginia became my girlfriend and the visions of creating a magazine grew. I'd initially begun thinking in terms of a jazz magazine because there was a huge Trad Jazz boom and Liverpool was a thriving centre. There were clubs such as the Cavern, the Liverpool Jazz Society and the Temple Jazz Club and promoters such as Albert Kinder regularly booked artists of the calibre of Chris Barber and Lonnie Donegan at the Empire and Pavilion Theatre.

One local promoter said he'd advance me £25 to launch the jazz magazine, but he never did.

By this time my thoughts were developing in a new direction. My experience writing for Frank Comments had taken me to places around Liverpool such as Wilson Hall, where local rock 'n' roll groups used to play. I began talking to members of groups who dropped by the Jacaranda and sensed that something unique was happening in Liverpool. The rock 'n' roll scene was larger than anyone – even the groups themselves – realised.

The little red notebooks I carried around with me began to fill up with information on venues, promoters and groups.

I decided to write to national newspapers, such as the Daily Mail, to inform them that what was happening in Liverpool was as unique as what had happened in New Orleans at the turn of the century, but with rock 'n' roll groups instead of jazz.

No one took any notice. Liverpool, it seemed, was isolated. It didn't have any media that could reach out nationally.

Historically, Liverpool had lost a great deal of power and prestige when the Manchester Ship Canal was built, allowing a lot of trade to bypass Liverpool and go straight to Manchester. Manchester became the capital of the North and was home to both Granada Television and the BBC TV Studios, in addition to radio stations and the northern editions of the national newspapers. Most North-West news on TV, radio and in the press had a Manchester bias. In comparison, Liverpool seemed to be almost a backwater. As a result, what was happening there developed without anyone realising it and without any undue outside interference.

Having received no reaction to my appeals to the press to cover what was happening, I decided to do something about it myself. Instead of a jazz magazine, I'd write about the local rock 'n' roll scene.

Although I'd received my National Diploma in design, I was still at the art college, having become the first student of the new Graphic Design course and later winner of the Senior City Art Scholarship. John Lennon had hoped to enter the Graphic Art department with me, but the lecturer, Roy Sharpe, wouldn't accept him.

Money was still a problem, but Dick Matthews, a friend from the Jacaranda, introduced me to a civil servant Jim Anderson, who offered to lend Virginia and me the £50 we needed to launch the project.

By this time I'd decided on a fortnightly newspaper, completely devoted to the music of Merseyside, which would also be a 'what's on' of every musical event during the fortnight.

Virginia's support is what really kept me going and ensured that the visions in my head became a reality. She gave up her job to work full-time on the project and Jim found us an office above a wine merchant's shop in Renshaw Street.

Jim, Dick, Virginia and I entered the tiny attic office room carrying a typewriter, a desk and a couple of chairs, which Jim had provided us with. Dick also took out his camera and promised to cover the local music scene for the new paper.

Sitting in the Jacaranda with John and Stu, I'd tell them of our progress. By that time they'd left the college and were about to go to Germany. I asked John if he could write a biography of the Beatles for the new paper, which I could run in the first issue. When the Beatles returned from Germany, John gave me the biography, written in his own inimitable style, which I entitled 'On The Dubious Origins Of Beatles, Translated From the John Lennon.'

By this time of course, I was friendly with all members of the group. As well as knowing Paul and George from college days and attending their early gigs, I also got to know Pete Best, who joined them at the Jacaranda. They were the group I was closest to and were the ones I was obviously going to promote the most.

Sitting alone in the office at about two in the morning, I was attempting to think of a name for the new paper. Having decided that I'd cover the entire Merseyside region – Liverpool, the Wirral, Southport, Crosby, St. Helens, Widnes, Warrington, Runcorn and so on – I suddenly visualised it as a policeman's beat. The image of a copper walking around a map of the surrounding area came into my head, along with the name 'Mersey Beat.'

The reaction to Mersey Beat was literally phenomenal locally and all 5,000 copies of the first issue sold out. The three main wholesalers, WH Smith, Blackburn's and Conlan's, took copies; I delivered copies personally to another two dozen newsagents, in addition to the main local venues and musical instruments and record stores.

At North End Music Stores (NEMS), when I asked to see the manager, Brian Epstein came down from his office. I showed him the publication and he agreed to take a dozen copies. He phoned me soon after to tell me how surprised he was that they sold out almost immediately. He ordered more – and more – and more.

For the second issue he placed an advance order for twelve dozen copies, an incredible amount of copies for a single publication in one outlet.

That issue, published on 20 July 1961, devoted the entire front cover to the Beatles recent recordings in Hamburg under the headline 'Beatles Sign Recording Contract!' There was also a photograph of the Beatles by Astrid Kirchherr, which Paul McCartney had brought back from Germany for me, together with Astrid's permission for me to use any of the Beatles pictures she'd taken as publicity for the group.

Brian Epstein invited me to his office for a sherry and wanted to discuss the groups he'd read about in Mersey Beat. He was incredulous that such a thriving music scene existed all around him, which he'd been unaware of. He was also amazed at the number of young people who came into his store just to buy copies of the paper.

Brian asked me to describe the local scene and was particularly interested in the Beatles cover story and the fact that a local group had made a record. He immediately booked advertising space and asked if he could review records. I appointed him record reviewer, beginning with issue No. 3 and his column was headed 'Stop the World – and listen to everything in it. Brian Epstein of Nems.'

His advertisements and reviews shared the same pages as the articles and photographs about the Beatles and he was particularly impressed by Bob Wooler's article about the group in the 31 August issue. Over the months he liked to discuss the stories in Mersey Beat with me and then asked if I could arrange for him to visit the Cavern to see the Beatles. I did this and he visited the club, less than 100 yards from his store, during a lunchtime session on Thursday 9 November.

When he published his autobiography, A Cellarful Of Noise, in 1964, he claimed that he first heard of the Beatles when a young man called Raymond Jones came into his store on 28 October 1961 and ordered a copy of the Beatles single (the one which was the subject of the front cover in July). The story is so neat that writers who haven't really examined the facts chronologically love to cite it. It's the old story of having to choose between the truth and the legend and opting to go for the legend.

I'm well aware that Mersey Beat readers went to NEMS to ask for copies of the Beatles single, but this was only after Mersey Beat printed the cover story in July.

The fact that Raymond Jones and others went into NEMS to ask for the record or not is beside the point. I had been discussing the group with Epstein for months and he had read all about them in Mersey Beat as they were the group I plugged most in the paper.

At least Paul McCartney recognises the truth and in his official biography Many Years From Now, he wrote: "Brian knew perfectly well who the Beatles were – they were on the front page of the second issue of Mersey Beat, the local music paper. Brian sold twelve dozen copies of this issue, so many that he invited the editor, Bill Harry, into his office for a drink to discuss why it was selling so well and to ask if he could write a record review column for it. He is unlikely to have missed the 'Beatles sign recording contract' banner headline, reporting their session with Tony Sheridan for Bert Kaempfert."

On the group's return from Germany, Paul gave me a copy of the single in question. The only other spare copy he gave to Bob Wooler, who began playing it at the local venues. I still have the record, personally signed by them all (probably the first record the Beatles signed personally), but there is no indication that they are on it.

There is a photograph of Tony Sheridan on the cover and the only words are: 'Tony Sheridan. My Bonnie. The Saints (When The Saints Go Marching In)'

There is no mention whatsoever about The Beatles and it would have been impossible for Epstein to trace the record, as he said he did, on this information alone. Even if he had the catalogue number, he would have been told this related to a single by Sheridan only.

The Mersey Beat newspaper became a catalyst for the scene and groups, managers and anyone connected with the music took to visiting the office. Initially the Beatles were the most frequent visitors, helping Virginia out on the typewriter or phone; even Ringo used to drop in when he was visiting the nearby dole office in Renshaw Street.

Soon, groups began calling themselves Beat groups instead of rock 'n' roll bands and venues which had been advertising 'Twist sessions' and 'jive sessions' began calling them 'Beat sessions', while the 'jive hives' were now being called Beat clubs.

Once the Beatles had achieved their initial success on record and the papers were looking for a tag to identify the movement they first began to call it the 'Mersey Sound' and 'The Liverpool Sound'. Some years later they adopted the name of the paper and 'Mersey Beat' became part of the English language.

As the world's first alternative music paper, the first 'What's On', Mersey Beat introduced many innovations which were later adopted by the national music press. It also created a wonderful range of early photographs of the Beatles for posterity. No other group achieving their initial success would have had such a large photographic record of their early career.

Initially Dick Matthews took all those wonderful shots of the Beatles at the Cavern for me. I made arrangements with various professional photographers and paid them with advertisements, publicity and recommendations in exchange for exclusive photographs for Mersey Beat. I did those deals with the professional studios of Peter Kaye, Harry Watmough and Graham Spencer.

As the policy of Mersey Beat was to introduce innovation, the photographers were encouraged to do what the London showbiz photographers didn't do – leave the studio and take shots on location or during performances on stage.

The Beatles had originally been portrayed brilliantly in Germany by Astrid and Jurgen Vollmer, and Mersey Beat created a whole range of unique photographs of them performing in Liverpool.

There was an undoubted editorial bias in their favour and this caused Bob Wooler to come to the office one day to complain on behalf of the other groups. He said that Mersey Beat was plugging the Beatles to such an extent that we should rename the paper 'Mersey Beatle', and in fact I later introduced a special section called just that.

When we decided to run a poll to establish the No. 1 group in Liverpool, we received a huge response. Virginia and I spent many hours sorting out the votes. When we'd finished, Rory Storm & the Hurricanes had more votes than anyone else. However, we noticed that a large bundle of their votes had been written in the same handwriting in green ink and posted from the same area at the same time, so we disqualified the green ink batch, which made the Beatles No. 1 and Rory Storm & the Hurricanes No. 4.

Our famous cover of issue No. 13 with the headline 'Beatles Top Poll' established them once and for all as the top group in the north of England – a fact that Brian Epstein was quick to capitalize on.

The paper's circulation kept increasing issue by issue and began to stretch throughout the country, covering groups in Manchester, Birmingham, Sheffield and Newcastle. We were also to champion the Rolling Stones.

What gave Mersey Beat the edge was 'the bulge', which Americans refer to as the 'baby boom'. There were more babies born in the few years towards the end and immediately following the Second World War than at any time in history. Those babies became teenagers in the 1950s.

In previous decades, there was no real awareness of 'teenagers' (a term which only emerged in the 1950s). In Liverpool, for instance, youngsters were mini-replicas of their parents. Fathers would look on with pleasure when their sons reached a certain age and started to accompany them to the local pubs for their first pint. Sons would also follow fathers into the business or union they belonged to, and youngsters would dress exactly like their parents.

Suddenly, there was an awareness of being young, and young people wanted their own styles and their own music, just at the time they were beginning to earn money, which gave them spending power.

On Merseyside, Mersey Beat was their voice. It was a paper for them, crammed with photos and information about their own groups, which is why it also began to appeal to youngsters throughout Britain as its coverage extended to other areas.

The newspapers, television, theatres and radio were all run by people of a different generation who had no idea what youngsters wanted. For decades they had manipulated and controlled them (see the scene with George Harrison and Kenneth Haig in 'A Hard Day's Night'), but now the youngsters wanted to create their own fashions.

What existed on the banks of the Mersey between 1958 and 1964 was exciting, energetic and unique, a magical time when an entire city danced to the music of youth.

1. Before the Boom

LIVERPOOL had achieved a degree of credibility as a breeding ground of talent in the fifties, prior to the emergence of the Mersey Sound and the Beatles.

In those days artists had to go to London to establish themselves, but it is worth noting the Mersey artists who recorded prior to Howie Casey & the Seniors – becoming the first Mersey band to do so.

The late Lita Roza was the first solo artist to top the British charts, as mentioned in the chapter 'Liverbirds'.

Another Mersey chart-topper was Frankie Vaughan, who was born Frank Abelson in his grandmother's house at 37 Devon Street, Liverpool on 3 February 1928, his father an upholsterer, his mother a seamstress. Frankie took his surname after his Russian grandmother kept calling him "my number vorn grandson" with her efforts to say "one" sounding like "Vaughan."

His grandmother had come to England from Russia at the age of 21 with her two children while her husband went on to live in America.

Frankie was to describe the area he was reared in as "a real Cohen and Kelly district, a place where the Jews and the Irish have rubbed shoulders for years."

Frankie attended Harrison-Jones School and also joined the choir at Princes Road Synagogue, although he was more interested in sport.

The family were evacuated when their home was bombed, with Frankie initially being sent to Endmoor, near Kendall, Westmoreland, but reunited with the rest of his family in Lancaster where he was sent to the Lancaster Boys' National School where he was taught boxing.

It was here that Frankie developed his life-long interest in the boys' club movement and he was later to give the entire royalties from three of his hits – 'Seventeen', 'The Green Door' and 'Something In The Bank, Frank', to the movement.

At the age of 14 he won a scholarship to the Lancaster School of Art where he studied for three years to gain a Master of Arts degree – and he also captained the soccer eleven.

After gaining his degree he was to join the Royal Army Medical Corps during his stint at National Service. On being demobbed he became a student teacher at Leeds College of Art. During a Rag Day show he performed a medley of Al Jolson numbers and was spotted by BBC producer Barney Coleham who advised him to become an entertainer. He also gave him a letter of introduction to Billy Marsh of the Bernard Delfont Agency in London.

Initially, Frankie didn't bother with it, being much more interested in art and design. Myra, one of his three sisters, introduced him to her friend Stella at the Locarno Ballroom, Leeds and the two became engaged 15 months later.

At one point Frankie sang with a big band in Leeds and was offered a long-term contract, but rejected it in favour of design. When he received some money for a furniture design he decided to go to London to see if he could sell further designs in the capital.

He was unsuccessful, but while there he found the letter of introduction and went to the Delfont Agency to see Billy Marsh and successfully auditioned. He was then offered a ten minute spot at the Kingston Empire. His performance ignited the audience, he was moved to the top of the bill and the theatre manager phoned Marsh to come along and see Frankie's act. As a result, he was booked as the bill topper in Manchester at a staggering £100 a week.

When he began touring he was told by variety artist Hetty King to change his style of dressing, which she considered sloppy – she advised him to adopt top hat and tails, which he did.

By this time Marsh had suggested that Frankie change his surname to one which had a better ring to it and Frankie remembered his Granny's favourite expression "You are my number vorn" – and Frankie Vaughan was born.

Eager to earn enough money to get married, Frankie studied the careers of British and American artists and saw that the big stars made their names in records, television or radio. He decided to stop touring the small provincial theatres and tried to break into the recording and television market, initially without success.

Despite that, he and Stella were married on 6 June 1951 and took a tiny two-roomed flat in Soho.

Finally, he managed to be given an opportunity with HMV by recording with the Ken Mackintosh Orchestra on the numbers 'Strange' and 'My Sweetie Went Away.' He received a penny per record and the disc sold 8,000 copies after being plugged on Jack Jackson's 'Record Round-Up.' His next release 'No Help Wanted' was played on 'Housewives Choice' and soon several disc jockeys, including Jean Metcalfe and Sam Costa, were playing his records. As a result he was given a top-of-the-bill tour on the Moss Empires circuit, Britain's major theatre group – at a huge salary.

The married couple were able to move to St John's Wood. Frankie had been advised to keep his marriage secret with the words, "The fans won't like it if they knew you were married. They prefer their stars to be single." But when his son David was born in October 1953, he announced it to the world.

1955 saw Frankie starring in Wildfire, a major ice show at Earls Court, having to learn to skate and sing at the same time, singing songs such as 'Give Me The Moonlight, Give Me the Girl.'

This song, which he discovered in a Glasgow music store and sang on stage for the first time in a top hat borrowed from an undertaker, became Frankie's signature tune and led to him being given the nickname 'Mr Moonlight.'

He then made his film debut in Ramsbottom Sings Again, which starred Liverpool comedian Arthur Askey. Television shows and more recordings followed and Frankie was also able to utilise a lot of his spare time working on behalf of the Boys' Club's movement.

25th May, 1956 saw the birth of his daughter Susan, during his appearances in Blackpool and after the show he rushed down to Queen Charlotte's Hospital in London to see his newly born daughter.

He then received a call from film actress Anna Neagle and director Herbert Wilcox inviting him to join a discussion on a new film they were making. Frankie told them about his early life in Liverpool and the problems youngsters had, especially those who were waiting to do their National Service. As a result Neagle and Wilcox asked him if he'd be interested in starring in a film based on his experiences.

Jack Trevor Story penned the script and the film was called These Dangerous Years. The character of Dave Wyman suited Frankie down to the ground and he performed several numbers in the movie, including 'These Dangerous Years', 'Cold, Cold Shower' and 'Isn't This A Lovely Evening.'

In the meantime, he had two major chart hits, 'The Green Door' and 'The Garden of Eden' and prior to the film's world premier at the Forum in Liverpool in June 1957, appeared on a tour of leading theatres and starred in the BBC TV series The Frankie Vaughan Show, the first time that a pop star had ever been given his own series by the BBC.

To promote the film, called 'Dangerous Youth' in America, he travelled to the States and appeared on The Ed Sullivan Show and The Perry Como Show and was also offered starring roles in a Hollywood musical and a Broadway show, but rejected them.

He returned to Britain for his Frankie Vaughan Show which was to open for four weeks at the Palace Theatre, London, where it broke box office records.

His next film for Anna Neagle and Herbert Wilcox was Wonderful Things, in which he played a Gibraltar fisherman who arrives in London to seek his fortune. Frankie then returned to America to appear on The Big Record Show, The Dick Clark Show and The Ed Sullivan Programme and was immediately asked to do return engagements, although he interrupted his American trip to return to London to be presented with an award as 'Show business Personality of the Year' by the Variety Club of Great Britain.

His next film for Neagle and Wilcox was The Lady Is A Square in 1959. In 1960 he left for America to star in Let's Make Love with Marilyn Monroe, during which he sang the numbers 'Hey You With The Crazy Eyes' and 'Incurably Romantic.' There were rumours that he rejected her advances, but the story is probably apocryphal.

He didn't really want a Hollywood career and preferred to remain close to his family in Britain.

Frankie's other films included Escape In The Sun (1956), The Heart Of A Man (1959) and The Right Approach (1960).

During the 1960s, following an appearance in Glasgow, he was appalled at the level of violence in the city and met with members of gangs to ask them to put aside their weapons. He became personally involved in raising funds, making appearances and trying to help youngsters in Easterhouse, on the outskirts of Glasgow and will be remembered for his work on The Easterhouse Project.

Frankie also found success in London's West End in 1985 when he starred in the stage musical 42nd Street. He suffered pains in his abdomen but turned down medical help as he wanted to continue working. However, he developed peritonitis and had to leave the cast of the show. He also suffered from a ruptured artery in October 1992 and later underwent six operations because of heart conditions.

In 1965 Frankie was awarded an OBE for his services to the Boys' Club's movement and he was also to receive a CBE in 1996.

During his career he issued over fifty singles. Among his chart entries were: 'Istanbul' (No. 11); 'Happy Days And Lonely Nights' (No. 12); 'My Boy Flat Top' (No. 20); 'The Green Door' (No. 2); 'Garden of Eden' (No. 1); 'Man On Fire' (No. 6); 'Gotta Have Something In The Bank, Frank' (No. 8); 'Kisses Sweeter Than Wine' (No. 8); 'We're Not Alone' (No.11); 'Kewpie Doll' (No. 10); 'Wonderful Things' (No. 22); 'Am I Wasting My Time On You' (No. 25); 'That's My Doll' (No. 28); 'Come Softly To Me' (No. 9); 'The Heart Of A Man' (No. 5); 'Walkin' Tall' (No. 28); 'What More Do You Want' (No. 25); 'Kookie Little Paradise' (No. 31); 'Milord' (No. 34); 'Tower Of Strength' (No. 1); 'Don't Stop Twist' (No. 22); 'Hercules' (No. 42); 'Loop De Loop' (No. 5); 'Hey Mama' (No. 21); 'Hello Dolly' (No. 18); 'Someone Must Have Hurt You A Lot' (No. 46); 'There Must Be A Way' (No. 7); 'So Tired' (No. 21); 'Nevertheless' (No. 29).

Frankie died of heart failure on Friday, 17 September 1999 at his home near High Wycombe. He was 71 years old.

He had once said: "I am lucky to have a talent, lucky to have met such a wonderful girl as my wife Stella, lucky to have such a wonderful family, and lucky to have a job I adore."

The third Liverpool artist to top the British charts on more than one occasion in the Fifties was Michael Holliday.

Michael was born Norman Milne in a terraced house in Easby

Road (off Stanley Road) in Kirkdale, Liverpool on 26 November 1928.

It was while he was working as a van driver in Liverpool that he fell in love with a girl called Margie, who was to become his wife.

He said: "She was the first girlfriend I had. We met like thousands of couples – in a dance hall. She worked in a bank."

From a seafaring family, Mike then joined the Merchant Navy during World War II.

He said, "Margie was a little annoyed but I had to save up some money to get married and thought this was the best way. For £17 a month I had to scrub the decks, wash the dishes and peel the spuds."

During a stopover in New York he won a talent contest at Radio City Music Hall. The win gave him confidence to begin singing when he returned to Liverpool. He was to change his name to Michael Milne by deed poll.

He became singer/guitarist with an orchestra, performing at holiday camps. It was said that when he originally auditioned for a job, he was too nervous to face the bandleader and he locked himself in a bathroom and auditioned there while the leader waited outside and listened – but Mike was able to secure the job for £5 a week.

He was to say: "Those first few nights singing in public were the most nerve-wracking in my life. For the first four nights I sang sitting down in a chair. I suppose that is how I got the tag 'the man with the sitting down voice.' Anyway, on the fifth night I decided to stand up and sing in front of the band. I rose from my chair, walked slowly to the microphone, and then…I froze. So I walked back to my chair again feeling terrible."

It was while at an Albert Hall reunion that he was introduced to bandleader Eric Winstone and joined his band.

He was later spotted by Columbia A&R man Norrie Paramor, who signed him to the label in 1955. Mike then took his mother's maiden name to become Michael Holliday.

He hosted his own television show, Relax With Mike, in which the studio set was a mock up of a flat with a rocking chair and sofa and he wore a sweater and open-necked shirt while he sang in a relaxed style – pre-dating other TV shows such as The Val Doonican Show.

At the time a critic commented: "He's the most relaxed singer I've ever heard," while another said, "This fellow has got what I call a 'sitting down' voice." Yet, although he gave the appearance of being relaxed, Mike suffered from stage fright and eventually had a nervous breakdown in 1961.

Radio and television work became regular, including nine appearances on The Six-Five Special and he also had an acting role in Life Is A Circus, directed by Val Guest and featuring the 'Crazy Gang', in which his romantic interest was actress Shirley Eaton. He recalled: "Another nervy experience. I had some love scenes with Shirley and I felt a proper Charlie as the technicians were looking on."

He also sang the theme to Gerry Anderson's 'Four Feather Falls,' providing the singing voice for Sheriff Tex Tucker.

Michael's style of crooning was in the vein of Bing Crosby and Perry Como. In fact, he was often compared to Crosby, his hero, and the two met and became friends in California in 1959 and later they met again when Crosby came to London.

When his records were no longer selling, with his marriage on the rocks and plagued by tax problems, he became very depressed. He arrived in the early hours of the morning at a club owned by his friend, former boxer Freddie Mills. Freddie told him, "You're late. You've missed the show. Come back tomorrow night."

Mike told him, "There won't be a tomorrow night," and the same evening, 29 October 1963, he took a drugs overdose. He was rushed to a hospital in Croydon, Surrey, but died. He was only 38-years-old.

In 2004 a biography was published, written by Ken Crossland, called 'The Man Who Would Be Bing.'

During the Fifties, British singers mainly recorded cover versions of American hits.

Mike's 1956 singles releases were: 'Sixteen Tons' c/w 'The Rose Tattoo'; 'Nothin' To Do' c/w 'Perfume Candy and Flowers' which reached No. 20; 'Hot Diggity' c/w 'the Gal With The Yaller Shoes' which reached No. 13; 'Runaway Train' c/w 'Ten Thousand Miles' which reached No. 24; 'I Saw Esau' c/w 'Yaller Yaller'; 'Love Is Strange' c/w 'My House Your House'; 'Four Walls' c/w 'Wringle Wrangle'; 'It's The Good Things We Remember' c/w 'All Of You'; 'Old Cape Cod' c/w 'Love You Darlin''; 'The Story Of My Life' c/w 'Keep Your Heart' which topped the British charts; 'Rooney' c/w 'In

Love' which reached No. 26 in the charts; 'Stairway Of Love' c/w 'May I?' which reached No. 3; 'I'll Always Be In Love With You' c/w 'I'll Be Lovin' You Too', which reached No. 27; 'She Was Only Seventeen' c/w 'The Gay Vagabond'; 'Careless Hands' c/w 'My Heart Is An Open Book'; 'The Girls From County Armagh' c/w/ 'Palace Of Love'; 'Dearest' c/w 'Moments Of Love'; 'For You, For You' c/w 'Life Is A Circus'; 'Starry Eyed' c/w/ 'The Steady Game' which became his second British chart-topper; 'Skylark' c/w 'Dream Talk' which reached No. 39; 'the One Finger Symphony' c/w 'Little Boy Lost' which reached No. 50; ; 'Stay In Love' c/w 'Catch Me a Kiss'; 'I'm The One Who Loves you' c/w 'Miracle Of Monday Morning'; 'Dream Boy Dream' c/w 'I Wonder Who's Kissing Her Now'; 'I Don't Want You To see Me Cry' c/w 'Wishin' On A Rainbow'; 'Have I Told You Lately That I Love You' c/w 'It Only Takes A Minute; 'Laugh And The World Laughs With You' c/w 'Iron Fence'; 'Between Hello And Goodbye' c/w 'Just To Be With You Again'; 'Drums' c/w 'Can I Forget You'; 'Dear Heart' c/w 'My Year Of Love'; 'May Last Date (With You).'

His album releases were: 'Mike', 1960; 'Holliday Mixture', 1961, 'Happy Holiday', 1962.

Mike's first chart-topper was the Burt Bacharach/Hal David number 'The Story Of My Life', released on Columbia DB 4058 which was No. 1 in the British charts for two weeks from 14 February 1958. The number had originally been a hit for Marty Robbins in America, but Michael beat other British covers of the song by Alma Cogan, Gary Miller and Dave King.

His next and final British chart-topper was 'Starry Eyed', penned by Mort Garson and Earl Shuman. Michael's version was issued on Columbia DB 4378 and was No.1 for one week on 20 January 1960.

The first major Liverpool figure of the rock 'n' roll age was Billy Fury. Strangely enough, despite his huge following, Billy never topped the British charts.

He was born Ronald Wycherley on 17 April 1941. His parents were Albert and Jean and he also had a brother, Albert, three years younger than himself, who became a pop singer, calling himself Jason Eddie.

Prior to the Beatles, Billy was Liverpool's most successful pop artist.

In a small Liverpool studio in 1958 Ronnie cut several songs and sent a demo tape and picture to impresario Larry Parnes. He then went to a Parnes Extravaganza Show at the Essoldo, Birkenhead, for a successful audition. Parnes was to rename him Billy Fury.

Billy became Decca's biggest-selling artist of the time, with 26 hits between 1961 and 1966. During this period he spent 268 weeks in the charts. His hits included 'Halfway To Paradise', 'Jealousy', 'I'll Never Find Another You', 'Last Night Was Made For Love', 'Once Upon A Dream', 'Like I've Never Been Gone', 'Wondrous Place' and 'In Summer'.

Fury was reared in the same area of Liverpool as Ringo Starr, the Dingle, where he attended St Silas's Junior School and Dingle Vale Secondary School, along with Ringo and Fury's best friend, Billy Hatton, who was later to become a member of the Fourmost.

On 10 May 1960, Billy and his manager, Larry Parnes, attended an audition at the Wyvern Club in Seel Street, Liverpool. Parnes had been impressed by the Liverpool bands appearing in a Gene Vincent concert and had asked one of his assistants, Mark Foster, to contact local club owner Allan Williams to arrange an audition.

He wrote: "Duffy Power will be touring Scotland from June 2nd to 11th inclusive and Johnny Gentle will be touring Scotland from June 16th to 25th. For these two periods, as agreed, we are willing to pay your groups £120, plus the fares from Liverpool."

The letter also added: "We will make arrangements for Mr Parnes to come and audition your groups to select the most suitable. He will also bring Billy Fury as Billy will want one of these four groups for his own personal use. Incidentally, the idea of Billy wanting a group from his own home town will provide several interesting press stories and publicity tie-ins."

There were actually five, not four, Mersey groups at the audition: Gerry & the Pacemakers, Cass & the Cassanovas, Cliff Roberts & the Rockers, Derry & the Seniors and the Silver Beatles. The Silver Beatles had been added to the list at the last minute because of Stuart Sutcliffe pleading with Williams to let them audition.

During the afternoon, The Silver Beatles' bass guitarist Stuart Sutcliffe drew Fury's portrait and John Lennon asked for and received his autograph. Although Fury didn't get his backing group, the Silver

Beatles were chosen to tour Scotland with Johnny Gentle. Billy himself decided that he liked The Silver Beatles best, although Parnes hadn't liked the appearance or age of their drummer Tommy Moore.

All four Beatles went to the Empire Theatre, Liverpool on Sunday 21 October 1962, prior to their Cavern appearance that evening, to see Billy perform at a show there.

Fury made his film debut in 1962 in Michael Winner's Play It Cool and also starred in I've Gotta Horse in 1965.

The singer had been plagued by ill health since he was a child, when rheumatic fever had left him with a weak heart. Several tour appearances had to be cancelled due to his recurring heart problems and he was hospitalised on a number of occasions, which caused him to cease live performances in 1967 and spend most of his time on a farm, breeding horses.

He appeared with Ringo Starr in a cameo role as Storm Tempest in That'll Be The Day in 1973, performing 'Long Live Rock', a number written specially for him by Pete Townshend. During the filming there was a jam session with Ringo on lead guitar, David Essex on bass, Graham Bond on drums, Harry Nilsson on tambourine and Billy Fury on vocals.

Billy's heart finally gave out on Friday 28 January 1983, at a time when he was in the process of recording a new album and had just had a new single enter the charts.

His chart history included his debut hit single 'Maybe Tomorrow' which reached No. 22 in the British charts, then entered a second time, reaching No. 18. His other entries were: 'Margo', No. 8; 'Colette', No. 9; 'That's Love', No. 19; 'Wondrous Place', No. 25; 'A Thousand Stars', No. 14; 'Don't Worry', No. 40; 'Halfway To Paradise', No. 3; 'Jealousy', No. 2; 'I'd Never Find Another You', No.5; 'Letter Full Of Tears', No.32; 'Last Night Was Made For Love', No. 4; 'Once Upon A Dream', No. 7; 'Because Of Love', No. 18; 'Like I've Never Been Gone', No. 3; 'When Will You Say You Love Me', No.3; 'In Summer', No.5; 'Somebody Else's Girl', No. 18; 'Do You Really Love Me Too', No.13; 'I Will', No. 14; 'It's Only Make Believe', No. 10; 'I'm Lost Without You', No. 16; 'In Thoughts Of You', No. 9; 'Run To My Lovin' Arms', No. 25; 'I'll Never Quite Get Over You', No. 35; 'Give Me Your Word', No. 27; 'Love Or Money',

No. 57; 'Devil Or Angel', No. 58; 'Forget Him', No.59.

Other Mersey artists who were active on the recording scene in pre-Beatles days included Lance Fortune.

The singer was born Chris Morris in Birkenhead in 1940 and he originally studied classical piano. He became interested in pop music when he received a guitar at Christmas 1956.

While at Birkenhead School he led a vocal/instrumental group the Firecrests with himself on lead vocals. The other members were Dave Williams, Barry Ezra, Gavin Melville and Brian Wrench.

They even cut a few tracks at a local radio/recording shop, Allanson's in Borough Road, Birkenhead, recording 'That'll Be The Day', 'I Knew From The Start' and 'Party' (two of their tracks 'Come Go With Me' and 'That'll Be the Day' have emerged on the CD compilation 'Unearthed Merseybeat.')

Chris began his studies at a Welsh University, but also travelled to London with former band mate Barry Ezra to find fame and fortune. Chris managed to appear at the 2i's Coffee Bar, but Barry had no success and returned to Liverpool to join Vince Earl & the Zeroes.

At the time, Lance recalled: "I had a problem on my mind, whether I should try show business or not. I know it's precarious, and if it had not been for a holiday in London, I would still be studying for a geography degree at Aberystwyth University."

He visited the 2i's Coffee Bar in Old Compton Street where he met the owner Tom Littlewood, who became his manager and immediately booked him to appear for six weeks at the famous venue.

Musician Ian Hunter recalled: "(At) the Two Eyes Cafe on Old Compton Street I met Wee Willie Harris there and saw Lance Fortune downstairs - with the Shadows backing him."

It was actually Larry Parnes, not Littlewood, who gave him the name Lance Fortune, a name Parnes had originally coined for Clive Powell who rejected it and became known as Georgie Fame instead.

Parnes had offered him £5 to appear in one show and told him, "I'll bill you as Lance Fortune." Lance gave up his scholarship at the University to take up singing full time, although his father, an insurance executive, was against it. As Lance Fortune he appeared on a Gene Vincent tour although for some dates which clashed with him appearing in the film London Lights, singer Keith Kelly deputised for him. He recorded with Joe Meek. The record was based on a German song 'Alle Madchen Wollen Kussen' ('All Girls Want Kisses'), which had been given English lyrics by Marcel Stellman.

Under the name 'Be Mine' and with a string arrangement by John Barry (using the pseudonym Johnny Prendy), Fortune took the record to No. 4 in the British charts following its release on Pye 7N15240 in January 1960. 'Action' was on the flip.

Meek had been inspired by the Buddy Holly hit 'It Doesn't Matter Anymore' to try pizzicato strings, and was the first single in Britain to use this style – although its release was delayed by several weeks and Adam Faith's single 'What Do You Want' was then issued before it, leading disc jockey Keith Fordyce wrote of 'Be Mine': "A mighty catchy tune, a good teenage lyric and a terrific bubbling rhythm in the string arrangement that takes over where 'What Do You Want' leaves off."

Lance Fortune's follow-up 'This Love I Have For You' only reached No. 26 in the British charts and he had no further hits.

He toured with the Everly Brothers and embarked on a short solo career, and there was even a 'Lance Fortune Night' at the Lyceum Ballroom in the Strand, but he had no further hits and was to comment: "I gave up singing for a while and was involved in running a club in Plymouth." That's where he first met a vocal group the Stagerlees who were often booked at the club.

Lance began singing again and was offered a stint in Hamburg and decided to take the Stagerlees with him. When their bass player left, Lance became a member of the group, who were now a trio.

The other members were drummer/vocalist Bill Covington, who had previously been with the Rusticks, a group managed by Brian Epstein and Tony Griggs on bass guitar.

The trio based themselves in Sheffield where they were voted 'Most Popular Group' by the local newspaper in 1964.

When Covington left, Lance and Tony continued as a comedy duo called Stag & Lee. Lance had to retire from show business after suffering a stroke.

The third Merseyside artist to be signed to impresario Larry Parnes was Johnny Gentle, who was born John Askew on 8 December 1936 in a terraced house in Nightingale Square, off Scotland Road,

Liverpool. He became an apprentice carpenter and in 1957 made his own guitar. He says: "I saw a woodwork magazine, which had an article on how to make a guitar in editions spread over three months.

"After I completed the guitar I took lessons to play. My tutor was amazed at the sound of my guitar. He always played it when I came for my lesson."

He recalls: "Being an apprentice meant learning how to use your carpentry tools correctly, learning how to boat build and going to night school to learn the theory of carpentry. My best friends at school, Peter Reilly and Stan Phythian went into the army, although several lads I knew served apprenticeships at Harland & Wolff."

He teamed up with Bobby Crawford and the two began making appearances at local social clubs. Johnny recalls: "We sang Everly Brothers' songs, 'Bye Bye Love', 'Wake Up Little Susie', 'Bird Dog' etc and we would go to a club in Walton on Saturday afternoons and audition for the agents looking for acts for the working men's clubs, that's how we got our bookings."

When his apprenticeship ended in 1958, Johnny became a ship's carpenter on a cruise liner. Following the initial voyage, he entered a talent competition at Butlins under the name George Baker – but the contest was won by Jimmy Tarbuck. By that time John had changed his name again to Ricky Damone. He says: "I first changed my name to Ricky after Ricky Nelson and Damone because I thought it was showbusiness sounding."

He moved to London and worked on a building site while writing to record companies and agencies. He says: "After winning a competition at the Locarno Ballroom I was given some contacts in London by the band leader Jan Ralfini whose son worked for Pye Records.

"I wrote to Larry Parnes who gave me an audition with Philips Records and signed a contract for six records."

When Larry Parnes decided to sign Johnny up he initially suggested that he call himself Tim McGhee. Johnny didn't like the name so Parnes said: "Your name is Johnny and you're a quiet guy – so how about Johnny Gentle?"

Parnes also appointed him a tour manager – another famous Scouser: Hal Carter. Johnny's debut record was the self-penned 'Wendy', but it wasn't successful. He followed with 'Milk', but it only managed to reach No. 28 in the charts. An EP 'The Gentle Touch' followed.

In 1960 Parnes co-promoted an event with Liverpool coffee bar owner Allan Williams at Liverpool Stadium. Initially it was to have a bill topped by Eddie Cochran and Gene Vincent, but Cochran was killed in a road accident.

With Vincent now topping the bill, Williams also featured local bands Cass & The Cassanovas, Rory Storm & the Hurricanes and Gerry & the Pacemakers.

The event took place on 3 May and Parnes saw the potential of the Liverpool bands and thought it might be a good idea to use one of them as a backing band for Fury and find others to back Duffy Power and Johnny Gentle on tours.

An audition was held at the Wyvern Club in Liverpool on 10 May which resulted in The Silver Beatles being selected to back Johnny on his Scottish tour.

Their fee was £120, which was to include their fares from Liverpool. At the time the group comprised John Lennon, Paul McCartney, George Harrison, Stuart Sutcliffe and Tommy Moore.

Gentle, then twenty-years-old, has been quoted as saying: "When I first saw them I wondered what on earth Parnes had sent me." But he was later to deny he'd said this, claiming that he immediately liked their youth and enthusiasm.

The tour began on 20 May 1960 at the Town Hall, Alloa, Clackmannashire. Other gigs were on 21 May at the Northern Meeting Ballroom, Church Street, Inverness; on 23 May at the Dalrymple Hall, Fraserburgh, Aberdeenshire; on 25 May at St Thomas's Hall, Keith, Banffshire; on 26 May at the Town Hall, Forres, Morayshire; on 27 May at the Regal Ballroom, Leopold Street, Nairn, Nairnshire and on 28 May at the Rescue Hall, Peterhead, Aberdeenshire.

The group name was never actually used in the promotion of the tour, as the billing read 'Johnny Gentle and his group'. However, three members of the band decided to use stage names.

Paul used the name Paul Ramon, George adopted the name Carl Harrison and Stuart called himself Stuart de Stael.

It has been suggested that John called himself Johnny Silver, but he denied this. Johnny first met the group half an hour before they were due to go on stage together and they had time for only twenty minutes of rehearsals before their performance. The promoter, Duncan McKinnon wasn't impressed with the show but Johnny explained that they needed rehearsal time together and, after practising the next day, the stage show improved.

McKinnon had also complained about their stage gear, so Johnny gave George a black shirt to wear, as Paul and John were wearing black shirts. It was the nearest they got to a uniform appearance on stage. Johnny says: "Duncan was more like a farmer than a man who put on shows in dance halls."

The repertoire for the Scottish tour was: 'It Doesn't Matter Anymore', Buddy Holly's 'Raining in My Heart', Presley's 'I Need Your Love Tonight', Ricky Nelson's 'Poor Little Fool', Clarence Frogman Henry's 'I Don't Know Why I Love You But I Do', Eddie Cochran's 'Come On Everybody' and Jim Reeves' 'He'll Have To Go.'

Johnny had a room to himself and The Silver Beatles shared two rooms. Sometimes they were put in different hotels. Johnny recalled the best hotel they stayed in was in Inverness, overlooking the river.

It was while they were at the hotel that he played a song he'd written called 'I've Just Fallen For Someone' to George and John.

Gentle was having difficulty with the middle eight and John came up with something he'd written which fitted in. Johnny decided to use Lennon's middle eight in his song and he actually recorded the number for Parlophone the following year under the name Darren Young.

The record sold about 3,000 copies. Says Johnny: "The middle eight words that John wrote to the song were:

We know that we'll get by,
Just wait and see,
Just like the songs tell us,
The best things in life are free.

"He also gave the tune to the middle eight. As Darren Young I recorded 'I've Just Fallen For Someone' as a one-off as I was beginning to think that Johnny Gentle was not bringing me much luck record wise."

Gentle was to say that, despite their rawness as a group, he was impressed with them and urged his manager to sign them up.

However, Parnes specialised in representing solo singers and wasn't interested in the problems associated with managing bands.

Parnes commented: "Johnny used to phone me virtually every night and say, 'Come up to Scotland and see these boys. I've given them a spot in my act and they're doing better than I am.' He was very honest, I always said that if I'd found the time to go up to Scotland he might have been the fifth Beatle. Who knows?"

Johnny says: "I enjoyed the tour. I found The Silver Beatles good company and was disappointed when they were not available for my second tour of Scotland, but used another Liverpool group Cass & the Cassanovas. Later they split up and became the Big Three. They were also good fun, with typical Scouse humour."

Following the tour, Johnny appeared with them once more. He visited Merseyside and on July 2 dropped into the Jacaranda Club with his father. He was told that the group was appearing that night at the Grosvenor Ballroom, Liscard, and went over to the gig and joined them on stage and said: "When I sang with the Beatles at the Grosvenor we ran through the complete Scottish repertoire."

Gentle asked Parnes to book them again as his backing band, but they were appearing in Hamburg at the time.

His singing career was unsuccessful, despite changing his name to Darren Young. He also joined vocal outfit the Viscounts for a time.

He moved to Jersey for a while, but couldn't maintain a living as a singer and in the early 1970s began his own joinery business.

This proved to be very successful. Johnny married and became the father of two children, Gavin and Donna – and is now a granddad and lives in Kent.

Happily ensconced in Kent, he had a brief return to the limelight when the 'Beatles Anthology' was released and the press became interested in that first Scottish tour. He also participated in the BBC radio show The Beatles In Scotland and Merseyside rock historian Ian Forsyth then persuaded him to put his story down in print. The result was 'Johnny Gentle & the Beatles: First Ever Tour', published in 1998.

Johnny concludes: "I still gig now and then. I think it would be good if somebody could do a cover version of the song I collaborated with John Lennon on, 'I've Just Fallen For Someone.'"

Michael James Cox was born in Liverpool on 19 March 1940 and educated at Quarry Bank School.

Without his knowledge, his four younger sisters wrote to TV impresario Jack Good about their brother and Good gave him an audition for 'Oh Boy!' Good was impressed and booked him to appear on the show in April 1959 when he sang a cover of Ricky Nelson's 'Never Be Anyone Else But You.' Good also recorded Mike on a couple of singles for Decca, although they were unsuccessful.

He was then to sign to Joe Meek's tiny Triumph label and released 'Angela Jones', a number which John D. Loudermilk had written and which Marty Wilde had suggested he record. Mike sang the number on the TV show 'Wham!' and it went straight into the charts.

There was a huge demand for the record, but as it reached No. 7, Triumph just couldn't keep up with the public's demand for the record, not having the infrastructure or distribution network of the major record labels and what could have been a Number One hit for Michael, stalled when there weren't enough copies to cope with the demand. Meek realised that his label couldn't compete with the majors and decided to work with them as an independent, dropping the Triumph label. However, it was too late for Mike with 'Angela Jones.'

The number had reached No. 7 in the charts in June 1960 with a chart life of 13 weeks and his follow up 'Along Came Caroline' reached No. 42 on October 1960 with a chart life of two weeks.

Despite the disappointments, Mike recorded regularly for several years with different labels and his discography includes: 'Angela Jones' c/w 'Don't Want To Know' Triumph RGM 1011; 'Along Came Caroline' c/w 'Lonely Road' HMV POP 789; 'Teenage Love' c/w 'Linda' HMV POP 830; 'Sweet Little Sixteen' c/w 'Cover Girl' HMV POP 905; 'Young Only Once' c/w 'Honey 'Cause I Love You' HMV POP 972; 'Stand Up' c/w 'In April' HMV POP 1065; 'Don't You Break My Heart' c/w 'Is That A Cannon I Hear' HMV POP 1137; 'Gee What A Party' c/w 'Say That Again' HMV POP 1220; 'Rave On' c/w 'Just Say Hello', HMV 1293; 'Gypsy' c/w 'It Ain't Right' HMV POP 1417.

During his recording years he became popular in both Denmark and Sweden and toured the Scandinavian countries, backed by Joe Meek's the Outlaws as his backing band (one of the members was Ritchie Blackmore).

Lack of success as a singer led him attend drama school and take up a career as an actor, changing his name to Mike James following a stint on a Ouija board. Among his acting roles as Mike James were parts in An Age Of Kings in 1960, Where The Bullets Fly in 1966 and The Butterfly Ball in 1979.

He then began singing again, appearing on cruise ships where he met his future wife. He next began performing in America and eventually emigrated there. In 1981 he moved to New Zealand, his wife's birthplace and continues to work there as Mike James.

At a time when British artists failed to reach the American charts, there was one Liverpool singer who attained a Top 5 entry in the States under the name Russ Hamilton.

The singer/songwriter was born Ronald Hulme on 19 January 1931 (some reports say 1932 or 1933) in the Everton district of Liverpool.

He served his National Service in the Royal Air Force during the Korean War and on his return to Britain he became a Redcoat at various Butlins Holiday camps, including Brighton and Blackpool. At that time he did numerous impressions of various stars ranging from Al Jolson to Frankie Laine.

He had formed a skiffle group at Butlins and was then signed to the Oriole label, who changed his name to Russ Hamilton and he had his first hit in 1957 with his own composition 'We Will Make Love,' backed by John Gregory & His Orchestra. The number was inspired by the break-up with his girlfriend Pat Hitchin.

Russ now became one of the very first successful singer-songwriters to emerge from Liverpool. The number, issued on Oriole CB 1359 reached No. 2 in the British charts on 24 May 1957 and had a chart life of 20 weeks. Then a remarkable thing happened. The single was issued in America, but a mistake had been made and it was the 'B' side 'Rainbow' (another self-penned number that he claimed to have written in a matter of minutes), which was released as the 'A' side on Kapp 184.

The single raced up the charts and rested in the No. 4 position on 5

August 1957 with a chart life of 17 weeks. This was the highest position a British artist had reached in the American charts and Russ became the very first artist from Liverpool to have an American hit. It is also interesting to note that each of two different sides of the same single became hits on both sides of the Atlantic!

The sales of the two sides combined topped a million and he received a Gold Disc. Russ also received an Ivor Novello Award in 1958 for his song writing activities.

At the time he was working at a holiday camp in Clapton, Essex and due to the success of the record, had to commute between America and the holiday camp!

Interest in America led to Elvis Presley contacting him by phone and congratulating him on his hits. Russ appeared on The Patti Page Show and The Big Record Show. He was then asked to appear on The Ed Sullivan Show but had to turn it down as he had commitments back in England.

His next release 'Wedding Ring', also inspired by Pat Hitchin, was issued on Oriole CB 1388 where it reached No. 20 in the British charts on 27 September 1957, with a chart life of six weeks.

However, it made no impact on the American charts and as far as Stateside success went, he was a 'one hit wonder.'

All sides of his two hit singles were issued in 1958 as an EP on Oriole EP 7005. Simply called 'Russ Hamilton', Russ was backed on all tracks by the John Gregory Orchestra.

His album 'We Will Make Love' was issued in 1959. In 1960 he signed with MGM and was invited to record in Nashville, Tennessee where he was backed by Chet Atkins and the Jordanaires on some of his sessions.

Among the songs he penned were 'Little One', 'I Still Belong To You', 'I Had A Dream', 'My Mother's Eyes', 'Reprieve of Tom Dooley.' He became a regular on the TV show 'Six Five Special' and also appeared in the film version of the show performing another of his songs 'I Had A Dream.'

His complete British discography is:

'We Will Make Love' c/w 'Rainbow', reaching No. 2 in 1957, Oriole CB 1359; 'Wedding Ring' c/w 'I Still Belong to You', which reached No. 20 in 1957, Oriole CB 1388; 'Little One' c/w 'I Had A

Dream, 1958, Oriole CB 1404; 'I Don't Know Why' c/w 'My Mother's Eyes', 1958, Oriole 1406; 'Tip Toe Through The Tulips' c/w 'Drifting And Dreaming', 1958, Oriole 1451; 'September In The Rain' c/w 'I Wonder Who's Kissing Her Now', 1958, Oriole CB 1459; 'Things I Didn't Say' c/w 'Strange Are The Ways Of Love', 1958, Oriole CB 1465; 'The Reprieve Of Tom Dooley' c/w 'Dreaming Of You', 1959, Oriole CB 1492; 'My Unbreakable Heart' c/w 'I Found You', 1959, Oriole CB 1506; 'Smile, Smile, Smile and Sing, Sing. Sing' c/w 'Shadow', 1959, Oriole CB 1508; 'Mama' c/w 'Things No Money Can Buy, 1960, Oriole CB 1527; 'It's A Sin To Tell a Lie' c/w 'Folks Get Married In The Spring', 1960, Oriole CB 1531; 'Gonna Find Me A Bluebird' c/w 'Choir Girl', 1960, MGM 1096; 'The Lonesome Cowboy' c/w 'My Love', 1961, MGM 1150; 'Take A Chance On Me' c/w 'I Stand Around', 1962, MGM 1150; 'Valley Of Love' c/w 'Loneliest Boy In Town', 1963, Ember EMBS 184; 'We Will Make Love' c/w 'No One Can Love Like You', 1964, Ember EMBS 193.

The fact that record companies persevered with further recordings, despite lack of success is something that would never happen today.

Russ appeared on a television show with the Rolling Stones and now that the Beatles were conquering the world, he decided to call it a day, saying: "There are new kings of Liverpool."

A sad note to this tale of one of Liverpool's first musical heroes, who admits to being young and naive at the time, is the fact that despite selling so many records and having written the hit songs, he ended with little money which he says was caused by "bad management" and greedy song publishers.

I don't think he included Paul McCartney in this category, because at one time Paul owned Russ' songs!

Sadly, Russ passed away at his home in North Wales on 11 October 2008. He was 76-years-old.

2. The Capital of Music

WHY Liverpool? What was the reason Merseyside became the incredible musical dynamo that eventually led to it being called the capital city of popular music?

That's a question I've been asked hundreds of times over the decades and it's one that has no simple answer.

In fact, I began such an investigation in 1962 in Mersey Beat by asking musicians "Why Liverpool?" and, as a result, may have been partly responsible for one of the controversies that have developed over the years which led to people saying that Liverpool had the edge because it was a seaport and that youngsters obtained records which weren't available in Britain due to Cunard Yanks.

'Cunard Yanks' was the epithet given to Merseysiders who went to sea on Cunard ships, mainly to New York.

There are several sites detailing the history and stories surrounding the Cunard Yanks, the Merseyside men, many of them young, who sailed the Cunard ships from Liverpool to New York. During the 1950s there were approximately 25,000 Liverpool men and women who worked, mainly in unskilled positions, on the Cunard ships as cooks, waiters, kitchen porters and stewarts.

One site reveals: "Before the cultures began to merge (American and British)...as they did in the late Fifties...we still were the guys who had it all...Because we dressed in American style...brought home their music...their clothes... and in a lot of cases... even their mannerisms... And all things American... And again... because most of us sailed with Cunard from Liverpool...we were called 'Cunard Yanks'... a lot of lads from Southampton filled the same criteria."

Incidentally, if the Cunard seamen and women brought the American records to their relatives in Southampton, why wasn't there a similar music scene there?

The maritime influence on Merseyside had waned by the time the Mersey Sound began to emerge, the Cunard Building at the Pier Head was sold to Prudential and Cunard had re-located to Southampton.

There is evidence that Cunard Yanks were providing records to Mersey youngsters in the Fifties, but by the time 1960 had turned around, the music in the repertoires of the Mersey groups were basically from records readily available in record stores throughout the country.

On the other hand, Kingsize Taylor, leader of the Dominoes, who had a particularly strong repertoire of American numbers, supports the Cunard Yanks theory, saying: "Rock and Roll in its various forms, was coming into the UK from 1954, and 90% of it was from Merchant Seamen or US forces."

He also comments: "It is a well documented fact that the Beatles' early rock numbers were all copied from the Dominoes. This fact was admitted by Pete Best during an interview I gave for the biography he was filming."

Another Mersey musician who supports Ted Taylor's assertion is Jose McLaughlin, who says: "As regards my early repertoire – I was very fortunate in the fact that my dad had his cafe Joe Mack's Cafe, in Shaw Street. He was ex WWII Navy, and a lot of his wartime mates were in the merchant navy. They used to call in quite regularly, along with other Cunard Yanks, and they knew that my dad was a singer who loved jazz and blues, so they brought him rare records from the USA.

"So as a youngster, I heard Josh White, Muddy Waters, Wynone Ryder, Louis Jordan, Elvis's Sun Records, The Dave Brubeck Quartet, very early Motown, the Burnette Brothers etc. along with records by Chuck Berry, Little Richard, Jerry Lee Lewis, Fats Domino, Elmore James, Howlin' Wolf, Count Basie, Duke Ellington, Jimmy Rushing, Joe Williams and lots of obscure race artists.

"So my first band, the Timebeats, had a very eclectic repertoire of rock 'n' roll, blues, R&B and some jazzy stuff, which seemed to go down well with the audiences. This initial eclectic mix has stayed with me all my life."

Cavern disc jockey Bob Wooler, when asked if he ever got any records from Cunard Yanks, said: "No, and no again, this is another of those myths about the Cunard Yanks, as they said – I never received any records from sailors at all! My collection was bought. Besides, you could order any obscure records in those days – you never had to ask any sailors!"

Radio Merseyside's Spencer Leigh, having interviewed hundreds of Mersey musicians over the past few decades, is adamant that the Cunard Yanks had nothing to do with the Mersey Sound and says, "It's a good, romantic story that's persisted for more than forty years but it remains untrue."

When I interviewed John McNally of the Searchers for the 'Why Liverpool?' piece in 1962 he told me that he got records from his brother, who went to sea. I was aware the Hank Walters had said that he got his records from seamen and made an assumption which I included when I wrote about it in the sleeve notes to the first 'This Is Mersey Beat' album and perhaps people assumed that this was how all the bands selected their repertoires.

I was also to interview Chris Curtis of the Searchers for a feature I called 'Chris – And His Mammoth Record Collection.'

This established that in the case of the Searchers, it wasn't John who provided the records, it was Chris Curtis. Chris told me about his record collection. "I have boxes and boxes of records in the house and I've just lost count of the number. There must be hundreds and hundreds. I'm particularly interested in collecting records that haven't 'made it' in the States – and Soul records are my favourite."

Chris carried numerous records with him in a large case which also held a portable record player – and he was constantly playing the records. He said: "We choose most of our own records from these lesser known American discs and, in fact, every one of our A sides, with the exception of 'Sugar and Spice' were chosen in this way – we also use a lot of these numbers on our LPs."

Chris also told me that his favourite artists were Bessie Banks, Dee Dee Warwick, Lou Johnson, Jackie de Shannon and Anita Franklyn, a Gospel singer.

There were also other sources where groups traced the numbers they wished to perform.

Chris Huston, guitarist with the Undertakers, told me: "Liverpool groups didn't get their material from sailors. We spent hours searching through piles of records on the stalls at the flea markets every time we went down to London. They were apparently records that had come mostly from the PX stores on the American Air force bases. In fact, I got my first James Brown, Lonnie Mack, Major Lance and Joey Dee albums from market stalls."

Johnny Byrne of Rory Storm & the Hurricanes told me: "That's a myth about the groups receiving copies or having records from Cunard Yanks. We certainly never got any material that way and I doubt that the Beatles did. Most group material was gleaned from the records (although some on limited release) that were issued at that particular time (1958-1961). Chuck Berry, Jerry Lee etc, were available and groups took their material from these and lesser-known artists with material that we were able to play and adapt that suited all the groups' limited styles."

Earl Preston, for instance, was given records by his brother-in-law, who was an American serviceman from the Burtonwood base near Liverpool. The Chants also told me that their Doo Wop numbers were obtained from records they received from friends at the same Burtonwood base.

Jim Clarke, former member of the Dimensions, recalls: "My brother Norman was in the army and he had an American friend who was based at Burtonwood Airbase just outside Liverpool (I would be about 11 then) and our Norman would bring him back to our house every Saturday night and he would stay over and he used to bring his country music LPs with him, (we would listen to them all Sunday until he went back to camp) so that's how I was introduced to country music."

The Beatles entire repertoire at the time, apart from Lennnon & McCartney originals, came from records that were readily available in local record stores and they used to seek out numbers for their repertoire at NEMS.

They would drift into the Whitechapel store following a lunchtime gig at the Cavern and listen to discs in the record booths. Like the other Mersey groups, they competed to find good numbers to include in their sets and often referred to the 'B' sides of the singles rather than the popular 'A' sides.

Pete Best told me that they dropped into NEMS regularly to listen to records: "Normally we all went there together and used to do the same thing every time: come in, walk over to the record counter, look at the list of new releases and listen to them. We'd make our decision about a number there and then."

Anyone researching the Beatles' repertoire would discover that there were no numbers they played which weren't available on records in British shops.

When disc jockey Paul Gambaccini asked Paul, "Did the Cunard Yanks have anything to do with introducing you to these records?" Paul told him: "I don't think so."

Groups competed to try and find numbers which other bands didn't have in their repertoire. On John's wedding night the group were appearing in Birkenhead on a bill with the Remo Four.

When the Remo Four began to play one of the numbers that the Beatles were including in their set, John jumped on stage to argue with them, but they told him where to get off! Brian Epstein also found the Merseybeats listening to a particular song and asked them if they'd do him a favour and not use it in their act as he wanted the Beatles to perform it.

In an editorial I suggested that Paul listen to a Peggy Lee album and I also suggested that some group should record 'Hippy Hippy Shake.'

When the Beatles appeared on the all-Beatles edition of 'Juke Box Jury' at the Empire Theatre in Liverpool, the Swinging Bluejeans version of 'Hippy Hippy Shake,' was played and John Lennon commented: "The boys nearly made it before. I like Bill Harry's version as well!"

This was typical of John's comments which were enigmatic to the populace in general. He was referring to my suggestion about recording the number. As a result, youngsters all over Britain were going into record shops that weekend asking for Bill Harry's version of 'Hippy Hippy Shake!'

Incidentally, John liked the Alabama R&B singer Arthur Alexander, who first made an impact in 1961/2 with songs such as 'Anna', 'Soldier Of Love', 'A Shot Of Rhythm And Blues', 'You Better Move On' and 'Go Home Girl'. In fact, Alexander's use of the word 'girl' in his songs became common lyric parlance and had an influence on

John Lennon's lyrics. In 1962 John introduced four songs popularised by Alexander into the Beatles act, and sang lead vocals on all of them: 'Anna (Go To Him)', 'A Shot Of Rhythm And Blues', 'Soldier Of Love (Lay Down Your Arms)' and 'Where Have You Been All My Life?'

The Beatles recorded 'Anna', which was included on their debut album 'Please Please Me', and 'Where Have you Been All My Life?' is to be found on the Star Club albums. The group performed 'A Shot Of Rhythm And Blues' and 'Soldier Of Love' on their BBC Radio appearances.

It can't be disputed that the American rock 'n' roll and R&B records that inspired Mersey groups were available in British record shops. Drummer Paul Chiddick comments: "I have two elder sisters, Florence and Rosa, who were born in 1941 and left school in 1956 – and that's when they got their 'Dansette' record player, which first got me listening to pop music.

"They both got married in 1960 so I had a good four years of pop music being played in the house. The records my sisters bought included Elvis, Buddy Holly, the Everly's, Cliff etc. Others I remember include the Kalin Twins, Johnny Tillotson, Little Richard, Connie Francis, Roy Orbison, Eddie Cochran etc."

Personally, I consider that the Cunard Yanks aspect had little influence on the Mersey Sound, and I give more credence to the proliferation of venues for the groups to play in and the enterprising local promoters.

One of the main catalysts that sparked off the Mersey music scene was skiffle music – and that was down to Lonnie Donegan.

Many aspiring musicians were inspired to form skiffle groups after seeing Lonnie perform at the Pavilion in Lodge Lane, others took their inspiration from his major hit 'Rock Island Line' and he also impressed Paul McCartney and George Harrison following his Empire Theatre appearances. Donegan's Liverpool appearance sparked Paul's desire for a guitar and his father, Jim, bought him one for £15.

Paul was in the audience of Donegan's 1956 Empire concert and he became inspired. Also, during a school lunchtime he'd gone down to the theatre to glimpse his idol and noticed that Donegan was writing notes to the employers of factory girls, explaining why they were late – they'd spent time in their dinner hour waiting for him. Paul was very impressed by the gesture and felt that this was the way that stars should behave.

A 14-year-old George Harrison, who'd originally met Paul on the bus on the way to the school they both attended, went round to Paul's house to look at his teach-yourself-to-play book. George recalled: "We learned a couple of chords from it and managed to play 'Don't You Rock Me Daddy'O".

The Donegan appearance also sparked off George's desire for a guitar and he bought a second-hand one from Raymond Hughes, a boy in school, for £3, which his mum had lent him.

George's brother Harry was to say: "Lonnie Donegan was appearing at the Empire and of course George just had to go. In fact, he borrowed the money from our parents so that he could see every single show! Anyway, he found out where Lonnie was staying, which happened to be in a house in Speke, so George went round and hammered on the door until he came out and gave George his autograph. Of course, he immediately raced home to show everyone."

During an interview in the Sixties, George was to comment: "Lonnie and skiffle seemed made for me…it was easy music to play if you knew two or three chords, and you'd have a tea-chest as bass and washboard and you were on your way."

They were similar to the comments he made to Hunter Davies in the official biography of the Beatles, when he told them that Lonnie Donegan was the first person to make an impression on him musically: "I'd been aware of pop singers before him, like Frankie Laine and Johnny Ray, but never really taken much interest in them. I don't think I thought I was old enough for them. But Lonnie Donegan and skiffle just seemed made for me."

The king of skiffle was also a catalyst for the 16-year-old John Lennon. He'd listened to the music on Radio Luxembourg and thought that it wasn't difficult to play, so he asked his Aunt Mimi if she could get him a guitar. He also bought a 78rpm record of 'Rock Island Line', which he later sold to a schoolmate, Rod Davis. Rod was also inspired by Donegan and bought a banjo for £3 from an uncle and joined John Lennon's new skiffle group, the Quarry Men.

Included in the Quarry Men's repertoire were several skiffle numbers popularised by Donegan, including 'Rock Island Line', 'The Cumberland Gap', 'Midnight Special', 'Railroad Bill' and 'Worried Man Blues'.

Ringo Starr also entered the music world during the skiffle era when he joined the Eddie Clayton Skiffle Group in 1957.

Donegan, once known as 'the king of skiffle', was born Anthony James Donegan on 29 April 1931 in Glasgow, the son of a violinist in the National Scottish Orchestra. When he completed his army service in 1949, he began playing in various jazz bands. His stage name allegedly came about in 1952, when he was appearing on the same bill as legendary blues guitarist Lonnie Johnson in London and the compere mistakenly announced him as 'Lonnie Donegan' – he decided to keep the name.

During the same year he joined Ken Colyer's Jazzmen on guitar and banjo, where he was reunited with a former army buddy, Chris Barber.

During the band's show he was given his own spot, accompanied by Colyer on guitar, Barber on bass and Bill Colyer on washboard, performing the style of music generally known as 'skiffle.'

Donegan had a massive hit with 'Rock Island Line' in 1956 and during the next six years enjoyed a total of 32 chart hits. He sparked off a skiffle boom and during its height it was estimated that there were 5,000 skiffle groups in the country. However, when the skiffle boom died, the musicians on Merseyside decided to keep on performing and their new inspiration was American rock 'n' roll.

In the meantime, we can observe the influence of another British artist as a seminal influence on the Beatles, and on John and George in particular. He was the ukulele master George Formby, who also became a major post war film star in Britain. George Formby was born George Booth Jr in Lancashire in 1904.

The entertainer was born blind, but later regained his sight following a coughing fit. In the 1930s and early 1940s he became the No.2 box office star in Britain after Gracie Fields. He starred in more than twenty films and had numerous best-selling records.

He was a favourite of both John Lennon and George Harrison, who admired his expertise on the ukulele.

John Lennon's mother Julia played ukulele, influenced by Formby, and John first learned to play a stringed musical instrument using a ukulele. John's admiration of George Formby began in his early years.

As a child he would spend holidays with his cousin Stan Parkes in Fleetwood and, together with their other cousin Leila, would travel to Blackpool by tram two or three times a week to see the summer shows.

Stan recalled: "Formby was a big influence on John's mother and me. Of course, it was our grandfather George Stanley who could play the banjo and ukulele.

"When George Formby came on the scene with his stage acts and then his comedy films, we were all thrilled because members of the family could play the same instruments. After seeing a Formby film, John would come out of the picture boasting, 'My mother can play banjo and ukulele just like him'.

"Before I went to live in Fleetwood I travelled from Preston to Fleetwood by a Ribble double-decker bus. John often travelled with me on the top deck as we passed by George Formby's house. He and his wife Beryl sat in deck chairs in their front garden, and they waved to us on the bus and we waved back.

"John, our cousin Leila and I went to all his shows in Blackpool whenever we got the chance. We felt we knew him personally."

In the video of John's song 'Free as a Bird', released posthumously, there is a tribute to George Formby. The video ends as the curtains come down in a theatre where a performer (Alan Randall, a Formby impersonator) is playing a banjolele on stage and takes a bow. The message heard at the end of the song is George's catchphrase, "It's turned out nice again", played backwards!

George Harrison admired Formby so much that he became an honorary President of the George Formby Appreciation Society. On Sunday 3 March 1991 he turned up at the annual George Formby Convention at the Winter Gardens, Blackpool.

The compere announced him to the Formby fans: "After some persuasion I'd like to introduce Mr George Harrison who says he's nervous."

George came onto the stage and said: "I thought I'd retired from all this years ago. You'll have to bear with me as I'm not certain I know the right chords, but you're all welcome to join in."

He then played Formby's 'In My Little Snapshot Album', a song from Formby's 1938 film I See Ice, on his ukulele.

In the evening, at the convention finale he was joined by his wife Olivia and son Dhani, together with Derek and Joan Taylor and publisher Brian Roylance and he went on stage with his ukulele once again.

This was George's last ever public appearance and in a 1991 interview he recalled memories of his mother singing George Formby songs at home and how he had developed an enthusiasm for Formby and the ukulele for the first part of his life.

George also recorded an interview with BBC Radio for the Formby tribute programme 'The Emperor of Lancashire.'

The influence of Formby is also obvious in George's posthumous album 'Brainwashed' in which the ukulele is heavily featured.

The only song not penned by George himself was 'Beneath The Devil And The Deep Blue Sea', penned by Harold Arlen, but which was an old George Formby song featured in one of his films.

Jeff Lynne, who produced 'Brainwashed' was to talk of George's love of the music of Formby.

He even mentions that George taught him how to play the ukulele. Lynne recalled that George had pulled all the song bits from George Formby movies and had them put on reel to reel and he told Jeff at least ten times that it was comedy but also very good music.

The ukulele is a four-stringed instrument that evolved from the Portuguese cavaquinho on islands in the Pacific Ocean and was patented in Hawaii in 1917. It resembles a little acoustic guitar.

One of Formby's favourite ukuleles was a Ludwig which he first used during the filming of Feather Your Nest in 1936, six years after production of the Ludwig ceased. He also used it on his famous 'Leaning on the Lamppost' number and a total of thirteen times in his 22 films. He also played the Ludwig on his last public appearance on BBC TV, The Friday Show three months before his death on 6 March 1961. George used it to entertain an estimated three million troops during the war years.

George's fiancée Pat Hewson put all his musical instruments up for sale later the same year, although the Ludwig failed to sell. It was also put up for auction in the mid-1960s and was bought by Rex Blake of

Sheffield. After his death, it was auctioned in June 1988 and purchased for £2,700 by a non-Formby fan.

Two weeks later a member of the George Formby Society paid him £3,500 for it and it was displayed at the Warrington Museum Exhibition in 1991.

George then bought Formby's Ludwig for a price estimated to be between £25,000 and £35,000. It is rumoured that Paul McCartney now possesses the instrument.

George had been buying ukuleles for years and had them in virtually every room of his house. His son Dhani became an accomplished player. George was to say: "It is hard to play a ukulele banjo without smiling."

He loved playing the instrument and at Terry Gilliam's party on 26 November 2000, he began playing George Formby songs on his uke, accompanied by Michael Palin and Terry Jones on spoons.

During Paul McCartney's 'Back In The US' tour, Paul stepped on stage strumming a ukulele and singing 'Something' in honour of George. He said: "The minute I thought of George I thought of the ukulele because he was such a fan of the instrument."

Formby himself suffered his first heart attack in 1952 and had his second heart attack prior to his marriage to Pat Hewson (his first wife Beryl had died of leukaemia) and died in hospital on 6 March 1961.

His funeral was held at St. Charles' Church in Aigburth, Liverpool and more than 100,000 mourners lined the route when his coffin was driven to Warrington Cemetery to be buried in the family grave.

Following the death in the popularity of skiffle, the numerous Merseyside skiffle bands began to turn to rock. The James Boys evolved into Kingsize Taylor and the Dominoes, the Quarry Men into the Beatles and so on.

In those days British radio meant the BBC with its Home and Light programmes. Rock 'n' roll music was rarely played and programmes such as 'Family Favourites', 'Worker's Playtime' and 'Desert Island Discs' held no appeal to youngsters.

Therefore, groups on Merseyside competed with each other to find rare and unique American numbers to add to their repertoires.

Gerry & the Pacemakers, for instance, had 150 songs in their repertoire and, as an example of musical influences; here is a list of numbers performed by the Beatles in 1960: 'Ain't She Sweet'; 'All Shook Up'; 'Apache' (which they say is the only Shadows number they performed); Bad Boy; Be-Bop-A-Lula'; Begin The Beguine; 'Blue Moon of Kentucky'; 'Blue Suede Shoes'; 'Bony Moronie' ;'Carol'; Cathy's Clown'; 'Clarabella'; 'C'mon Everybody'; 'Corrine, Corrine'; 'Crying, Waiting, Hoping'; 'Dance In The Street'; 'Dizzy Miss Lizzy; 'Don't Forbid Me'; 'Don't Let The Sun Catch You Cryin''; 'Fools Like Me'; 'Glad All Over' (the Carl Perkins number, not the Dave Clark Five hit); 'Gone, Gone, Gone'; 'Good Golly Miss Molly; 'Hallelujah, I Love Her So' (when Derry Wilkie recorded this number he sang 'In the evening when the sun comes up'!); 'The Harry Lime Theme'; 'Heavenly' 'Hey, Good Lookin''; 'High School Confidential'; 'Honey Hush'; 'Hound Dog'; 'Hully Gully'; 'I Forgot To Remember to Forget'; 'I Got A Woman'; 'I Remember' ; I'm Gonna Sit Right Down And Cry (Over You)'; 'It's A Long Way To Tipperary'; 'It's Now Or Never'; 'It's So Easy'; 'Jailhouse Rock'; 'Johnny B. Goode'; 'Lawdy Miss Clawdy'; 'Lend Me Your Comb'; 'Little Queenie'; 'Long Tall Sally'; 'Love Me Tender'; 'Love Of The Loved'; 'Lucille'; 'Maybe Baby'; 'Mean Woman Blues'; 'Midnight Special'; 'Money (That's What I Want); 'Moonglow'; 'Nothin' Shakin' (But The Leaves On The Trees)'; 'Ooh! My Soul'; 'Over The Rainbow'; 'Peggy Sue'; 'Ramrod'; 'Raunchy'; 'Red Sails In The Sunset'; 'Reelin' And Rockin'; 'Rock And Roll Music'; 'Searchin'; 'September Song'; 'Shakin' All Over'; 'Shimmy Shimmy'; 'Short Fat Fanny'; 'Shout'; 'Slow Down'; ''Summertime'; 'Sure To Fall (In Love With You)'; 'Sweet Little Sixteen'; 'Teenage Heaven'; 'Tennessee'; 'That'll Be The Day'; 'That's Alright (Mama); ;Think It Over'; 'Three Cool Cats'; 'Three Steps To Heaven'; 'Too Much Monkey Business'; 'True Love'; 'Tutti Frutti'; 'Twenty Flight Rock'; 'Well...(Baby Please Don't Go)'; 'What'd I Say'; 'Whole Lotta Shakin' Goin' On'; 'Words Of Love'; 'The World Is Waiting For the Sunrise'; 'You Are My Sunshine'; 'You Don't Understand Me'; 'You Were Meant For Me'; 'You Win Again'; 'Youngblood'; 'Your True Love.'

They were covers of numbers by Elvis Presley, Chuck Berry, Carl Perkins, Buddy Holly, Larry Williams, Gene Vincent, the Everly Brothers, Ray Charles, Jerry Lee Lewis, Little Richard, Eddie Cochran and the Coasters.

Elvis was one of the major seminal influences on the young John Lennon, causing his Aunt Mimi to say: "It was Elvis Presley, Elvis Presley, Elvis Presley. In the end I said, 'Elvis Presley's all very well, John, but I don't want him for breakfast, dinner and tea.'"

John said: "Nothing really affected me until I heard Elvis. If there hadn't been Elvis, there would not have been the Beatles."

It was John who performed 'Hound Dog', 'Jailhouse Rock', 'Blue Suede Shoes' and 'I'm Gonna Sit Right Down And Cry (Over You)', while Paul performed 'All Shook Up' 'Blue Moon Of Kentucky' and 'That's All Right (Mama)'. Stuart Sutcliffe performed 'Love Me Tender'.

George Harrison was to comment: "I remember at school there was all that thing about Elvis. When a record came along like 'Heartbreak Hotel' it was so amazing. We know Elvis is great. He stopped being a rocker and they made him go into the army, and by the time he came out he was a lean, healthy American, doing clean, healthy songs and films. But basically he's got such a great bluesy voice."

Paul McCartney was to say: "Every time I felt low, I just put on an Elvis record and I'd feel great, beautiful."

Despite the Beatles early fascination with Elvis, Presley didn't have much impact on the repertoires or performances of the hundreds of other Mersey bands. Perhaps it was because they were real rock 'n 'rollers and, as George said: "He stopped being a rocker."

No one who had heard it can forget John Lennon's blistering version of 'Twist and Shout.' This was originally a hit by the Isley Brothers, another seminal influence for Mersey bands and yet another American favourite to appear in Liverpool.

When the Isley Brothers came to Liverpool they were interviewed by Mersey Beat. Ronald Isley was to say: "In America there just aren't any groups like your British ones. Back home we have vocal groups and instrumental ones, but very rarely do we have a group who play instruments and sing at the same time like the Beatles."

Kelly Isley also remarked: "That doesn't mean that Americans who play instruments can't sing – but I think the nearest thing to a beat group we've got in America is the Beach Boys. I don't know why we've been so slow in catching on – it used to be Britain copying American trends – but now it seems to be the other way round."

Another of the major musical influences on the Liverpool groups at the beginning of the 1960s was the Tamla Motown label, created in Detroit by Berry Gordy Junior in 1959. Berry had originally derived the name Tamla from a Debbie Reynolds film Tammy, and Motown was an abbreviation of the nickname of Detroit: Motor City. Berry actually used the name Tamla as a label in America in 1959 and Motown in 1961. The name Tamla Motown was used on the European releases.

In Britain in 1962, Tamla Motown was distributed by a small record label, Oriole, and the largest market for the records by the Detroit groups was on Merseyside.

At that time I began to feature Motown regularly in Mersey Beat, profiling the artists and reviewing the latest releases. Oriole Records began to take half page advertisements due to the interest aroused by the label in Liverpool.

When I received the latest Motown singles I'd take them down to the Cavern and ask Bob Wooler to play them. When I took 'Fingertips' by Little Stevie Wonder, Ringo was there and asked me if he could have the record. I gave it to him. When, shortly after, he told me that it was his favourite record I told John Schroeder of Oriole who arranged for a complete Tamla Motown collection to be sent to Ringo.

The Tamla Motown numbers were included in the repertoire of the Liverpool bands. They adapted the songs to fit in with the developing Liverpool sound, the basic three guitars/drums/harmony line-up which produced a hybrid sound, which I dubbed 'the Mersey Motown sound.'

This particular sound found its way on record when a number of Mersey acts recorded their own versions of Motown numbers. Faron's Flamingos recorded 'Do You Love Me' and 'Shake Sherry', Ian & the Zodiacs with 'Beechwood 45789', Beryl Marsden with 'When the Lovelight Starts Shining Through His Eyes,' Steve Aldo with 'Can I Get A Witness', The Trends with 'You're A Wonderful One', the Dimensions with 'Tears On My Pillow' and so on. Numbers such as 'Money' were also part of the repertoire of numerous Mersey bands such as the Searchers, Undertakers, Dominoes and All Stars.

The Beatles, in fact, featured three Motown numbers on their 'With The Beatles' album – 'Please Mr Postman' originally recorded by the

Marvelettes, 'You Really Got A Hold In Me', recorded by the Miracles and 'Money (That's What I Want)', penned by Berry Gordy.

One of their main heroes was the Motown singer/songwriter Smokey Robinson who was born in Detroit, Michigan on 19 February 1940. He founded the Miracles in 1955. While in London he spent an evening in the company of John and Paul at the White Elephant club on 29 November 1964. At the time the Miracles had already recorded 'You Really Got A Hold On Me', one of Smokey's songs which had been inspired by Sam Cooke's 'Bring It On Home To Me'.

Robinson was to comment: "When they recorded it, it was one of the most flattering things that ever happened to me. I listened to it over and over again, not to criticise it but to enjoy it." He also said: "They were not only respectful of us, they were down right worshipful.

"Whenever reports asked them about their influences, they'd go into euphoria about Motown. I dig them, not only for their songwriting talent, but their honesty."

Another track on their 'With The Beatles' album was penned by John in 1961. It was called 'All I've Got To Do' and John said it was his attempt to do a Smokey Robinson. In 1980, when recording 'Woman', Yoko said that John sounded like a Beatle, but he told her, "Actually, I'm supposed to be Smokey Robinson at the moment, my dear, because the Beatles were always supposing that they were Smokey Robinson."

George Harrison dedicated 'Ooh Baby (You Know That I Love You)' on his 'Extra Texture' album to Smokey Robinson. He also wrote about him in his song 'Pure Smokey' on the '33 1/3' album.

Another Detroit-born Motown artist who the Beatles admired was Mary Wells. When Mary entered the British charts with 'My Guy', the Beatles wanted her to appear on tour with them and she was booked to appear on their Autumn 1964 tour, making her debut with them on the bill at the Gaumont, Bradford on 9 October.

When the tour reached the Ardwick Apollo in Manchester, Virginia and I attended the gig and spent our time backstage with the Beatles.

I also took the opportunity of interviewing Mary, who told me: "I first heard that I'd be touring with the Beatles in September and I thought it was wonderful. I admire them very much and as far as I'm concerned, they're the best."

She also told me: "I'd just love to record a number by John and Paul and I think I'll ask them about it."

In fact I went round to see John myself that night and told him what Mary had said. He told me: "We've got a number which we think will really be suitable for her."

However, nothing transpired from it.

Differing from the Mersey-Motown sound was the straight Motown-sounding presentation of numbers by local black vocal group the Chants. I lent them my albums of the Miracles and the Marvellettes which they literally wore out by playing them so often!

Interestingly enough, Virginia and I visited the Motown Museum in Detroit with Mike and Rowena McCartney, escorted by Martha Reeves. I noticed they had a photo on display entitled 'Liverpool Meets Detroit': it was a photo of the Supremes with the Dave Clark Five!

Another influence was American girl groups such as the Shirelles with numbers such as 'Boys', 'Baby It's You', 'It's Love That Really Counts' and 'Everybody Loves a Lover', covered by local artists such as Cilla Black, the Beatles, Chick Graham & the Coasters, the Merseybeats, Beryl Marsden, Lee Curtis and others.

Incidentally, although I mentioned that the Beatles used to go to NEMS to listen to records and that the cover versions they performed in their act were all available at local record stores, there was one other source they were able to obtain records from: Ron Ellis, author of the Johnny Ace novels (Ace is a fictional Liverpool disc jockey/detective).

He was to tell me: "I had a pen friend in the States, Ronnie Kellerman who, oddly enough, was a friend of Jerry Lee Lewis and he sent me photos of Jerry Lee taken at his home with his family. Ronnie also used to send me albums that were not released over here by artists, who'd only had singles released in Britain, such as the Olympics with 'Western Movies' and Bobby Blue Bland with 'Turn Your Lovelight.'

"He also sent me record catalogues. I couldn't afford to buy many so I used to tape them then sell them on to groups who wanted the new material. Among my customers were the Beatles, the Searchers and Billy J. Kramer & The Dakotas.

"I was the one who approached the groups asking if they wanted to buy the American albums and I chose the Beatles and the others as they were the ones making the most money, so they were more likely to be able to afford them. John Lennon wrote me a list of albums he wanted.

"The records that John ordered were ones by the harder-edged R&B artists such as Dr. Feelgood, Inez & Charlie Foxx, Bobby Blue Bland, James Ray and Rufus Thomas. George went for the Coasters and Ben E. King. Ringo wanted everything in the catalogue, particularly the most obscure gospel albums. They all wanted Tamla Motown records which hadn't been released in this country."

However, this was in 1963 and the Beatles repertoire was soon to include most of their original material.

3. People and Places We Remember

ONE of the main reasons, I believe, that Liverpool had the edge over most other cities when it came to establishing a large and exciting music scene, was because of the proliferation of venues and the enterprise of a number of promoters.

As mentioned in my introduction, the amount of venues on Merseyside was vast, running into the hundreds. There were dances at ballrooms, swimming baths, ice rinks, synagogues, town halls, youth clubs, theatres, cinemas, restaurants and social clubs – and also on the Mersey ferries, most notably the Royal Iris.

Scores of churches also promoted the Christian groups in their halls. From 1963 onwards, for instance, the Christian group the Crossbeats had over 700 bookings, which affords some idea of the amount of venues open to the Merseyside Christian rock groups.

Some of the venues on Merseyside they appeared in included: St John & St James, Bootle; Netherton Methodist Church; St Andrews', Clubmoor; St Leonard's, Bootle; St David's & St Mark's, St Helens; Orrell Park Baptist Church; St Helens Parish Church; St Benedict's, Everton; Wellington Road City Mission; St Anne's, Aigburth; Emmanuel Church, Fazakerley; Dovecot Mission'; Angers House, Netherton; York Street Mission, St Helens; Garston Parish Church; People's Church, Everton; St Mary's, Upton, Birkenhead; Aigburth Methodist Youth Club; St Matthews, St Helens; York Street Mission, St Helens; All Hallow's, Allerton; West Kirby Methodist Church; Page Moss Baptist Church; Cheadle Parish Church; Orrell Park Baptist; Skelmersdale Christian Fellowship; St Catherine's, Birkenhead; Hoylake Evangelical Church; Speke Congregational Church; Gordon

Smith Institute, Liverpool Mission to Seamen; St Cutherbert's Everton; St Ambrose, Everton; St John's Waterloo; Little Neston Methodist Church; St. Mary's Church School, Bootle; Liverpool Dockside Mission; Holy Trinity, Walton Breck; Salvation Army, Clubmoor; Stanley Road Baptist Church, Bootle; Palm Grove Methodist Church, Birkenhead; Cheadle Parish Church; Holy Trinity, Formby; Hartington Road Congregational Church; St Simon & St Jude, Southport; St Mary's, Bootle; Huyton Congregational Church; All Saints, Stoneycroft; St Andrew's, Bebington; St Helen's Parish Church; St Philips Church, Litherland; Little Neston Methodist Church, Wirral; St Mark's, Newtown, Wigan; St Paul's, Hatton Hill; Emmanuel Hall, West Derby Road; St John's, Ainsdale; Brighton Road Methodist Church, Southport; St Ambrose Church, Liverpool; St Cyprians, Edge Hill; St John's, Widnes; St Phillips, Litherland; St Anne's, Aigburth; St Cuthbert's, Everton; St Philemon's, Toxteth and Warrington Independent Methodist.

In the early issues of Mersey Beat, I featured an Entertainment Guide which listed Jazz Clubs; Coffee Clubs; Jive Halls; Cabaret Shows; Clubs, General; Restaurants; Chinese Restaurants; Theatres and Bingo Clubs.

Some of the Jive Hives mentioned were: Aintree Institute; Blair Hall; Bootle Town Hall; David Lewis; Empress Club; Grosvenor; Hambleton Hall; Holyoake Hall; Jive Hive; La Mystere; Litherland Town Hall; La Scala, Runcorn; Lathom Hall; Mossway; Merrifield; Neston Institute; Orrell Park Ballroom; Quaintways; St John's Hall; Town Hall, Skelmersdale'; Valentine 'Rock' Club.

But this was only scratching the surface.

As far as the social clubs were concerned there were over 300 of them affiliated to the Merseyside Clubs Association. I featured these regularly in a column I called 'Clubland', penned by Ted Knibbs, manager of Billy Kramer & the Coasters. Virginia and I often dropped by the legendary 'Ozzie Wades' on a Sunday afternoon where artists performed before the club secretaries of the numerous clubs, which was more or less a 'showcase' for the acts to receive bookings.

Ted's first column featured the Walton Lane Social Club, affection-ately known as Ozzie Wade's, a reference to owner Ada Wade's late husband.

The venue had been opened since 1940 and had a stage, dance floor and three bars. Among the artists who had appeared there were Ken Dodd, Billy Fury, Johnny Gentle, Michael Holliday, Lita Roza, Joseph Locke and Russ Hamilton.

Eight years previously the club had also become the headquarters of the Merseyside Clubs Federation who had an affiliated membership of 131 clubs – which soon grew to more than 300 venues.

There are too many social clubs to be listed here, but here are a handful to give you some idea: MPTE Social Club, Finch Lane; Merseyside Civil Service Club; Childwall Labour Club; Stanley Abbatoir Social Club; Norgreen Club; N.U.R. 5 Club; R.N. Club, Waterloo; Deacon Road Labour Club; Willo Club, Devonshire Road; O.D.V.A. Social Club, etc.

Early in 1963 I began serialising 'The Beatles Story', interviewing everyone locally who was associated with the group. One feature in the series was headed 'The Man Who Discovered The Beatles.'

I began: "Numerous people have stepped forward and claimed to have discovered the Beatles. However, it is generally acknowledged that Brian Kelly was the first promoter to really have faith in the group, and their early appearances at Litherland Town Hall marked a turning point in their career.

"Their debut appearance at Litherland Town Hall was certainly the setting for their first major impact on the Mersey scene and Bob Wooler was to begin his prophetic article on the Beatles in August 1961 with the words: Why do you think the Beatles are so popular?

"Many people many times have asked me this question since that fantastic night (Tuesday 27 December 1960) at Litherland Town Hall when the impact of the act was first felt on this side of the River."

In the article I wrote on Brian, he told me: "I was organising a dance at Litherland Town Hall to be held on Boxing Day, 1960, but I was short of a group. I received a phone call from Bob Wooler who said. 'I've found a group for you at the Jacaranda and they're free. They want £8. Will they do?'

"Not at that price, they won't," I said. "A group won't increase my attendance enough to warrant that.

"Bob told me they were called the Silver Beatles and that they played at the Casbah, Hayman's Green. We finally agreed to pay them

£6. On their first appearance I was completely knocked out by them.

"They had a pounding, pulsating beat which I knew would be big box office. When they had finished playing, I posted some bouncers on the door of their dressing room to prevent other promoters who were in the hall from entering. I went inside and booked them solidly for months ahead.

"I had a huge poster made with 'The Beatles' written in large fluorescent lettering. The poster caused a certain amount of curiosity and I remember the first reaction to their name. 'Beatles – you've spelt it wrong, mister', 'Beatles – where've you dragged them from?' 'Beatles – who are they?'

"The group went from strength to strength at Litherland and built up a fantastic following. Even then, the song-writing talents of Lennon and McCartney were evident. On stage they'd say, 'Here's a song we've just written – if you don't like it you needn't clap.'

"They were the first really noisy group to appear on Merseyside – and amplifiers were insufficient to cope with their sound. I worked on the amplification for them – and received a great deal of business for Alpha Sound. Groups on Merseyside seemed to play wilder and louder and more of them approached me to help with their amplification."

Brian's story is interesting because he was probably the Liverpool promoter who booked them more times than anyone else, apart from the Cavern – and also helped to build their reputation at his venues prior to their residencies at the Cavern.

He was one of the handful of Liverpool promoters who helped to establish the network of local venues which provided Mersey groups with the opportunity to develop their music in front of live audiences on a regular basis.

Kelly promoted 'Beekay' dances, the first of which took place at the Savoy Hall, Bath Street, Waterloo on 11 May 1959. He then built up a number of other regular promotions at Lathom Hall, Seaforth; Alexandra Hall, Crosby; Aintree Institute, Litherland Town Hall and a venue in Skelmersdale.

Like several other promoters, Kelly would have bands appearing at 'auditions.' In other words, if he hadn't seen a band perform before, he would let them play at his venue for no fee as an 'audition.'

He first booked the Silver Beats for an audition at Lathom Hall on

Saturday 14 May 1960 on a bill that included Kingsize Taylor & the Dominoes, Cliff Roberts & the Rockers and the Deltones.

They passed the audition!

Kelly next booked them to appear the following week, on Saturday, 21 May. However, they never turned up because they had set off on their brief Scottish tour with Johnny Gentle.

As for their Litherland gig, it was their debut appearance at the venue. Kelly hadn't booked the Beatles since their failure to turn up at his Lathom Hall promotion, but Bob Wooler had talked him into booking them at a fee of £6.

Kelly then booked the Beatles for numerous other appearances at the venue during 1961.

As it was a late booking, their names for that first appearance didn't appear in the local newspaper advertisements, which had already been placed, announcing the Searchers, the Del Renas and the Deltones. Entrance to the gig was three shillings (fifteen pence).

Kelly managed to place their name on some posters with the tag: "Direct from Hamburg, the Beatles!" As they weren't all that well known in Liverpool at the time, this led to a number of members of the audience believing that they were a German group. Their line-up that night was John, Paul, George, Pete and Chas Newby.

Brian Kelly, impressed by the immense excitement the Beatles had generated, immediately booked them for a string of dates at all his main venues and Bob Wooler was later to devote an entire page of Mersey Beat to them, extolling their performance that night.

For the Monday, 7 August gig, the Litherland Town Hall classified advertisement in the Liverpool Echo carried the message: "Hear Pete Best Sing Tonight." Pete Best had been talked into performing the song 'Pinwheel Twist', while Paul took over on drums.

The Monday, 21 September appearance saw them share a bill with Gerry & the Pacemakers and Rory Storm & the Hurricanes.

On Thursday, 19 October, the Beatles and Gerry & the Pacemakers combined to make a single appearance as the Beatmakers.

Their Litherland Town Hall appearances during 1961 were on Thursday 5 and Thursday 26 January; Thursday 2, Tuesday 14, Thursday 16, Tuesday 21 and Tuesday 28 February; Thursday 2 March; Monday 17, Monday 24 and Monday 31 July; Monday 7

August; Thursday 7, Thursday 14, Thursday 28 September; Thursday 19 and Tuesday 31 October. Their last appearance at Litherland Town Hall took place on Thursday 9 November: Interestingly enough – earlier that day Brian Epstein had visited a Cavern lunchtime session to see the Beatles for the first time.

Kelly also booked the Beatles for a total of 31 appearances at Aintree Institute. They made their debut there on Saturday, 7 January 1961 and also appeared on Saturday 7, Friday 13, Saturday 14, Wednesday 18, Saturday 21, Friday 27 and Saturday 28 January; Wednesday 8, Friday 10, Wednesday 15 Saturday 18 Wednesday 22 and Saturday 25 February; Wednesday 1, Saturday 4, Wednesday 8, Saturday 11, Friday 21 and Friday 28 July; Friday 4, Saturday 12, Friday 18, Saturday 19 and Saturday 26 August; Saturday 2, Saturday 9, Saturday 16 and Saturday 23 September; Saturday 28 October; Saturday 11 November. Their last appearance at the venue took place on Saturday 27 January 1962.

Their fee for their Aintree Institute appearance was now £15 and by that time Brian Epstein had become their manager. Kelly paid them for the gig in coins. A furious Brian Epstein was to recall the incident in his biography and said they were paid "in sixpences and florins and even halfpennies and I kicked up an awful fuss, not because £15 isn't £15 in any currency, but because I thought it was disrespectful of the Beatles." As a result, Epstein ensured that they never appeared at the venue again.

Kelly also booked the Beatles for Alexander Hall in College Road, Crosby, although it was only for a single gig on 19 January 1961.

Brian Kelly died in 1993, which is why I suppose his contribution to the Beatles rise in Liverpool has never been fully acknowledged by the many people who have written books in the succeeding years.

Ray McFall was the most important promoter of the Beatles in Liverpool, booking them more times than anyone else in the world, and building their reputation at his club – the legendary Cavern club.

When original owner Alan Sytner decided to sell the Cavern Club in Liverpool, he received an offer from Ray, who worked on the accounts for the Cavern and another nearby jazz venue. Ray purchased the club from Sytner on 1 October 1959 for £2,750. Music had always been a leading interest in his life and his tastes ranged from the classics to all forms of pop music. Ray was born in the Garston area of Liverpool on 14 November 1926. His family settled in Maghull and he attended St. Mary's College, Crosby, cycling 11 miles every day to school. On leaving school he worked for the British-American Tobacco Company and then joined a firm of chartered accountants.

During the war he worked down the mines as a 'Bevan boy' between the years 1944 and 1948. He married in February 1952 and moved to London with his wife Shirley, but decided to return to Liverpool as an accountant two years later.

He began to work on accounts for the Sytner family and Alan asked him to handle the accounts of the Cavern club. He also worked as a cashier on Sundays at the Temple Jazz Club and fulfilled the same function at the Cavern on Thursdays and Saturdays.

When Sytner got married and moved to London, Ray became the new owner of the club. Once he'd taken control of the Cavern, Ray's new policies became an important factor in the development of the Liverpool sound. The Cavern had been primarily a jazz club and the local rock groups mainly played on the 'jive hive' circuit. After taking over the running of the club, McFall made a radical departure – he introduced rock 'n' roll. He also pioneered lunchtime sessions.

By the end of February 1961 he'd stopped the modern jazz nights as the musicians had failed to receive the support they'd deserved.

The club was now almost exclusively presenting rock 'n' roll, with the Swinging Blue Jeans running their customary guest night, during which the Beatles made their evening debut on 21 March 1961, with Johnny Sandon and the Remo Four and the White Eagles Jazz Band.

The Beatles also began their own series of resident nights on Wednesday, 2 August 1961 and made a total of approximately 274 appearances, their final one taking place on 3 August 1963.

Another innovation Ray introduced were the lunchtime sessions, he recalled, "I gave the idea a lot of thought and it seemed to me that working people would come into the club in the middle of the day if the supply of snacks was adequate and supply of music was appealing. I began on Tuesday 18 October with a straightforward record session. And I laid on plenty of hot dogs, soup, sandwiches and drinks. It worked. By Christmas we were open most lunch times with groups instead of jazz jam sessions to entertain the crowds."

As success began to spread across the Mersey scene, Ray undertook a policy of expansion and the Cavern soon became the most famous club in Britain.

McFall also launched a Junior Cavern club, membership of which cost sixpence (2.5p) with admission at two shillings (10p) for members and two shillings and sixpence (12.5p) for visitors.

The sessions took place between 1.00 p.m. and 4.00 p.m. each Saturday and featured two groups and Top Twenty discs, was strictly for 13 – 16 year olds and began on 1 February 1964, with a guest appearance by Billy J. Kramer who was promoting his latest single 'Little Children.'

Ray continued his expansion plans and launched a management/agency called Cavern Artists Ltd, and in November 1963 he bought the premises next door to the Cavern, extended the width of the club and began building a recording studio, Cavern Sound, which opened on 15 October 1964.

During alterations the old stage had to go and Ray had the idea of selling pieces of the original stage as 'Beatleboard' to Beatle fans who would like a souvenir of the stage on which the group had performed so many times. Beatleboard cost five shillings (25p) a piece, the proceeds being donated to Oxfam. There were so many requests from all over the world that it took four months to fulfil the orders.

On Saturday, 12 September 1964 there was a 'Caverncade' – a parade through the streets of Liverpool by groups on decorated floats. The proceeds again were donated to Oxfam.

There was even a half-hour weekly radio show which took place at the club. Called 'Sunday Night At The Cavern,' it was broadcast on Radio Luxembourg each Sunday at 10.30 p.m. commencing 15 March 1963. The show was hosted by Bob Wooler who played the latest chart records and introduced a group live from the Cavern stage each week.

Unfortunately, Ray had taken on too many enterprises and stretched his capital too far, with the result that he had to declare himself bankrupt, and the Cavern was sold.

While the Cavern had become famous, Ray had become something of a celebrity and began to travel widely. He joined the Beatles on their first trip to America, but while he was away, things began to deteriorate at the club, particularly in relation to the cash which was collected at the door each session, much of which became unaccounted for. Unfortunately, Ray couldn't salvage the situation and the club was never the same after he left, and it was eventually torn down to make way for an air vent for an underground railway in 1973.

A decade later, a new Cavern was rebuilt on the site of the old.

Ray moved down to London and resumed his career. He is now retired and settled in the South of England. For someone who was so important to the development of the Mersey Sound, it is unfortunate that he has never received any proper acknowledgement for his efforts from Liverpool, via any awards or honours from the city.

It's a fact that a number of the original promoters have passed away, so their stories remain untold, but it was through their efforts that so many venues were providing the work for the groups virtually every evening of the week.

Many refer to the late Charlie McBain as the pioneering Mersey promoter, with the venues he ran from 1956 onwards such as New Clubmoor Hall in Norris Green and Wilson Hall in Speke Road, Garston, Garston Swimming Baths, Wavertree Town Hall and Holyoake Hall. John's skiffle group the Quarrymen were booked by McBain for his New Clubmoor Hall venue on Friday 18 October 1957.This was a Conservative club where Paul McCartney made his debut with the Quarrymen. There was an audience of approximately 100 people that night.

Paul had tried to convince the group that they should have some sort of stage uniform and he suggested white coats. They couldn't really afford to buy any at the time so their manager Nigel Whally was able to borrow a couple of white jackets from the golf club where he worked. For the gig the group wore matching outfits with long-sleeved cowboy shirts, black string ties and black trousers. John and Paul wore the white sports coats.

The line-up that night comprised Colin Hanton on drums, Len Garry on tea chest bass, Eric Griffiths on guitar and John and Paul.

John, Paul, Len and Nigel caught the 81 bus from Woolton and Eric and Colin met them at the venue.

They were due on stage at 9pm and began with Paul singing 'Long Tall Sally'. On this occasion Paul played lead guitar for the first and only time – and it was a disaster.

Paul played the old Arthur Smith hit 'Guitar Boogie', but ruined the guitar solo because he was playing his guitar upside down and backwards, as he still didn't know how to restring a guitar for a left-handed person.

After the show, aware that his debut as a lead guitarist hadn't gone down too well, Paul tried to impress John by playing him an original number he'd written called 'I've Lost My Little Girl'. John responded by trying out a few tunes he'd written and sought Paul's opinion – the Lennon & McCartney songwriting team was soon to develop.

The group returned to the venue on 23 November 1957 and performed their third and last gig at the club on 10 January 1959. By that time the line-up comprised John, Paul, George Harrison, Colin Hanton and John Lowe.

McBain, affectionately known as Charlie Mack, also booked the group for his Wilson Hall venue and the second gig for the Quarrymen in which Paul was present took place on Thursday 7 November 1957. The line-up comprised John Lennon, Paul McCartney, Colin Hanton, Eric Griffiths and Len Garry.

Nigel Whalley was with them, but had to leave half way through the night due to an asthma attack. They were each paid 50 shillings. Two teddy boys, Rod and Willo, were determined to beat up John.

The Quarrymen next appeared on 7 December 1957. When the Quarrymen appeared at the hall on 6 February 1958, Paul had been trying to convince John to allow George Harrison to join the group and arranged for him to hear George play. It was a most unusual audition, George performed 'Raunchy' for them on the upper deck of a bus. George was fourteen years old at the time, although it was shortly before his fifteenth birthday, and John thought he was too young.

Vic Anton, Dave Forshaw, Wally and Audrey Hill, Les Dodd, George and Jimmy Blott, Doug Martin and Jimmy McIver, Sam Leach, Ralph Webster, Jim Turner, Ron Ellis, Les Ackerley, Billy Gillin, Bobby Meadows, Jeff Hogarth, Ken Hignett, Gordon Vickers, Maurice Linacre and Jack McGee were also among the other promoters who helped to keep the Mersey Sound alive locally.

Dodd was a dance promoter from Wallasey, 'over the water' from Liverpool, who had been promoting dances at the Grosvenor Ballroom, Liscard and the Institute, Neston since 1936 via his company, Paramount Enterprises. He ran '21 plus' nights weekly in two halls, strictly for adults, with advertisements which declared 'No Jiving! No Rock 'n' Roll! No Teenagers!"

But the impact of young music on Merseyside was so strong that Dodd reluctantly began booking local groups on Saturday night 'swing sessions', at the Grosvenor – and Thursday evening dances at the Institute.

Allan Williams had formed Jacaranda Enterprises, a part-time agency to book a few groups locally and the first gig he arranged for the Silver Beatles was via Dodd.

It took place at the Institute, sited in Hinderston Road, Neston, Wirral in Cheshire, on 2 June 1960. Dodd booked them for six Thursday night gigs at the venue. He also booked them for his Grosvenor Hall dances, beginning on Saturday, 4 June 1960.

Both venues became noted for violence and a 16-year-old boy was nearly beaten to death in front of the Beatles at the Institute during one of their sessions. They were also quite nervous when they turned up at the Grosvenor without Tommy Moore – who had quit as their drummer – only to find a tough local teddy boy called Ronnie joining them on stage to play drums and telling them he was going to join the group!

From June to August 1960, all the Silver Beatles' bookings – with the exception of a single Jacaranda coffee bar appearance – were for Les Dodd at his two venues. This came to an end when Wallasey Corporation cancelled Dodd's season at the Grosvenor due to the violence. The group had been due to play there on Saturday, 6 August, but Dodd had to cancel their appearance as the venue was now closed to rock 'n' roll.

Wally Hill and his wife Audrey, were also notable promoters, running an organisation called Peak Promotions with events at Blair Hall, Walton every Saturday and Sunday; Holyoake Hall, Smithdown Road every Saturday; the David Lewis, jive sessions on Fridays and Columba Hall Widnes, Thursdays and Saturdays.

Regular groups at these gigs included Mark Peters & the Cyclones, the Counts, the Ravens and the Seniors. It's promoters like Wally Hill who kept the scene active. Like some of the other Merseyside promoters, he hasn't figured much in the written history of the local music scene because he only booked the Beatles a handful of times.

However, as an example of his contribution to the scene, here are some of the groups he booked into his venues in September, 1961: Mark Peters' Cyclones; Carl Vincent's Counts; Frank Knight's Barons; Robin's Ravens; Derry's Seniors; Foo Foo's Flashy Falcons; Clay Ellis' Raiders; Karl Terry's Cruisers; Ray's Del Renas; the Strangers; the Phantoms; the Black Diamonds; the Hi-Cats; the Travellers; the Cimmarons; Steve Bennett's Syndicate and the Wranglers.

The same lack of acknowledgement could be said for Doug Martin and Jimmy McIver who ran events at the Jive Hive, Crosby, the Masonic Hall, Skelmersdale and Mossway Hall, Croxteth, as they only booked the Beatles on one occasion – on 17 March 1961 at their Mossway Hall venue.

Doug and Jimmy originally started promoting dance bands around Seaforth, Litherland and Crosby in the early fifties at venues such as Litherland Town Hall and Lathom Hall.

In 1958, for local teenagers, St. Luke's Church Hall, Crosby, became known as 'the Jive Hive.' One of the first promotions there featured the Deltones, the Dominoes, the Bobby Bell Rockers and Al Storm & the Hurricanes (who were to become Rory Storm & the Hurricanes).

Recalling the Jive Hive, Johnny Guitar of Rory Storm & the Hurricanes said: "The place had a great atmosphere. It was a big hall with a wooden sprung floor and when the crowd used to jive in time together they would all bounce in unison.

"There was no alcohol served there and it was really friendly, no fights. Early on we would get the L3 bus from Stanley Road. Ringo would put his drum kit in the luggage rack. We would then get off at the shop nearest to the hall and lug all our stuff there. Later on, after we'd made a bit of money, we all drove there in new cars."

The Jive Hive closed in 1962 and is now known as the Crosby Comrades Club. Jim 'Jiver' McIver died in 1996.

Another local promoter was Sam Leach who first began booking groups into the Mossway Jive Club at Mossway Hall in 1958 and later went on to run various clubs such as the Cassanova Rock 'n' Swing Club.

Promoting under 'The Leach Organisation', Sam began to launch some innovative promotions such as the 'Rock Around the Clock' 12 hour session at the Iron Door Club (also called the Liverpool Jazz Society) in March 1961.

In 10 November of that year he launched the first of his Operation Big Beat promotions at the Tower Ballroom, New Brighton, a venue which had a 5,000 capacity. He ran other Operation Big Beat concerts at the Tower on 24 November and 8 December 1961.

One of the younger promoters was Dave Forshaw. He originally began promoting at Bootle YMCA, St. John's Hall, Bootle and various youth clubs to raise funds for various charity organisations.

He recalls: "In those days bands didn't have their own PA systems and most dances had to handle the PA systems from either Charlie McBain or Brian Kelly. Brian Kelly promoted dances including Litherland Town Hall, Savoy Hall and many more but he also ran his own PA hiring system at Alpha Sound and he looked after the north side of Liverpool."

"Charlie McBain was one of the oldest dance promoters on Merseyside and promoted so many venues it was unbelievable.

"In his last years it was mainly the likes of Wilson Hall, and the baths at Garston. I had my equipment from him. After seeing the way I ran my dances, Charlie asked me if I had ever thought of doing it myself. I said yes but I didn't have any money to cover losses if that were to happen. He said that if I was prepared to promote and run the dances with him he would cover any losses and we would just go 50 50. Consequently I ran St Johns Hall from 1957 until 65 or 66, booking all the Merseyside groups.

"In 1960 I was lucky enough to be at Litherland Town Hall. Brian and myself had become good friends as dance promoters and he had given me a free pass to any of his dances and this was reciprocal.

"At that time the Beatles were doing one of their first performances after Hamburg.

"Obviously on that night I was so impressed by the way they performed, by their sound, the songs and the music which was fantastic.

"The thing that stood out for me at the time was the fact that they were wearing jeans and leather coats. Jeans in those days were not allowed in dancehalls, we banned them because they were classed as working men's clothes and we thought people wearing them would cause trouble because they weren't wearing a suit. In those days we made people wear ties coming in - and they took them off inside!

"At the end of their performance the girls and fellahs that were there were absolutely made up and the girls were raving about the Beatles.

"At the end of the night they all tried to get back into the rear changing rooms to see them, meet them, greet them or whatever, but Brian Kelly had put a doorman outside the door to stop the people going inside. He later said he did it to stop other promoters booking them, but that so-called story was wrong because the only promoter who was there at the time was me.

"As I knew the doorman at the time I was able to go behind and took the opportunity to book the Beatles for six pounds ten shillings for the first booking, then for ten pounds ten shilling for the next two, if they were okay. Obviously they were and the first booking was at St John's Hall on January 6 1961. Their amazing pulling power drew in an extra 192 people to be precise to our normal crowd, the club was full.

"It just proved that from their few performances since they were back from Germany, they'd already obtained that cult following that was to become tremendous over the years.

"On with the Beatles on that night 6 January were the Searchers who I paid £4 to. I think another audition group at the time was called the Diablos, I think they were paid one pound fifty to play the first half hour or something like that and again I was the MC/Compere as well as running the dance and organising it.

"From then on I tried to run many other dances and did so quite successfully at various venues. As well as St John's we did the Church Institute at Ellesmere Port, Fazakerley Hall, Sampson & Barlows in Walton, Rainhill Village Hall, the Merrifield Club in Old Swan, Bootle YMCA and the original Sampson & Barlow's which was on Stanley Road, Bootle. At these times, as well as the Beatles, we were booking all the groups and popular ones at St Johns were local bands such as the Searchers, the Dennisons, the Remo Four, Dale Roberts & the Jaywalkers and Ian & the Zodiacs."

Once Brian Epstein became manager of the Beatles he also began promoting at the Tower Ballroom, part of his plan to associate the Beatles with established names by putting them on bills with Little

Richard, Joe Brown and Bruce Channel. The most famous club on Merseyside was the Cavern. It's been a long and winding road since the time in 1961 when Brian Epstein phoned me and asked if I could arrange for him to visit the Cavern for the first time, so that he could see the Beatles.

I contacted Ray McFall and arranged for Brian's name to be left at the door, then phoned Brian and told him he could visit the club during the lunchtime session on 9 November. Accompanied by his personal assistant Alistair Taylor, Brian walked down those eighteen steps – and the rest is history! However, as the Cavern's history has been so exhaustively documented in magazines and books, I'll mention some of the other venues.

As far as the title 'birthplace of the Beatles' is concerned, arguably that name really belongs to the Casbah, a cellar club in West Derby Village where the Quarrymen were to re-form and appear as resident band in 1959 (catch a Beatle fan out by asking which club in Liverpool with six letters beginning with C was the birthplace of the Beatles?)

Also, as far as the city centre was concerned, Allan Williams had opened a club exclusively devoted to rock 'n' roll called the Top Ten in December 1960, but it was burnt down a short time before the Beatles were to begin a residency there. Other city centre jazz clubs which turned to rock 'n' roll before or at the same time as the Cavern were the Mardi Gras, the Downbeat and the Iron Door Club.

Another major Mersey venue was the Tower, New Brighton which was named because it originally featured a huge tower which was patterned on the Eiffel Tower in Paris. Work began on it during June 1896 and it was completed in 1900. The tower was the highest structure in Britain and stood 567ft. Four lifts took half a million sightseers to the top during the first year with the view taking in the Isle of Man, parts of the Lake District and the Welsh hills.

During the First World War, for security reason, trips to the top of the Tower were suspended. The Tower was neglected, turned rusty and the owner couldn't afford the renovations so it began to be dismantled in 1919. The Tower building contained one of the largest ballroom facilities on Merseyside which was able to accommodate up to five thousand people.

George Harrison's grandfather was once a commissionaire at the ballroom. During the days of the burgeoning Liverpool Sound the venue began to be used for a series of spectacular dance promotions, the first beginning on 10 November 1961 under the name 'Operation Big Beat.'

The show opened at 7.30pm and the Beatles appeared at 8pm. They then fulfilled another engagement at Knotty Ash Village Hall before returning for their second Tower appearance that evening at 11.30 pm.

The first Operation Big Beat event drew an audience of 3,000 people. The groups appearing were the Beatles, Rory Storm & the Hurricanes, Gerry & the Pacemakers, The Remo Four and Kingsize Taylor & the Dominoes.

Operation Big Beat 2 took place on the evening of Friday, 24 November 1961, with the Beatles once again topping the bill. The other local groups who appeared were Rory Storm & the Hurricanes, Gerry & the Pacemakers, the Remo Four, Earl Preston & the Tempest Tornadoes and Faron's Flamingos.

Late night transport had to be arranged with the various local authorities as the event took place between 7.30pm and 2.00am. Tickets cost 6/- (30p).

An added treat for the audience was the appearance of Emile Ford, who'd had several chart hits, including 'What Do You Want To Make Those Eyes At Me For' and 'Slow Boat to China.' He got up on stage and sang with Rory Storm & the Hurricanes while American singer Davy Jones joined the Beatles on stage and sang two numbers with them.

The Beatles returned to top the bill again on Friday, 1 December 1961 at a six-group extravaganza which attracted 2,000 people.

The other bands were Rory Storm & the Hurricanes, Dale Roberts & the Jaywalkers, Derry & the Seniors, Kingsize Taylor & the Dominoes and Steve Day & the Drifters. There was also a 'Mr Twist' competition.

The next Tower promotion, The Davy Jones Show, took place on 8 December 1961 and featured South African singer Danny Williams, whose current hit 'Moon River' was No. 4 in the British charts. Once again the headliner was Davy Jones, backed by the Beatles, who had also provided backing for him earlier that day at the Cavern.

The other acts were Rory Storm & the Hurricanes, Gerry & the Pacemakers, Earl Preston & the TTs and the Remo Four. The compere was Alan Ross. The second heat of the 'Mr Twist' competition also took place.

On 15 December five bands were featured on a five-and-a-half-hour show. The Beatles topped the bill. The event also saw the appearance, for one night only, of former top Liverpool band Cass & the Cassanovas. When Brian Casser had originally left the group (did he go or was he pushed?) the remaining three members continued as the Big Three. On this evening's bill Casser joined the Big Three under the old name for a special one-off reunion performance.

Saturday 3 December featured Alf Tweedle's Super Jazz Band, The Swinging Bluegenes and Tony Osbourne & his Orchestra.

The Boxing Night Ball featured the Beetles (that was how the posters advertised them), Rory Storm and Tony Osbourne and his Band.

The first bill of the New Year was on Friday, 12 January 1962 on an extravaganza called 'Twist Around The Tower', advertised as: "The Greatest Show on Merseyside. Starring that horrible hairy Monster Screaming Lord Sutch (X certificate) and his horde of Savages, with Philips recording artists Mel (King of Twist) Turner and the Bandits.

"Also Mersey Beat Poll Winners the Beatles (After 11.30pm), Rory Storm & the Hurricanes, the Strangers. We introduced the Twist to Merseyside, now we present another lead – a sensational Twist exhibition team, Mr Twist & the Twistettes."

Bill toppers Screaming Lord Sutch & the Savages failed to turn up.

The Beatles' next Tower appearance took place on Friday, 19 January, followed by a special Pre-Panto Ball on Thursday, 15 February. Panto Day was an annual event in Liverpool, organised by students at Liverpool University. They would parade around the city on huge decorated floats, dressed in costumes, collecting for local charities. On the Panto Day evening, all students who had taken part in the event were invited to a special Panto Day Ball.

Local promoter Sam Leach capitalised on the publicity by putting this bill on the eve of Panto Day, with Terry Lightfoot and His New Orleans Jazz Band, co-headlining with the Beatles. It drew an audience of 3,500 people.

The Beatles then appeared twice at the Tower on 16 February, initially at 9 pm, followed by a set at 10.45pm. They appeared at the Tower again on 23 February and on 2 March they appeared at another Tower event, billed as the 'Mad March Rock Ball.'

The Beatles (their name on the posters was The Beetles) appearance on Friday, 6 April was their last Tower appearance prior to their season at Hamburg's Star Club. The two headliners were Emile Ford & the Checkmates and the Beatles. The other bands were Gerry & the Pacemakers, Howie Casey & the Seniors, Rory Storm & the Hurricanes and the Big Three. Adding some novelty were the Original Kingtwisters.

There were plenty of activities at the Tower, apart from the major promotions. Friday, 1 June was 'Big Beat Night' starring Rory Storm & the Hurricanes, the Kansas City Five and Lee Curtis & the Detours. Every Monday there was a 'Teenagers Disc Night', with a 1/6d entrance fee. Commencing Thursday, 7 June was a 'Pick The Pops', a competition with various cash prizes. Every Saturday was 'Twist 'N' Trad Night' with Les Osbourne & his City Slickers Jazz Band, the Swinging Bluegenes 'plus Top Rock and Trad guest groups', with an admission charge of 5/-. The next Beatles appearance there was on a promotion financed by Brian Epstein and organised and compered by Bob Wooler. It was the first of a series of planned prestige gigs by Epstein to place the Beatles on a bill with name artists.

For this appearance on Tuesday, 21 June 1962, the bill was topped by Bruce Channel. Channel had had a massive hit with 'Hey Baby' and he was backed by harmonica player Delbert McLinton & the Barons. The Beatles were advertised as "Parlophone recording artistes, and stars of the BBC's 'Teenager's Turn.'" Bolton group the Statesmen were next on the bill, followed by Mersey groups the Big Three and the Four Jays.

Incidentally, it's interesting how people's memories recall events.

Decades later Delbert McLinton, in an interview, was to comment on the event, "The Beatles were the opening act on about four of the shows we did…we were in New Brighton the first night we played with them, at a place called the Castle. It was an old castle, if I remember right, because when you looked out of the dressing room window it was a sheer drop to the ocean."

As we know, the Beatles only appeared on one show with Channel and McClinton, the Tower was not called the Castle and it overlooked the River Mersey, not the ocean.

However, during the evening it was said that John Lennon chatted with McClinton, who showed him how to play the harmonica passage from 'Hey Baby.' When the Beatles came to record 'Love Me Do', John used the style McClinton had taught him.

The next Operation Big Beat promotion took place on 29 June with the Beatles topping the bill. Ten local groups were featured in a five and a half hour spectacular. Another Beatles appearance took place on 13 July.

The next Brian Epstein presentation at the Tower featured Joe Brown & the Bruvvers headlining over the Beatles on 27 July. The other acts on the bill were the Statesmen, the Big Three, Steve Day & the Drifters and the Four Jays.

For their appearance at the venue on 17 August the Beatles had drummer Johnny Hutchinson sitting in with them as Pete Best had been ignominiously sacked a few days previously.

Operation Big Beat IV took place on Friday 3 August, but the Beatles were appearing at the Grafton Ballroom that night. The bill comprised Lee Curtis & the All Stars, Billy Kramer & the Coasters, The Four Jays, Faron & the Flamingos, The Mersey Beats, Kansas City 5 with Freddy Fowell, Earl Preston & the TTs, Gus Travis & the Midnighters, Clay Ellis & the Raiders and Sonny Kaye & the Reds.

Operation Big Beat V on Friday, 14 September was another five and a half hour marathon featuring six local groups headed by the Beatles. Later the same month the Beatles appeared at the Tower on 21 September. The occasion was advertised as 'Rory Storm's Birthday Night' and apart from the Beatles and the Hurricanes, the other bands were Billy Kramer & the Coasters, the Big Three and Buddy Dean & the Teachers.

The next event was another five and a half hour extravaganza pro-moted by Brian Epstein and starring Little Richard and 12 local acts on Friday, 12 October. The NEMS Enterprises presentation was another Bob Wooler production and, apart from the Beatles, Lee Curtis & the All Stars appeared with their new drummer Pete Best.

Other acts on the bill were the Big Three, Billy Kramer with the

Coasters, the Dakotas with Pete MacLaine, the Four Jays, the Merseybeats, Rory Storm & the Hurricanes and the Undertakers.

On 23 November the Beatles appeared on the bill of the 12th Annual Lancashire and Cheshire Arts Ball. Also appearing were Billy Kramer & the Coasters, the Llew Hird Jazz Band and the Clan McLeod Pipe Band.

The Beatles appeared again on 1 December and their last Tower appearance during 1962 was on 7 December when they topped the bill on a line-up of seven local bands.

Bob Wooler was to present a special Easter Monday Show on 15 April 1963 headlined by Gerry & the Pacemakers. The other acts were Billy Kramer & the Dakotas, Peter Jay & the Jaywalkers, Shane Fenton & the Fentones and Jimmy Powell Takes Five.

The Beatles final appearance at the Tower Ballroom took place on Friday, 14 June 1963 on a special NEMS Enterprises presentation of their 'Mersey Beat Showcase' series. The Beatles were supported by Gerry & the Pacemakers and five other groups.

The building was destroyed by fire in 1969 and only the shell was left. It was demolished and a housing estate now occupies the former site.

Chris Huston, former member of the Undertakers, recalls when the group were booked for an 'Operation Big Beat' promotion in 1962.

"The PA system was supplied by Alpha Sound, which was Liverpool promoter Brian Kelly's company. He supplied the PAs for practically all the major clubs and dances on Merseyside. Renting or leasing them to the various venues. By today's standards the PA system that was used at the Tower was laughable. It consisted of a black painted, open-back wooden speaker enclosure at each side of the stage, each having 2 x 12" speakers. That was it! There were no stage monitors at all. This being another concept whose time had not yet arrived.

"Luckily, guitar amplifiers weren't all that big either, so there was a sort of tenuous balance between the instruments and the vocals, although the instruments always seemed to win out, in the end."

I have only basically covered the main Beatles appearances at the Tower, but, of course, there were rock shows constantly being promoted on virtually a weekly basis by people ranging from Lewis Buckley to Bob Wooler.

Buckley usually featured a chart artist along with several local groups. One example was his bill of The Springfields, the Coasters, Johnny Templar & the Hi-Cats and Tommy Quickly & the Challengers on Saturday, 23 March 1963 and another included the Bachelors, the Remo Four with Johnny Sandon, the Chants, The Dennisons and Four Hits and a Miss on Friday, 7 June 1963.

An interesting one was Bob Wooler's 'Thank Your Lucky Stars' promotion on Thursday, 17 May 1962. This was headlined by Jerry Lee Lewis, backed by the Echoes with a bill which also included ten local bands.

At one time, manager Tommy McArdle gave me access to the files in the Tower, a valuable archive of history which, sadly, was destroyed in the fire. Brian Epstein also asked me to design the poster for the Joe Brown/Beatles show at the Tower, and I obliged.

There were numerous other promotions at the Tower including a special tribute to the Searchers by the Lord & Lady Mayor of Birkenhead, which I took photos of. The most memorable moment was when Little Richard appeared. Virginia and I were accompanied by our photographer Les Chadwick and I asked Richard if we could take a photo of him and the Beatles. This took place in the band room and I gathered them all together for the historic photograph.

Les also took some other shots for me, including one of Richard with members of the Chants and Sugar Deen with Richard.

Paul McCartney spotted Joe Ankrah at the gig and invited him and his group the Chants to the Cavern where the Beatles provided backing for them. At another gig Paul was so impressed by the sight of Iris Caldwell, dancing with the Kingtwisters in a costume which displayed her legs in fishnet stockings, that he began dating her.

Virginia and I attended virtually all of the Tower Ballroom promotions and particularly remember the night when Jerry Lee Lewis was on. After the show we accompanied him for a drink and a chat at the Witch's Cauldron. At the time he was being hounded by the press because the news of his marriage to his young cousin was in the headlines.

Lathom Hall is a venue situated in Lathom Avenue, Seaforth, Liverpool L21 which was originally built in 1884 as a cinema. It became one of several venues, including Litherland Town Hall and

Aintree Institute, promoted by Brian Kelly. It was standard practice in Liverpool to offer groups 'auditions', which would actually take place at a live show. In other words, the promoter would regularly have groups playing for free with the enticement that he might book them.

Under the name the Silver Beats, the group who were later to become the Beatles auditioned for Kelly at Lathom Hall during the interval on Saturday, 14 May 1960 on a bill which included established Liverpool bands Kingsize Taylor & the Dominoes, Cliff Roberts & the Rockers and the Deltones.

As a result of their brief performance, Kelly booked them for the following week, on Saturday, 21 May. He advertised the event, which was the first time the group had officially appeared in an advertisement. Despite the fact that they'd only auditioned, the advertisement billed: "Silver Beats, Dominoes, Deltones."

In spite of the top billing they didn't turn up for the gig. Instead they left on a tour of Scotland backing Johnny Gentle without informing Kelly who, as a result, didn't book them again for several months until Bob Wooler talked him into it.

Drummer Cliff Roberts recalled the Silver Beats' appearance that first night on 14 May and said they were a scruffy bunch whose drummer hadn't even brought his kit and asked if he could borrow Cliff's.

Roberts had a brand new Olympic kit that he hadn't even used on stage himself, so he naturally refused. However, he agreed to play with the Silver Beats and they performed six numbers together: "Four rock 'n' roll standards that all of the groups played, and two originals that they had to teach me."

He says that the group then disappeared and he didn't see them until eight months later when they appeared on the bill at the Alexandra Hall, Crosby on Thursday 19 January 1961, where, says Roberts: "They wore black leather, had brand new instruments and played brilliantly."

All their subsequent appearances at Lathom Hall took place during the first two months of 1961, by which time Kelly was paying them an average of eight pounds and ten pence a performance. Their appearances at the venue took place on 20, 21, 28 and 30 January and 4, 6, 10, 11 and 25 February. Their last performance on Saturday 25 February took place on George Harrison's eighteenth birthday (or so

George believed at the time. It was many years later that he discovered he was actually born on 24 February).

It was at Lathom Hall that an incident occurred with troublemakers.

In 1966, Neil Aspinall was to recall that the group was often a target for gangs who would shout insults at them because they were either looking for a fight or were annoyed that their girls fancied the foursome. For the sake of peace, the group ignored the taunts.

"But it wasn't easy," said Neil. "At Lathom Hall...two troublemakers followed Stu Sutcliffe into the dressing-room muttering things like 'Get your hair cut, girl!' John and Pete saw this and went after them.

"A fight broke out and John broke his little finger...It set crooked and never straightened."

Pete Best was also to recall the Lathom Hall incident. He said: "When we'd done our session and came off, we changed, which didn't take an awful lot of time because we basically played in what we stood up in. Stu went out, followed by John and myself.

"These lads started a fight with Stu after picking on him. We got to know about it because some people ran back to the side of the stage where we had come from and said, 'Stu's getting the living daylights knocked out of him.'

"So John and I dashed out. We threw a couple of punches, sorted things out and pulled Stu back in again. Then we turned to the lads and said, 'What the hell's going on? What the hell are you picking on him for? He hasn't done anything. We're only here to do a job, we're playing; so go away and behave yourselves.' And it was left at that.

"The fact that John and I had pitched in and got involved made these lads feel a certain amount of respect for us....as a result of the fight John broke a little finger. He still managed to play for a couple of gigs after that. He hadn't complained ...the next time we saw him he had a splint on it.

"When people talk of Stu being beaten up, I think it stems from this incident. But I don't remember Stu getting to the stage where he had his head kicked in, as some legends say, alleging that this caused his fatal brain haemorrhage.

"For as long as I was with the band I can only remember two incidents when fists were thrown and Stu was involved. The Lathom Hall incident aside, the other occasion was at the Top Ten Club, and that was between Paul and Stu. Paul took the mick out of Astrid and Stu lost his temper and took a swing at him."

Stuart was never injured during the Lathom Hall gig, but this is where another apocryphal Beatles story had its origins. In the book 'The Man Who Gave the Beatles Away', by Allan Williams and Bill Marshall, journalist Marshall admitted that he just took the bones of Williams' memories and elaborated on them, exaggerating the violence, swearing and sex.

In the book he writes: "It was on such a night that Stuart Sutcliffe received the injuries, which I believe hastened his death a couple of years later. Stuart was attacked outside Litherland Town Hall, where the Beatles played regularly, and was kicked in the head by a local thug. From then on he complained to me often of severe headaches."

This is hindsight presuming too much. According to Stuart's mother, who Stuart revealed everything to; his headaches only began following a fall in Hamburg.

Despite the fact that Allan's story was not corroborated (Did Stuart actual play at Litherland Town Hall with the group?), it was taken up and elaborated on by writers and began to take on a life of its own.

Even more bizarre is Albert Goldman's accusation in 'The Lives of John Lennon' that John was responsible for Stuart's death. "He had gotten into a quarrel with Stu at Hamburg…suddenly John was seized by one of his fits of uncontrollable rage. He lashed out with hands and feet…when he came to his senses he looked down and saw Stu lying on the pavement."

Goldman said that, as a result, John felt completely responsible for Stu's death. This is complete fiction, but of such stuff, myths are made.

One of Merseyside's most luxurious and comfortable venues at the time was the Downbeat Club in Victoria Street, owned by Jim Ireland who also ran the Mardi Gras. The club was licensed and membership was restricted to over 18s. It was open four nights each week: Wednesdays, Thursdays, Saturdays and Sundays, and between two and three groups were featured each night.

Len McMillan, who had been manager of the club since it first opened, told Mersey Beat: "At first we featured only jazz groups and bands, with a beat group now and then.

"Eventually when the beat boom started we switched over to solely beat groups."

Among jazz greats who appeared there were Johnny Dankworth, Ronnie Ross, Tubby Hayes, Kenny Baker and Bruce Turner, and the club also featured most of Merseyside's top groups, including the Swinging Bluejeans, the Remo Four and the Escorts.

The decor of the club was designed by Liverpool artist Bob Percival, who also painted the murals. Stage designer Sean Kelly, who designed the sets for the 'Maggie May' musical, was so impressed with the Downbeat's decor that he made sketches and took photographs for ideas for the beat club scenes in the musical.

The club, which accommodated about 350, was also the first in Liverpool to use ultra violet lights which spot-lit white clothes.

It was the only beat venue in Liverpool which was open during the entire afternoon, incidentally, for the sale of drinks and snacks to members.

Prices of admission to the club, which regularly featured such groups as Cy Tucker's Friars, Earl Preston's Realms and the Kinsleys, varied from 4s to 5s with guests paying 1s extra.

The Mersey Sound produced a fantastic crop of new clubs, but one of the most popular with Merseyside teenagers first opened its doors years earlier.

It was 28 September 1957 when the Mardi Gras in Mount Pleasant opened its doors to Merseyside teenagers, and in the years since a glittering array of top beat and jazz stars appeared there.

Club membership was confined to over 18s and the club's two floor premises held between 700-800 people – the dance floor alone accommodated 300. Open four nights a week – Tuesdays, Fridays, Saturday and Sundays –the club had two bars, one on each floor, and a snack bar on the second floor.

The club's dance floor and bars, with walls decorated with Beat City murals done by Liverpool artist Bob Percival, appeared on television and cinema screens all over the Continent.

Dutch Avro TV televised a programme and a film in the Look At Life series featured the Swinging Bluejeans at the Mardi Gras. Film cameras were again at the club when location shots were filmed for a Rank feature film.

On average 12 different groups a week played at the club, and famous personalities who visited the Mardi Gras while in Liverpool include Frank Sinatra Junior. Amongst the top line stars who appeared there were Kenny Ball, Johnny Dankworth and Muddy Waters – and the Count Basie band played an informal session there.

Owner of the Mardi Gras was Jim Ireland, who was also manager of the Swinging Bluejeans, the Escorts, Earl Preston's Realms, Cy Tucker's Friars and Billy Kinsley's the Nameless Ones. The club was also the headquarters for the Theatre and Philharmonic presentations of Roberts and Ireland, who brought such jazz stars as Louis Armstrong, Ella Fitzgerald, Miles Davis, Thelonius Monk and Dave Brubeck to Liverpool.

Roberts and Ireland also presented a rhythm and blues and gospel package show at the Philharmonic, which included Sonnie Terry and Brownie McGhee. Average charge for admission to the club for members varied from 2s 6d on Tuesday nights to 6s on Saturday nights, with guests paying 1s extra.

Also of note were the actual ballrooms such as the Rialto, Locarno, Grafton, Orrell Park Ballroom, the Plaza and Majestic.

In the case of the Majestic, it was situated in Conway Street, Birkenhead. When it opened in 1962 it was a 'luxury venue' compared to some of the cellar clubs and local halls the Mersey groups had been appearing in. It was one of 28 ballrooms around Britain run by the Top Rank organisation.

When the Beatles made their debut there on Thursday, 29 June 1962 it was their first ever appearance at a Top Rank venue. The Majestic rapidly became one of the top Merseyside venues, open throughout the week and presenting several groups each evening – for instance, the Saturday, 15 December 1962 bill comprised the Beatles, the Fourmost and Jenny & the Tall Boys.

The venue was managed by Bill Marsden and his office became a meeting place for various members of the Mersey scene who would gather in Bill's office for a drink to chat about the business. This group generally comprised Brian Epstein, Virginia and I, Joe Flannery and Ted Knibbs. During one of the evenings Flannery tried a joke by putting a call to the office and claiming it was Colonel Tom Parker trying to contact Brian Epstein.

The Beatles complete appearances for 1962 were: 29 June, 3 July, 12 July, 28 July, 17 August, 24 August, 8 September, 28 September, 15 October, 22 November, 29 November, 15 December. The 1963 appearances were: 17 January, 31 January, 21 February and 10 April.

On their 17 August 1962 appearance their drummer was Johnny Hutchinson. Following their 15 December 1962 show there was a special 'Mersey Beat Awards Party' at which I presented them with their very first award, the Mersey Beat shield for being voted No. 1 group on Merseyside in the Mersey Beat poll. The Top 20 groups in the first–ever Mersey Beat Poll were:

1. The Beatles
2. Gerry & the Pacemakers
3. The Remo Four
4. Rory Storm & the Hurricanes
5. Johnny Sandon & the Searchers
6. Kingsize Taylor & the Dominoes
7. The Big Three
8. The Strangers
9. Faron & the Flamingos
10. The Four Jays
11. Ian & the Zodiacs
12. The Undertakers
13. Earl Preston & the TTs
14. Mark Peters & the Cyclones
15. Karl Terry & the Cruisers
16. Derry & the Seniors
17. Steve & the Syndicate
18. Dee Fenton & the Silhouettes
19. Billy Kramer & the Coasters
20. Dale Roberts & the Jaywalkers

The second Mersey Beat Poll Awards at the Majestic took place on 15 December 1962. Agents, promoters, musicians and various local personalities were crammed into the ballroom for the event and the top ten groups from the poll played one number each.

Unfortunately, this meant that the bands weren't given an opportunity to check their instruments and Christ Huston of the Undertakers found that the strings on his guitar had been de-tuned and he had to mime his way through the number.

In addition to the groups in the Top Ten, other artists appearing included Alby & the Sorrals, Steve Day & the Drifters, the Blue Mountain Boys and the Shades, plus other entertainers such as Mike Coyne, Tony Kennedy and Pat Delaney.

Pat was, of course, the famed Cavern doorman who also delivered our copies of Mersey Beat. He performed Al Jolson numbers in minstrel make-up. Virginia and I, when we originally heard that Pat was an Al Jolson fan, arranged for him to perform as Jolson before 2,000 people at the Gaumont (formerly the Trocadero where Julia Lennon had been an usherette) Camden Street which was due to screen a reissue of The Jolson Story. Pat was initially nervous and was actually physically sick before the show – but when he went on stage he gave a great performance to an enthusiastic audience.

The show was compered by Bob Wooler, who was presented with 'The GB Entertainments Award for An Outstanding Contribution To the Local Entertainment Scene' by Alan Watts, manager of Freddie Starr & the Midnighters. I was also presented with a special award by Joe Flannery, manager of Lee Curtis & the All Stars.

Apart from the awards to the Top Ten groups, there were various other awards. Brian Epstein presented a 'Nems Enterprises Award' to Billy Kramer & the Coasters for being 'The Top Non-Professional Group' and Bob Wooler presented an award each to The Blue Mountain Boys and Johnny Sandon in recognition of their services to the local Country Music scene. And it was Virginia who had suggested a special award for Beryl Marsden as 'The Most Outstanding Female Artist of the Year'.

For the Beatles' 17 January 1963 appearance all tickets had been sold out in advance and 500 angry fans queuing outside were unable to see the show as the hall only had a 900-capacity and was already full. As a result, for the Beatles' next appearance, there was an innovation: two separate performances. Although it was common to have two performances at a theatre concert, it had never been done before in a ballroom.

In 1964 a new manager, John Glass, took over the running of the ballroom and he received a telegram from the Beatles for the second anniversary which congratulated the Majestic on "its bi-centenary, or something."

Personally, my favourite Liverpool club was the Blue Angel.

I remember sitting with Allan Ginsberg who described his excitement at being in Liverpool. The combination of its energy and the personality of its people inspired him. The club was swarming with members and visitors. Apart from Liverpool artists such as the Beatles and Gerry & the Pacemakers, there were representatives of the media, ranging from the Saturday Evening Post to Man About Town, a TV team, a German film crew and leading journalists such as Nancy Spain, George Melly and Derek Taylor. No wonder Ginsberg was to say: "Liverpool is at the present time the centre of the consciousness of the human universe."

The club, affectionately known as 'The Blue', was the after-hours watering hole of us all during the heyday of the Mersey scene.

Situated next to an antiquarian bookshop at the top of Seel Street, near the city centre, it had previously been operating as the Wyvern Social Club. Allan Williams, who ran the nearby Jacaranda club in Slater Street, took over the premises in 1960.

I'd been spending a lot of time at the Jacaranda, along with John Lennon, Stuart Sutcliffe, Paul McCartney, George Harrison and Pete Best, who were playing some gigs in the coffee bar basement.

Allan had co-presented a rock 'n' roll concert at the Liverpool Stadium with Larry Parnes. Gene Vincent topped the bill and several local acts had supported. Parnes was impressed with the groups and mentioned to Allan that he was looking for a backing band for Billy Fury. Auditions, organised by Allan, were set up at the Wyvern.

On 10 May 1960, the groups who auditioned were Cass & the Cassanovas, Derry & the Seniors, Gerry & the Pacemakers, Cliff Roberts & the Rockers. The Silver Beetles (whose drummer at the time was Tommy Moore) were a last minute addition to the occasion due to Stuart Sutcliffe asking Allen to give them a chance.

When it was time for the Silver Beetles to play, their drummer hadn't turned up, so Johnny Hutchinson sat in with them for the first few numbers. Moore then arrived and took over.

The Silver Beetles appealed to Fury, but Parnes told him the drummer wasn't suitable. Not only had he turned up late but he was dressed differently from the other group members and was at least ten years older than them. However, Parnes booked them on a short tour of Scotland backing Johnny Gentle.

He also booked Howie Casey & the Seniors to back another of his acts, but it was cancelled at the last minute. As Casey and his band had given up their day jobs to appear on the tour, Howie and singer Derry Wilkie turned up at the club to give Williams a serious talking to.

But Allan was always able to talk himself out of a hole and persuaded them that he would drive the group down to the 2i's Club in London. They were able to perform at the 2i's where they were spotted by German club owner Bruno Koshmider. As a result they became the first Liverpool band to be booked into Hamburg.

Williams' dream was to operate a sophisticated night club. He'd visited the Blue Angel club in London and decided to adopt the title, decorating the main stairway with a huge blow-up of Marlene Dietrich from 'The Blue Angel' film. The Blue opened on 22 March 1961 with cabaret artist Alma Warren, backed by the Terry Francis Quartet.

The club achieved a degree of media attention because Allan granted membership to his friends at the Press Club, in particular to Bill Marshall the local rep for the Daily Mirror newspaper. Press stories included the tale of the female snake charmer who lost her snake at the club – and the real bullfighting sessions which took place with a baby bull. The Beatles and ourselves weren't initially granted membership as Allan didn't want elements of the local music scene around – he was trying to build an affluent and sophisticated clientele.

However, the club didn't succeed as a cabaret venue (unlike the Cabaret Club in Duke Street) and Allan dropped his veto on the Beatles and other groups. By that time Virginia and I had launched Mersey Beat and the local rock 'n' roll scene was now attracting attention.

For the next few years the Blue became one of the most interesting clubs in the world. Initially the place was crowded with members of groups who'd arrive shortly before midnight after finishing gigs around the city. Other showbiz personalities such as Tommy Steele, the Bachelors and Bruce Forsyth dropped by when they were in Liverpool.

Playwright Alun Owen told us he regularly visited Liverpool from his home in Wales to recharge his batteries. He had an 'ear' for dialogue and used to carry a notebook to jot down the phrases he heard, examples of the famous Scouse wit.

Virginia had heard Pat Davies, Ringo Starr's girlfriend and Cilla Black's mate, utter the words "Who knitted your face and dropped a stitch?" Virginia told Alun and he used it in his stage musical Maggie May.

In fact, the Blue was the setting for the after-show party when 'Maggie May' made its debut in Manchester. We all drove back to Liverpool and poured into the Blue. On the ground floor there was a grand piano, with fruit machines on either side.

I was playing one of the machines with Judy Garland and she told me she'd like to sing – could I find someone to play the piano?

No problem, I thought, with a club full of musicians – but no one would volunteer (despite 'Over The Rainbow' being one of the songs in several Mersey group repertoires), so we missed the golden opportunity of a special performance from Judy. As the night progressed Allan had an argument with the legendary singer and told her to leave the club and never darken its doors again! He even ran after her car and kicked it!

I'd become friendly with the Rolling Stones soon after the Beatles had visited them in Richmond and when I heard they were playing in Southport, phoned their hotel, told Mick I was in the Blue and invited them down. They drove over from Southport in their van, with their equipment, and got up on stage and gave us a show.

The Blue was a compact club, entered through a large copper-coloured door, guarded by a bouncer. The ground floor had a grand piano, various fruit machines and a corner bar, with a door leading onto a patio. The basement featured a larger bar, a stage and a passage leading to the Gent's toilet. The first floor sported two rooms, one with a large statue of a nude woman, the other with Sans Souci, a casino run by Barry Chang, Allan's brother-in-law. The second floor harboured the Ladies room and an office. Live entertainment was provided by resident bands and there were regular jam sessions.

John Lennon and I usually drank in the downstairs bar. At one time I asked him if he had a song he could give to Beryl Marsden, a 15-

year-old singer who was Liverpool's equivalent of Brenda Lee. He said he had one in mind, 'Love Of The Loved.' Next time I asked him about it he was apologetic: Brian Epstein had told him that as manager he would decide who would be given the Lennon & McCartney songs and he wanted to use them for his own stable of acts.

There were various resident bands who played at the Blue, including the Escorts (at the time Ringo Starr's cousin was in the band and it was Ringo who arranged their residency) and the Nocturnes. Alun Owen liked the Nocturnes and they were hired to appear as the Beat group in the stage musical Maggie May. Another friend of ours, Geoff Hughes, who worked as a salesman in the car showroom next to the Mersey Beat office, also managed to get a part in Maggie May.

Another of the resident bands were the Masterminds, who were signed up by Stones manager Andrew Loog Oldham following the night I'd got them to back Cilla.

Each night there were up to thirty members of the various local groups down at the Blue. There were always lots of girls. I remember Rory Storm and Ringo Starr with two girls, who looked like twins with their jet black fringed hair – Ringo was to marry one of them, Maureen Cox. John Lennon was also going out with another girl, Ida Holly, while he kept his marriage to Cynthia a secret. Cilla and her mate Pat Davies were regulars, as was Marie Gurion, who later married Justin Hayward of the Moody Blues.

Apart from the Beatles, regulars included the Bluejeans, the Hurricanes, Freddie Starr, Billy Kramer, Mark Peters, the Dennisons, the Chants, the Big Three, the Undertakers, the Searchers, Derry Wilkie, Howie Casey, the Mojos and Faron's Flamingos.

By the end of the 1960s the Angel was closed, but it was reopened as a drinking club under various names. In recent years the club re-adopted the name the Blue Angel and plays hosts to guests at the annual Mersey Beatle conventions.

Groups would also play in coffee bars, the most famous of which was the Jacaranda, originally opened by Allan Williams in September 1958 and situated at 23 Slater Street, Liverpool L1.

At the time coffee bars were very fashionable and this particular area of Liverpool was honeycombed with them. Quite close to the 'Jac' was a coffee bar called the Studio, frequented by the models and students from Liverpool College of Art; local painter Yankel Feather ran the Basement, directly to the rear of Mount Pleasant Register Office where John and Cynthia were married; 50 yards from the Jac, in Duke Street, were the Zodiac, the Kinkajoo and Boomerang Coffee Bars; in Mount Pleasant was Streates, where poetry readings were held – and there were many more.

Allan saw an advertisement in the Liverpool Echo which read "suitable premises for a club" and went to Slater Street. The premises to let were formerly occupied by Owens Watch Repair Shop and the lease was owned by a man in the sweetshop next door who demanded an extra £150 for 'goodwill and fittings.'

Allan raised the money and managed to engage a group of West Indians to play in a steel band by offering them ten shillings (fifty pence) each. They were called Lord Woodbine and His All-Steel Caribbean Band. Steel bands were scarce in Britain at the time and they proved to be a popular attraction at the club.

Shortly before opening the club, Allan had been trying to think of a suitable name. He eventually decided he'd call it the Samurai, because he'd recently seen the film 'Seven Samurai', when a friend, Bill Coward, who'd just read a book called 'The Jacaranda Tree', suggested Jacaranda.

The clientele was mixed – solicitors, doctors, art students, musicians – and two of the girls who served there as waitresses, Mary Larkin and Terry Sharrock, found themselves on the cover of the first issue of Mersey Beat after their photograph had been taken with the rock 'n' roll star Gene Vincent.

The ground floor had a large glass window looking out onto Slater Street and there were small padded benches and coffee tables, a tiny kitchen, an outside loo for Gents and steps leading to the tiny basement where the steel band played and steps leading upstairs to the Ladies loo.

Among the art students who went there were John Lennon, Stuart Sutcliffe, Rod Murray, Rod Jones and myself while among the musicians were Paul McCartney and George Harrison, Gerry Marsden, Casey Jones, Adrian Barber, Rory Storm and Johnny Guitar.

At one time Allan asked Stuart to paint some murals, which he did, together with Rod Murray.

Stuart and Rod had already painted a mural on the walls of Ye Cracke pub in Rice Street – a dock scene with cranes, and also a wall at the Territorial Army rooms in Norris Green. They received a little help from Rod Jones. Rod Murray tells me that they didn't receive any money, but Allan gave them a bottle of Vodka.

Years later, when the murals were rediscovered during a refitting of the premises, Allan Williams claimed that they were painted by John Lennon and Stu, but this wasn't so. John and I watched them painting but didn't participate.

When Lord Woodbine left the steel band to open a club of his own, the remaining quartet, Everett, Otto, Bones and Slim began to call themselves the Royal Caribbean Steel Band. Williams was to comment: "The boys were so black and the Jac basement dance floor so dark, that you couldn't see them until they smiled."

One night Williams arrived at the club to discover that his star attraction hadn't turned up. They'd gone to Hamburg!

The steel band had Monday evenings off, so Williams urgently needed a band to fill the vacuum and he decided to book John's group for the Monday evening spot. At the time they were still trying to decide on a name. Casey Jones, a regular at the club, suggested they call themselves Long John and the Silver Men! John and Stuart in particular were regulars at the club and Alan was able to book them for a series of appearances, for a relatively low fee.

The group, we'll call them the Silver Beatles for the moment, made about a dozen appearances between May and August 1960. They were crammed into a corner of the stone-floored basement as there wasn't any room for equipment; their girlfriends had to sit opposite them on chairs holding broom handles to which the microphones were attached.

Their first appearance at the Jac took place on Monday, 30 May while on Monday, 13 June drummer Tommy Moore appeared with them for the last time. It was during that period that they backed poet Royston Ellis to a 'poetry to rock 'n' roll' session.

In later years the club was turned into a late night drinking club called the Maxie San Suzie then, following the death of John Lennon and the subsequent resurge of interest in the Beatles, it reverted back to its original name, with a flamboyant giant placard above the club premises which featured a painting of the group in their Sgt Pepper personae and the words 'The place the fab four first played' which is, of course, inaccurate. It has since received further refurbishments, both inside and out.

John, Rod, Stuart and I would often take time off from the college to sit for hours in the Jac, mainly by the glass window. I remember it was 4d for toast and 5d with jam on it. Next door to the Jac was the Marlborough pub where we sometimes dropped in if we could afford a beer. Since the coffee bar didn't have a drinks license, Bob Wooler, who always carried a hip flash of whiskey, used to go to the toilet to have a nip!

The Jac was where I first commissioned John to write a piece about the Beatles for Mersey Beat and was where I saw Stuart for the last time. He'd come over from Hamburg with Astrid and introduced me to her. They were both dressed in black which contrasted with their extremely pale pallor.

The Jacaranda is now a popular bar (drinks are served, unlike the non-alcoholic original) and occasionally presents groups and karaoke nights. Of course, the venue has been extended and extensively refurbished over the years and bears no resemblance to the actual coffee bar as it existed in the days when we hung around there. Publicity still makes out that John and Stu painted the murals there, which is untrue.

The final mention of a venue goes to the Royal Iris. This was the famous Mersey ferry which presented regular dances on board each week as it sailed up the River Mersey from the Pier Head.

Independent promoters also ran events aboard and Ray McFall, owner of the Cavern, rented the vessel for a series of 'Riverboat Shuffles.' The Beatles were to appear on four of them.

Before being taken out of service in the late Eighties, the Royal Iris sailed to London and held some special cruises down the Thames with entertainment provided by several original exponents of the Mersey Sound such as Faron's Flamingos.

Apart from venues already mentioned and excluding all the social clubs and Christian venues, here are just some of the other places on Merseyside which provided regular work for groups, which led to the birth of more than 500 local outfits in the Merseyside area:

St John's Hall, Tuebrook; Blair Hall, Walton; Village Hall, Knotty

Ash; Merseyside Civil Service Club; Heswall Jazz Club, Quaintway's Chester; Kingsway, Southport; YMCA, Birkenhead; Odd Spot Club, Bold Street; Plaza, St Helens; Majestic Ballroom, Birkenhead; Grafton Ballroom; Locarno Ballroom; Riverpark Ballroom, Chester; Rialto Ballroom; Floral Hall, Southport; Town Hall, Newton-Le-Willows; Club Django, Southport; Royalty Theatre, Chester; Civic Hall, Ellesmere Port; YMCA, Hoylake; Odeon Cinema; Pavilion Theatre; St Barnabus Hall; Allerton Synagogue; the Morgue; Childwall Labour Club; Alexandra Hall, Crosby; Winter Gardens Ballroom, Garston; Gateacre Labour Club; Lathom Hall; Orrell Park Ballroom; The Black Cat Club; the Peppermint Lounge, London Road; Bootle Town Hall; the Empress Club, New Brighton; the Grosvenor Ballroom, Wallasey; La Mystere, Magull; La Scala, Runcorn; the Merrifield, Old Swan, Neston Institute, Town Hall, Skelmersdale, Valentine Rock Club, Dale Street; the Kon Tiki Club, Wood Street; the Witches Cauldron; the Cubik Club; the Kraal Club; the Phoenix, Mount Pleasant; the Scorpion Club; Heaven & Hell, the Pink Parrot, the Mandolin Club; the New Shakespeare Club; the Beat Route Club, Crawford Avenue; Burton Chambers, Walton Road; Carr Mill, St Helens; West Derby Village Hall; the Black Cat Club, the Peppermint Lounge; the Glenpark Club, Southport; the Colony Club; Cambridge Hall, Southport; Casanova Club; Embassy Club, Wallasey; Greenbank Drive Synagogue; Hulme Hall, Port Sunlight; Lowlands; Macdonna Hall, West Kirby; Merseyview, Frodsham; Queens Hall, Widnes; Wavertree Town Hall; the Lantern, Aigburth Road; the Basement, Mount Pleasant; the Black Rose, South Castle Street; La Locanda, Duke Street; the Masque, Clarence Street; the Scorpion, Duke Street; the Mambo Club; the Starline Club; the Mandrake Club; Columba Hall, Widnes; Ivormar Club, Skelmersdale; the Beat Route Club, Crawford Avenue; Empress Club, New Brighton; Top Hat Club, Lockerby Road; Blue Penguin Club, Bootle, the Cazzie, Aigburth; the Marine Club, Southport; Club 21 New Brighton, Maggie May's, Seel Street; Witch's Cauldron, New Brighton, Heaven & Hell, Warrington, Civic Hall, Ellesmere Port, St Barnabus Hall; Driftwood Club, Ainsdale and many others.

4. The North South Divide

ONE of the reasons I decided to launch Mersey Beat was because there had been no acknowledgement in the media of the burgeoning music scene on Merseyside.

When I began to realise how extensive the scene was – and the fact that no one, even on Merseyside, seemed to realise it, I decided to do something about it.

I'd already gained a hint of the musical landscape on Merseyside helping to produce a magazine for Frank Hesselburg of Frank Hessy's music store, but I didn't realise initially just how big it was. Groups in different areas of Merseyside knew of promoters in their area, but weren't aware of the extent of the scene, the number of promoters or the wide range of venues.

Prior to publishing Mersey Beat I began to take notes and realised the uniqueness of the Mersey music scene even more. When I compared my information with Bob Wooler and published a list of almost 300 groups in the paper, the scene began to go overground and the publication became a catalyst.

My feeling that the Mersey scene was unique was confirmed by my visits to London at the time.

The repertoires of the Mersey musicians were numbers from the cream of American rock 'n' roll and R&B artists while generally, in the rest of the country, the music of Cliff Richard & the Shadows and the current artists in the British charts held sway. An example of the artists in the charts in 1962, for instance, indicates this.

On the other hand, Mersey groups were inspired by American artists such as Chuck Berry, Carl Perkins, the Drifters, Larry Williams, the

Coasters, the Crystals, Fats Domino, Betty Everett, Marvin Gaye, Jerry Lee Lewis, Little Anthony & The Imperials, Sam the Sham & the Pharoahs, Arthur Alexander, Joe Turner, the Isley Brothers and other rock and R&B artists.

In fact, the music of the Mersey groups was to revive the popularity of American rock artists such as Berry, Perkins and Lewis to such an extent that they all toured Britain – and Berry paid tribute by composing an instrumental, 'Liverpool Drive.'

Also, Bill Haley, when he arrived in Liverpool revealed to Mersey Beat that he'd just recorded a song called 'Liverpool' in Mexico, which is a tribute to the Mersey Sound and which he described as a 'semi-rock instrumental.'

(Incidentally, over the years there have been several mentions of Liverpool in American songs, including, 'Long Haired Lover From Liverpool' by Little Jimmy Osmond; 'In Liverpool' by Suzanne Vega and 'Going Down To Liverpool' by the Bangles).

The Animals were actually discovered appearing in the Cavern. Former Star Club manager Henry Henroid spotted them there and contacted recording manager Mickie Most. The Hollies, Freddie & the Dreamers, Herman's Hermits, Dave Berry & the Cruisers and Wayne Fontana & the Mindbenders were all Cavern regulars and each of them became major hit artists.

In fact, Freddie & the Dreamers heard the Beatles performing the James Ray number 'If You Gotta Make A Fool Of Somebody' at the Cavern, recorded it, and it became their very first hit, reaching No. 3 in the British charts.

Despite the euphoria and spectacular impact of the Beatles, the London media, while having no choice but to cover their amazing success, were harbouring hopes that a London band would appear as the saviour of the South and overshadow the Fab Four.

They believed their opportunity came with the success of the Dave Clark Five. Suddenly there were national newspaper headlines to the effect "The Tottenham Sound has Crushed The Beatles" and cartoons began to appear in papers such as the London Evening Standard portraying the Beatles as has-beens.

The campaign didn't work out, the Beatles held sway, although in fact, the Dave Clark Five became even more popular in the States than in Britain, becoming second only to the Beatles in US style fan fervour.

Ironically, the Dave Clark Five had their breakthrough in Britain by copying Faron's Flamingos version of 'Do You Love Me' and were promoted in America as 'the Liverpool group with the Mersey Sound.'

The Motown Museum in Detroit even has a photograph of the Dave Clark Five with the Supremes captioned 'Liverpool Meets Detroit.'

Bern Elliott & the Fenmen rushed back to London after hearing the Searchers perform 'Money' at Hamburg's Star Club and recorded the number, entering the charts with it. A&R men had refused to record Mersey groups performing the song.

The North-South divide in Britain is not so obvious today as it was in the days of the Mersey Sound. There was a definite and strong feeling in the north that Southerners had all the benefits and maintained control of the country.

Some Southerners regarded Northerners as people who wore clogs and lived in slum properties. There was also a hint of antagonism in the relationship between the two areas of Britain.

It was a major feat for any artist from the provinces to make a name in the music industry unless they decamped to London and were taken over by London-based managers or agents. Liverpool artists such as Billy Fury and Johnny Gentle, for instance, were 'controlled' by impresario Larry Parnes.

In those days there were no motorways and it was an eight-hour journey from Liverpool to London - and a major trek from Glasgow or Newcastle. With Mersey Beat I tried to capture London's attention with editorials such as 'London - Take A Look Up North!'

When the Beatles turned the British music industry upside down, they created a gap in the London power base through which a host of artists from the provinces passed through - from Sheffield, Birmingham, Newcastle and Manchester. Then London closed the gap once again.

Manchester group the Dakotas, who Brian Epstein engaged to back Billy J. Kramer, told me: "Liverpool is the biggest area for rock. The crowds are more appreciative, they respond and produce an infectious atmosphere which, we have found, has helped us to play better.

"If a group is bad, the audience will let them know it – which is a good thing. They find that they HAVE to improve.

"In Manchester and in other parts of the country, the audience seem only interested in top twenty numbers. Produce a carbon copy of a top twenty number and the crowd is satisfied. Yet, on Merseyside, a group can play in their own individual style whatever numbers they are interested in – and the audience will judge them on their own merit."

The Grades were the most powerful show-business family Britain has ever known.

Lou Grade had his power base in television with ATV, his brother Bernard Delfont not only ran the Moss Empires theatre chain, but Sunday Night At The London Palladium the premier television entertainment show and also The Royal Variety Show, whilst their other association with the Harold Davidson empire controlled the agency and management contracts of the majority of star names in film, television and record.

It was a case of having the power to make or break a name. In addition, the national press was based in London, as was the entire musical press (until Mersey Beat came along), together with all the record companies, music publishing companies, the BBC radio and television, offices of Radio Luxembourg and so on. It was not unnatural for the London press to want to see the Northern upstarts fade away and they quickly sought a London-based replacement.

Initially it was the Dave Clark Five. When 'Glad All Over' hit the No.1 spot there was media saturation.

Then, of course, it was the Rolling Stones - who, ironically, got their recording break via the Beatles. I was looking through an old issue of the Star Club News, published in August 1965. I contributed a column each issue free of charge in exchange for Manfred Weissleder providing me with colour transparencies of the Beatles performing at the Star Club.

The item read: "Three Mersey outfits failed to get singles into the charts because they couldn't get any major television promotion."

The Big Three recorded 'Bring It On Home To Me', Chick Graham & the Coasters recorded 'A Little You' and the Escorts recorded 'I Don't Want To Go On Without You'. Some months later the Animals, Freddie & the Dreamers and the Moody Blues had hits with the same numbers. Although those groups came from Newcastle, Manchester and Birmingham, as far as the media were concerned, they didn't come from Liverpool.

It reminded me of the suspicion I had at the time. There may well have been an understanding between London A&R men and the capital's media to undermine the impact of Mersey groups in favour of returning London to the forefront of the music business.

Certainly, talented Liverpool groups did find it difficult to receive any promotion once the initial euphoria surrounding the Beatles and Brian Epstein's stable of acts had settled.

London was the centre of the music business and there was a degree of resentment about the attention which had been given to the Mersey music scene. I know of a Liverpool manager of a stable of acts who was paid a large sum by a London agent for his acts - who were then virtually never heard of again. I had the feeling that the Liverpool scene had not been allowed to flourish as it should.

The talent remained in Liverpool, but it was simply condemned to isolation once more when London regained control of the music business. Yet whenever recording managers did take an interest in Liverpool, they always found it overflowing with talent. I continued to feel that Liverpool acts from the Mersey era could have continued to spin out hits for the rest of the decade, but they were literally sabotaged.

Let us look at a few examples.

Lee Curtis was signed to Decca and recorded 'Let's Stomp', the Bobby Comstock number that was popular with the group's fans. Yet the Decca A&R man sabotaged the number by forcing Lee to repeat the words 'Let's Stomp' a total of 36 times, which Lee felt ruined the recording and stripped it of any commercial impact. He was right; you only have to listen to the number to realize that a potential hit was rendered ridiculous by the endless repetition of the two words.

Lee then wanted to record 'Twist and Shout', but Decca refused, and later the same company made sure Brian Poole & the Tremeloes released the number and they topped the charts with it. Lee's group asked if they could record 'Money', but Decca refused to let Lee record it and later released the number by another of their Southern acts, Bern Elliot & the Fenmen.

Curtis then asked Decca if he could record 'Shout'. Decca refused and later released a single of 'Shout' with Lulu & the Luvvers, which established Lulu's career. Lee next requested that he be allowed to record 'It's Only Make Believe', but Decca once again refused and later released a version by Billy Fury, which charted.

No wonder Lee got fed up of Britain and settled in Germany for a time, recording several albums and singles there.

The Undertakers had similar problems when they signed with Pye and Tony Hatch was appointed their A&R manager. They wanted 'Mashed Potatoes' to be the 'A' side of their debut disc, but Pye refused and put it on the 'B' side, when it was obviously a stronger number than 'Everybody Loves A Lover'. They next wanted to record 'Money', but Pye refused and made them record 'What About Us?'

As mentioned, Southern group Bern Elliot & the Fenmen then recorded 'Money' and earned themselves a Top 20 hit.

Finally, Tony Hatch allowed the Undertakers to pick their own 'A' side, but only after Pye had forced them to truncate their name to the 'Takers. They recorded 'If You Don't Come Back' which began to sell in quantities enough to edge them towards the charts - but it was issued around the holiday period for the record plant, and production of the record ceased, making it impossible for them to have a chart hit.

I was amazed at some of the decisions taken by A&R men.

Liverpool was the largest market for Tamla Motown records in the early 1960s and Mersey groups adapted Motown numbers to their own style in what we called 'the Mersey Motown Sound.'

Virginia and I attended the recording session in London when Faron's Flamingos recorded a blistering version of 'Do You Love Me', which they'd arranged and adapted from the Contours, a Motown vocal act. When the tapes were played back, everyone was convinced that Faron's Flamingos would have a major chart hit and be on their way to establishing themselves nationally. Imagine the group's dismay when the record company put it on the 'B' side to a number called 'See If She Cares' and Faron's 'Do You Love Me' never got an airing.

Then Brian Poole & the Tremeloes and the Dave Clark Five recorded it, with the Tremeloes topping the charts and Dave Clark entering the Top Ten for the first time. Anyone listening to the versions can tell that they are basically copies of the Faron's Flamingos record and are quite unlike the original Contours version.

The Flamingos were so devastated that they disbanded.

Columnist Alan Smith stepped into the 'Do You Love Me' controversy in Mersey Beat: He mentioned that people had commented that Brian and his group were copying the Beatles 'Twist And Shout' and Faron's 'Do You Love Me.'

He writes, "Personally, I'm with the anti-Tremeloe brigade – even more so since speaking to Brian Poole recently. He quite candidly admits that his version of 'Twist and Shout' was influenced by the Beatles.

"'It's obvious', he says. 'You've only got to hear both versions to notice the similarity.'

"I pointed out that at one time he seemed to model himself on Buddy Holly, even down to the heavy, horn-rimmed glasses. 'That's right', was his comment, 'but we stopped that because everybody likes the big beat now.

"'Our policy is this: as musical trends change, we'll change.'

"Notice that he makes no mention of the Tremeloes trying to develop their own distinctive sound. The way I see it, he's admitting that he's ready to jump on whatever bandwagon comes along!"

Everyone agrees that the Big Three were one of Liverpool's greatest groups - but even their debut disc was sabotaged.

As detailed on 'The Big Three Story' elsewhere in the book, Decca refused to allow them to record 'Some Other Guy' at a proper recording session and issued a substandard version from a test recording.

There are numerous other examples of such treatment Liverpool groups received at the hands of London recording companies but what no-one can take away from Liverpool is the amazing chart record of 1963 when Liverpool acts held the No.1 spot in the British charts for 36 weeks.

Despite success of the Beatles and other bands, I wrote in the July 1964 issue: "London R&B groups receive more publicity than groups from Liverpool, Newcastle, Birmingham and most other parts of the country put together, in all other musical papers apart from Mersey Beat." This was obvious, wasn't it? London wanted to re-establish its status as the music capital.

In September 1963, Alan Smith, the Merseyside writer working for the New Musical Express in London, who also wrote a column for

Mersey Beat under the pseudonym George Jones, wrote: "Liverpool still has a good name around the disc and TV studios, thanks to the Beatles, Gerry & the Pacemakers, Billy J. Kramer and the Searchers. But time is running out.

"In all honesty I don't think it will be very long before the whole Liverpool bubble bursts. In some cases I can see that coming from the city will actually come to be a drawback.

"Don't take it that I agree with this situation – I'm just stating facts. The tide originally began to turn some time before June, when radio and TV producers started to complain about the seemingly-endless supply of Liverpool groups.

"One told me: 'They may have talent, but it doesn't help me when I have to prepare a balanced programme. I can't feature Merseyside acts all the time. It's getting to be like the old days - every time some-one held a talent contest; they were snowed under by skifflers.'

"Don't underestimate comments like these. They come from influential men in broadcasting, people who can have a marked effect on the tastes of the listening public.

"As time goes by I think we'll be left with a 'stable' of stars, including the Beatles, Gerry & the Pacemakers, Billy J. Kramer, the Searchers and a few others. But I think they'll lose the 'Liverpool' tag sooner or later, just as Billy Fury has done."

Several groups did realise that they would have to move to London to have any chance of success. They included the Kubas (aka Koobas), the Trends, Lee Castle & the Barons, the Nashpool Four, Paddy Klaus & Gibson and Beryl Marsden.

The fact that Mersey groups decamped to London upset a lot of people in Liverpool who felt that the Beatles and other groups had deserted them. Frankly, I don't think they had much choice, but arguably I also felt that Epstein could have used his influence to make Merseyside another music centre by encouraging record companies and music publishers to set up Northern offices in the area.

In Issue 55 I featured a story on the Escorts with the caption 'We'll Never Leave Liverpool', while a story on the same page about the Nashpool Four is headed 'Liverpool Group for London.'

An indication of this 'Deserting Liverpool' controversy was also found in Alan Smith's Mersey Beat column where he points out that there was near-hatred for Billy Fury in Liverpool: "I know it exists. I've heard the snide comments about his success and listened to yobbos who would like to beat him up", he writes. Alan says that, "One of the accusations often pointed at Billy is that he keeps his Liverpool background quiet, as if he were ashamed of Merseyside. This is far from the truth when you remember that just about every Fury fan in the country knows he once worked as a tug-boat hand on the river, and that he still regards Liverpool as home."

He says that there is something of a similar mistaken attitude growing among the Beatles' Liverpool fans. He mentioned this to John Lennon, who said: "The Liverpool fans made us, and I'll never forget it. We can't bear to do a bad show when we come home, because the audiences here are our biggest critics. They've seen us develop over the years. They know when we're bad."

In Mersey Beat I had a section called Mersey Beatles and in issue No.57 I ran the story: 'Big 'Beatles' Controversy' on the Mersey Beatles page.

This was filled with letters from readers following complaints on letters in the previous issue commenting on the lack of appearances by the Beatles in Liverpool, saying: "They are not our Beatles any longer." This resulted in a flood of letters fully supporting the lads, a number of which I used on this page.

One letter from Linda and Gloria in Birkenhead ends: "Unlike other stars they haven't moved to London, and we're quite sure they won't."

5. The Poetry of the Mersey Sound

IN the cultural landscape of the Sixties in Britain, just as the Beatles dominated the music scene, the Cavern dominated the club scene and the Spinners dominated the folk scene, so the Mersey Poets dominated the poetry scene.

It's appropriate that the biggest-selling poetry book of the Sixties was 'The Mersey Sound' by Adrian Henri, Roger McGough and Brian Patten.

Because I was interested in poetry myself, when John Lennon and I were sitting together in Ye Cracke in Rice Street one day I mentioned that I'd heard he'd written some poetry and asked if I could see some.

He demurred at first, I think he felt that being a poet didn't go with his macho image, but I managed to persuade him.

He had some pieces of paper in his pocket and showed me a piece he'd written. There was no title to it as I recall, but it read:

Owl George ee be a farmer's lad
With mucklekak and cow
Ee be the son of 'is owl Dad
But why I don't know how

Ee take a fork and bale the hay
And stacking-stook he stock
And lived his loif from day to day
Dressed in a sweaty sock

One day maybe he marry be
To Nellie Nack the Lass

And we shall see what we shall see
A-fucking in the grass

Our Nellie be a gal so fine
All dimpled wart and blue
She herds the pigs, the rotten swine
It mak me wanna spew!

Somehaps perchance ee'll be a man
But now I will unfurl
Owl George is out of the frying pan
'Cos ee's a little girl.

Our dual interest in poetry then began to be shared with our two other art school chums, Stuart Sutcliffe and Rod Murray and we obtained some books by the American beat poets, published by the City Lights bookshop in San Francisco. I noted that John was amused by a poem about the crucifixion, written by Lawrence Ferlenghetti. I particularly liked Allan Ginsberg's 'Howl' and used to walk the streets of Liverpool 8 reading it out loud.

We also frequently dropped into the Student's bar at Liverpool University as the Art College took part in the annual 'Panto Days' at the time. In fact, I was asked to assist in the production of Pantosphinx, the magazine which was produced to tie in with the charity event.

As a result we became friendly with a group of University students and used to drink with them in the Marlborough, next to the Jacaranda in Slater Street. I'd met Virginia at the Jac in March 1960. The Royal Caribbean Steel Band, who used to play in the basement, had absconded for Hamburg and Allan Williams, the bearded club-owner, who often used to wear a top hat at the time, asked John and Stuart to play in their place.

We used to watch them in the dark, cramped cellar as their girl friends Dot and Cynthia sat in front of them on chairs holding broomsticks to which their mics were attached!

Virginia and I would also then walk to Mount Pleasant to visit Streates, the club where Phil Tasker, Roger McGough and other local poets would be performing, noticing John and Cynthia and Paul and Dot necking in doorways as we passed.

On Friday, 24 June and Saturday, 25 June, 1960 the Beat poet Royston Ellis (advertised as 'Britain's foremost exponent of Beat Poetry') held a lecture 'Jazz and Poetry' in the basement coffee bar at the University during an Arts Festival.

After attending one of his lectures, during which Royston read some of his poems, John, Stuart, Rod and I retired to Ye Cracke to discuss it. I pointed out that we had an undue amount of cultural input from America – with American music, films, books, poetry and even comics being generally looked upon as more glamorous than the British creative arts.

A big influence at the moment was Jack Kerouac, the Beat poets and the American Beat generation, which had led to a section of British youth becoming 'Beatniks.' Yet John's poems, for instance, weren't copies of the American Beat poets, but had a particular 'Englishness' to them. We began to talk about Liverpool 8 and the talent in the area, artists such as Arthur Dooley and Sam Walsh, writers, art students, even the range of characters we met in pubs with their ready Scouse wit and tremendous sense of humour.

The main point we focussed on was the fact that creative people should draw inspiration from the environment around them and not from environments elsewhere which they had no experience of. Why try to copy the style of American writers and poets who were writing about their own surroundings and experience, when we had our own exciting city to inspire us?

Then and there we took a view that we would use our creative efforts to make Liverpool famous. John would do it with his music, Stuart and Rod with their painting and me with my writing. We also decided on a name for our little group – 'The Dissenters.'

Despite this, we'd taken a real liking to Royston, so John, Stuart and Rod invited him to stay at their Gambier Terrace flat for a few days while he was in Liverpool. They then went to the Jacaranda and provided musical backing to his poems in a Poetry-to-Rock session.

Royston tells me: "Unfortunately I don't remember what I performed at the Jacaranda and can only assume that we rehearsed at the flat beforehand. I based a chapter on the Jacaranda in a 1963 novel I wrote about a pop star called 'Myself For Fame' in which the Beatles feature as the Rythmettes.

"However, Paul told me in Paris when we met by chance in 2006 that he remembers one of the poems had the line 'Break me in easy' - he even recited it to me – so the poems came from my book 'Rave' published later in 1961. Incidentally, I dedicated my 1963 pamphlet of poems 'A Seaman's Suitcase' to Tony and Jet, Christine Keeler and the Beatles in admiration of their achievements."

Royston was born in Pinner on 10 February 1941, and while he was at the Gambier Terrace flat he introduced John, Stuart, Rod and I to our very first experience of a drug. He cracked open a Vick inhaler and showed us the strip of Benzedrine inside. It was nicknamed a 'spitball' and you chewed it. The amphetamine kept you awake all night in a state of excitement.

He tells me: "Yes, the Vick inhaler story has become part of drug legend. I was shown how to do that by a singer who later became Neil Christian and his guitarist, who used to accompany me in those days, Jimmy Page."

It was during this short stay that John and Stuart were trying to think of a new name for the group. They'd long since jettisoned the name the Quarry Men and at one time had called themselves the Moondogs. When we booked them for our art college dances I just referred to them as the college band.

It was Stuart who said they should think up a name similar to Buddy Holly's backing band the Crickets. As the Quarry Men and at the college dances they had included a number of Holly's songs in their repertoire. An obvious next step was to think of the name of insects and they came up with beetles (Ironically enough, Holly had originally considered using the name Beetles for his band before deciding on the Crickets).

Royston recalls that he suggested then that they put an 'a' into the word, making it 'Beatles', inspired by the Beat Generation (people who say it was associated with Beat groups are wrong, because the term Beat groups didn't come into being until after Mersey Beat had been published).

However, they didn't use that name straight away. During the next few months they used a number of variations, including the Beatals, the Silver Beats, the Silver Beetles, the Silver Beatles and finally, in August 1960, the Beatles.

Ellis recalled that in conversations with Paul he told him of his ambitions to be a 'paperback writer' and said that he used the phrase so often in his conversations, that perhaps Paul subconsciously recalled it when he came to write the song.

The Record Mirror reported that Ellis was thinking of bringing a Liverpool group called the Beetles to London to back him on his poetry readings, but nothing came of it.

Royston tells me: "My recollection of the Beatles with an 'a' is similar to yours. I recall discussing with John at the Gambier Terrace flat my plan to take John, Stuart, George and Paul to London to back me on my poetry reading performances. This was reported in the Record Mirror of 9 July 1960 – the first ever major musical press reference to 'the Beetles' with a follow-up in the next issue, 14 July 1960, in which I described the Beetles thus 'For some time I have been searching for a group to use regularly and I feel that the Beetles (most of them are Liverpool art students) fit the bill.'"

"Of course, they never got to London to back me but I do remember meeting Allan Williams in London and he said that John wanted me to go to Hamburg with them as compere. I declined and am alive to tell the tale!

"I asked John what name he was calling the group. He said the Beetles. I asked him how it was spelt and he said B-E-E-T-L-E-S.

"That's when I suggested that since they liked the Beats and I was a beat poet, why not spell it with an A.

"I recall cooking a meal at the flat one day which included frozen chicken pie. Somehow I managed to burn the chicken pie. It is that, I have always assumed, that gave rise to John's reference to 'a man on a flaming pie' suggesting they call themselves Beatles with an A – as you published in Mersey Beat the following year.

"John did make other references to me in subsequent writings, including 'Polythene Pam' and Paul in 'Paperback Writer' (based on my phrase "I want to be a paperback writer" which I stated when we were discussing what we wanted to be in life). I recall later, in Jersey, advising John how to get rid of crablice, and he made a reference to this in one of his stories. A great and incredible man!"

While discussing his appearance at Liverpool University, Royston showed me the original programme, which he retains, and comments: "In the same programme, in my writing on the back cover, is the name and address of a girl (Janice Collins, 47 Catherine Street, Liverpool, ROYAL 9547) who later came with her friend Cathy to London and stayed with me in a beatnik pad in Notting Hill Gate, where Colin Wilson was a frequent visitor as well as other poets and even, on one curious night, Billy Fury.

"Ah, happy days! You ask how long did I stay at Gambier Terrace. I don't remember but it was obviously a few days since I remember travelling around in a van with them and also beginning the affairs which continued later in Notting Hill with Janice and Cathy, who later lived with me in an astonishingly named village in Sussex, Balls Cross (To which address someone sent me a letter addressed to Bollocks Cross, which found me!)"

Royston did receive backing to his poetry: "I gave Jimmy Page his first stage and TV shows when he backed me reading my poetry and we are still firm friends."

He met the Beatles again in August 1963 when they appeared in the Channel Isles. John spent the night with Ellis and his girlfriend Stephanie at their flat in Guernsey, which was to inspire another of his songs. In his 1980 Playboy interview John commented that his song 'Polythene Pam', "was me remembering a little event with a woman in Jersey, and a man who was England's answer to Allen Ginsberg, who gave us our first exposure."

At the time Royston had taken a summer job as a ferry boat engineer on the island, which was actually Guernsey, not Jersey. Following the Beatles appearance on 8 August at the Guernsey Auditorium, Royston and his girlfriend took John back to the attic flat they were renting.

Although there was no hanky-panky, Royston, Stephanie and John all slept in the same bed and they dressed in polythene bags which they found in the room, more or less as a joke.

They'd actually been talking about leather, but couldn't find any leather to dress up in.

Royston recalls that in the poetry booklet of his which he'd dedicated to the Beatles, there was a poem with the lines: "I long to have sex between black leather sheets. And ride shivering motorcycles between your thighs."

Ellis travelled to the Canary Isles with Cliff & the Shadows during the filming of Wonderful Life and stayed there for a while. He left in 1966 to live in the Caribbean where he enjoyed success with a number of best-selling plantation novels under the pseudonym of Richard Tressilian. He later settled in Sri Lanka with a new profession as a travel writer.

With my enthusiasm for poetry I decided to organise and promote the North's first ever Poetry to Jazz event at the Crane Theatre on 31 January 1961. I borrowed £25 from the manager of Streates and began painting hand-made posters to place in all the appropriate venues and was surprised at the response. I'd received help and advice on how to book London musicians and poets from Johnny Byrne and Spike Hawkins, who had moved to Liverpool.

Anthony Barrell, one of my good friends from the University, wrote a piece about the concert in Sphinx, the University magazine. It read:

"'For the first time in the North', proclaimed the programme, but the attendance at this experimental concert did not suggest that people had come from far and wide to be in on it (although most of the local Weirds and Beards were there: God knows where some of them came from but wherever it was, they must have been there for at least a thousand years). The cosy Edwardian rococo setting of the Crane Theatre seemed to be an incongruity for what one might have expected to happen, but all was quiet and dark and the presentation was designed so that even the squarests could filter easily into the mood without breaking their prejudices all over themselves as they tried to dodge the shocks and jolts.

"The Concert began with 'Thirty Minutes of Modern Jazz' by the Art Reid Quintet, later amplified by two London jazzmen, Buddy Bound (trumpet) and Dick Heckstall-Smith (tenor), which gradually developed into a JATP-type jam-session, presumably to get us into the right mood. Smith and Bound showed the most originality and generally speaking the rest passed for 'Modern' jazz (although somebody might like to give a metronome to the drummer).

"Next, Phil Tasker, a Liverpool poet, looking brilliantly pale and Drained of Purpose, read some Liverpool poems (without jazz) which were very, very sad and quivering with the wounds inflicted by social injustice (although most hitch-hikers seem to have a rucksack full of goodies and the National Assistance to save them from actually starving).

"Such was the extent of his exasperated exhaustion that he couldn't find titles for the works. The programme hinted that it was going to be Strong Stuff, and no doubt it was supposed to be so, but nobody fainted, even when the microphone exploded in his face and there were clouds of significant smoke – it seemed we were cut off from The Light for a moment. Tasker's main conclusion was that 'nothing can exist outside Life except a belief in Nature', which if it isn't tautological, sounds pretty incontestable.

"Mark Hawkins (the youngest poet there) followed and gradually introduced the Art Reid Quintet into his poetry with a series of semi-topical jokes to jazz (napalm jelly roll blues etc). He used the jazz for punctuation marks, especially in his long 'jazz soliloquy' (in Jazz Stanzas). He used the ends of choruses to get his best punch lines in and everybody tittered like crazy. The contrivance showed wit and ingenuity and a liberal dose of facetiousness. He nodded his head in time to the jazz, which gave it all a sort of convulsive continuity.

"There was then a 'short' 20 minute interval before we were introduced by Mike Horovitz (of New Departures, Tomorrow, Oxford Opinion, Isis, The Times Literary Supplement and Radio Cologne) and Pete Brown (Evergreen Review, Chicago Poetry Review and Streates).

"Horovitz started with an elongated pun about trick-cyclists and painters, which was ingeniously constructed and poked lots of fun. His second poem professed to be anti-intellectual while it contained remarks like 'Kant didn't know what time it was, then he met Hume' which seemed to be lost on the sunglass brigade in the front row.

"He then made some very nasty comments on the work of Lionel Hampton (Hamp, HAMP, HAMP) like, 'sometimes his music makes for a kind of sickness.'

"In 'Bartok Funky Blues' he made excellent use of Heckstall-Smith's tenor sax and it was really jazz-poetry, although the finger-clickers (again in the front row) lost the beat. Unlike Hawkins, Horovitz was using the melody (if that's the right word for funk) as well as the rhythm to convey his meaning. So did Pete Brown, whose rendering 'Advertizement' was a sharp satire of subgoonery, followed by a lot of jokes about television materialism and middle-class sex in a brilliant picture of The Poet returning to an empty world, where 'someone had dropped The Bomb, or they found out they didn't have to and everybody died laughing.'

"The climax was the mammoth (50 mins) 'Blues For the Hitch-Hiking Dead', by Brown and Horovitz together. At times it was difficult to follow both jazz and poetry (prosy at that) and some people claimed that they didn't hear a word. Society with its 'Tudor roofs and Clark gables' (Horovitz), was travelling through and cut up on the way. Lack of vocal variation made it monotonous and the jazz was a good deal repetitive, although one passage read by Brown to a flute was very effective.

"Both Brown and Horovitz seemed to have a greater command over the language and seemed to be more aware of the possibilities of adding jazz. But it is fair to say that it is not quite clear if the medium is really poetry to jazz or jazz to poetry (as advertised). Hawkins certainly sounded like the latter but seemed to underestimate the ability of the musicians.

"Sceptics may cringe, but Bill Harry's effort is significant and it is to be hoped that this first won't be the last even if it only makes the local beats feel at home."

In fact, it was the first and only poetry to jazz concert which I organised. Although it proved to be popular and enjoyed a full house at the theatre, I lost money on it and had to wait for several months before I was even able to pay back the Streates manager his loan. At that time I was just living on a student grant.

I noticed that one of the photos in the Sphinx feature included a shot of Mal Dean. Mal was a good friend from the art college. I didn't read my poetry at Streates during those days, but Mal took me to the Net in his home town in Widnes where I built up a small following with my type of poems which, at the time were questions about life and our place in the universe, explorations of mysteries and the unknown powers of the mind.

In some ways the poems I wrote came from the long chats Stuart Sutcliffe and I had in his Percy Street flat (Phil Tasker, one of my favourite Liverpool poets, also lived in Percy Street. He was asthmatic and when I used to visit him he used to take more than the recommended doses of Bronchipax, which made him high!).

Stuart was interested in the mystical/religious writers such as Kirkegaard and both of us were intrigued by a specific statement by the philosopher: "Where am I? Who am I? How did I come here? What is this thing called the world? How did I come into the world? Why was I not consulted? And if I am compelled to take part in it, where is the manager? I would like to see him".

I suppose it was this that inspired my poems at the time. None of those type of poems of mine have survived, although I was to write some more poems in this vein towards the end of the decade, such as:

Call Me A Stranger

Call me a stranger
I have no name
Nor do I have a voice
I am the wind, the breeze in the trees
Born to this life without choice.
Call me a stranger
Though I live within
Hidden in dreams and the night
The wisdom of ages long in the past
The knowledge of second sight.

I am the hidden iceberg
Below the waves of the mind
The hopes and desires of a million years
The memory of all mankind.

Call me a stranger
Although you guess
That I am around you now
In the air you breathe
In the pain you feel
You know, but you don't know how.

Call me a stranger
When you close your eyes
And surrender to sleep each night
I am your vision, I come to you
As you dream, then I take flight.

The only poem that survived is one which is actually on the same page of the February 1961 issue of Sphinx as Tony's Crane Theatre review, a love poem to Virginia:

Virginia

Had I not met your eyes   your face

i would be sleeping still   dead

blind   living life   not knowing life

and sleeping years towards the grave

had I not seen your mouth   moving

lovely in your golden face   had

i not seen that   and your eyes

looking upon me   within their glow

a spell

there would have been no awakening

no crying sweet for breath of air

not known before   so cool

so full   fulfilling all   and

filling heart and lung and

soul   had I not known you

there would have been a

slumber still   and no aliveness

no yelling at the stars

for being there   and twinkling

down   those smiling dots above

had I not known your name

Virginia   words would have been

words and not the breath

of life   breathing me from

the years of dormant lostness

had not your auburn hair

touched my mouth   colour   sweet-

ness would have hid   and not

caressed my mind   life i

breathe with your fingers curled

in mine   and your sweet

smell around my mouth   lead   me to this world.

In 1961 Virginia and I were both involved in publishing Mersey Beat and I had already commissioned John to write me a piece about the Beatles. We were sitting in the Jacaranda when I asked John if he'd written the Beatles biog for me and, just like the time in Ye Cracke, he had it written on two scraps of paper in his pocket. He seemed a little unconvinced about it when he handed it to me.

Well, it certainly was the most unusual biography of a band I'd ever come across and I loved it. I had begun to understand most of John's influences. They included Stanley Unwin, who we often heard on the radio with his 'fractured English' and Lewis Carroll, who'd written John's favourite book 'Alice Through The Looking Glass' and the Goons, whose radio series 'The Goon Show' was a major joy to British youth.

I was delighted with the piece and immediately ordered John a coffee and toast (with jam on it!) Back in our tiny attic office in Renshaw Street I re-read the two scraps of paper. The piece was untitled but I decided to publish it word for word exactly as John had written it and I gave it the title 'Being A Short Diversion On The Dubious Origins Of Beatles, Translated From the John Lennon' and it graced page two of the first issue.

It was a thrill for me, in 1997, to see that this piece I'd commissioned John to write for me had been given a new lease of life because it inspired Paul when he conceived his 'Flaming Pie' album.

John was so pleased to see his work in print for the first time – and realised that I'd not changed a single word, which must have boosted his confidence – that he turned up at the office with a huge bundle of material.

It comprised stories, poems and drawings and he handed them to me and said they were mine to do whatever I wished with them. I decided to begin using the items as a column in each issue and I also coined a pseudonym for him 'Beatcomber', which I'd based on 'Beachcomber', the short, humorous column in the Daily Express newspaper.

They proved to be very popular, but a disaster occurred when we moved office from the tiny little attic to the floor below. When I opened my desk drawer to take out another piece of John's to use in another issue, the drawer was empty – all of his work had been misplaced and lost during the office change. We told John in the Blue Angel one evening and he cried on Virginia's shoulder.

At least I was able to save a number of John's creations for posterity, columns such as 'Small Stan' and 'Liddypool' and poems such as 'Tales Of Hermit Fred' and 'The Land Of The Lunapots.'

Incidentally, the Blue Angel is where I met Allen Ginsberg in 1965.

How ironic that we had been admiring his work while still at Art College at a time when our four Dissenters were vowing to make Liverpool famous – and here he was, in Liverpool and describing the city as "the centre of consciousness of the human universe."

Incidentally, there was the time Bob Dylan asked me to introduce him to Liverpool poets.

Saturday Evening Post writer Al Aronowitz arrived in Liverpool to write a story about the city for the magazine. Virginia and I acted as hosts and took him around the various venues ranging from the Cavern to the Blue Angel. Al kept telling us about his friend Bob Dylan, so I went to Nems, bought Dylan's albums and was hooked.

When Dylan came to Britain to tour, I went to his press reception in London. Dylan seemed to be rather bored with the media and the questions they were asking. I went up to him and told him I knew Al Aronowitz. He perked up and suggested we go outside for a chat.

Then I suggested I get hold of John and I phoned John up and handed the phone over to Dylan, who then told me that John had invited him to his house (this was the one in Weybridge). Dylan then asked me if I could take him around Liverpool when he appeared there at the Odeon and I said it would be a pleasure. He told us to meet him at the Adelphi Hotel after the show.

After the Odeon performance, Virginia and I went to the Adelphi and at the reception desk we were able to contact Bob who invited us to his room. The only other occupant was his manager Al Grossman. Bob asked if we could take him to meet some Liverpool poets.

We went to the Blue Angel and I asked Dylan what he'd like to drink. He asked for Beaujolais, but I had to tell him that the Angel didn't sell wine, only beer and spirits, so he suggested we go back to the hotel. Roger McGough and Mike McCartney were there, so I introduced them and Dylan said we should all go back to the hotel – and we were joined by the Poppies, a female trio who, I believe, Roger managed at the time. Back at the hotel we noticed that there was a box of bottles of Beaujolais on a table and we spent the entire night chatting, with Dylan telling me about a book he was writing called 'Tarantula.'

I did hear that Dylan had offered to record the Poppies, but I don't know if he ever did.

The Liverpool poets who gained most from the exposure granted their work in a book by Edward Lucie-Smith, which led to their poems being presented in a collected work in the Penguin Modern Poets series under the name 'The Mersey Sound' were Adrian Henri, Roger McGough and Brian Patton.

Adrian Henri was born in Birkenhead on 10 April 1932, spent a great deal of time in his early years in Rhyl and was initially to study art at King's College, Newcastle between 1951 and 1955 before teaching part time at Preston Catholic College.

In 1963 Adrian was one of the original founding members of Scaffold, along with Mike McGear, Roger McGough and John Gorman when they were originally called 'The Liverpool One Fat Lady All Electric Show', but he didn't actually participate in any part of their subsequent career once the outfit had changed their name to the Scaffold.

A great believer in performance, Adrian spent a great deal of his time reading his work in clubs and pubs, graduating to prestigious concert halls on both sides of the Atlantic. He remembers initially hiring a basement in Liverpool in which he could recite his poetry.

He then achieved fame as one of the trio of Mersey poets, along with Roger McGough and Brian Patten, whose work was featured in 'The Mersey Sound', one of the biggest-selling poetry books of all time, which continues to sell to this day. Adrian's contribution was 30 poems in the first 44 pages.

Paul Weller of the Jam was a fan of Henri and named a track of the groups' second album 'This Is The Modern World' after Adrian's poem 'Tonight at Noon', which contained a collage of words from the original poem.

However, while Roger and Brian moved away from Liverpool, Adrian loved the city too much and remained there; dedicated to paying cultural homage to the place he loved in his poems, paintings and music. Adrian created 'Happenings', performing them at the Cavern with the Clayton Squares backing him. The Roadrunners were another group who collaborated with Adrian and his 'Happenings.'

Adrian founded the poetry band called The Liverpool Scene, along with Mike Hart, Mike Evans, Andy Roberts, Brian Dodson and Percy Jones.

The outfit recorded four albums, which featured Adrian's poems. Interestingly enough, the first, 'The Incredible New Liverpool Scene' (CBS 63047) in 1967 was produced by John Peel, who was then working for the pirate radio station, Radio London.

Their other albums included 'The Amazing Adventures Of' (RCA Victor LSP 4189), 'Bread On The Night' (RCA Victor SF 8057), 'St Adrian & Co., Broadway and 3rd' (RCA SF 8100) and 'Heirloom' (RCA SF 8134), the latter, issued in 1970, containing rarities and outtakes.

The Liverpool Scene also went out on the road and opened for Led Zeppelin on their 1969 tour.

Adrian was also a founder member of Grimms in 1973. Apart from himself, the other members were Vivian Stanshall, Mike McCartney, Andy Roberts, John Gorman, Neil Innes, Brian Patten and Roger McGough. Their first album, simply called 'Grimms', was released on Island HELP 11 in 1973. Their second 'Rockin' Duck' was issued on Island ILP S9248 the same year and their third album 'Sleepers' was issued in 1974 on DJM DJLPS 470.

In 1973 a live reading of his performance was recorded at the Liverpool Academy of Arts and issued as an album the next year called 'Charivari.'

In 1998 Adrian suffered a stroke from which he never fully recovered and he had a quadruple heart bypass operation, following which he was told he would never speak or be able to walk again. He was in hospital for six months and hadn't engaged in art for two years. The nurses brought him a pen and sketchbook, but he could only scribble.

Adrian died in Liverpool at the age of 68 on 21 December 2000, following a long illness.

The night before his death he was awarded the Freedom of the City in recognition of his cultural contribution to Liverpool and was also given an honorary doctorate from Liverpool University.

Author Nell Dunn, who he collaborated on a book with, was to recall: "He told me how, after a gig, he had gone back to a girl's room in some desolate seaside town and lost his wallet. Forced to leave before breakfast in the morning, he walked by the grey waves and, hearing a seagull, looked up - and a piece of bread dropped into his open mouth."

Roger McGough was born in the Liverpool district of Litherland on November 9 1937 and was reared at the terraced family home, 11 Ruthven Road, now demolished. A Roman Catholic he was initially educated at Star of the Sea School, Seaforth (along with John Askew, later to be known as Johnny Gentle) and then attended the Catholic grammar school St Mary's College, Crosby.

Roger went to Hull University when he was seventeen where his love of poetry grew. He also joined a skiffle group Tinhorn Timmons & the Rattlesnakes, playing tea chest bass, as he describes it: "Take a large plywood chest, empty the tea leaves and tie a length of string from one corner to the top of a broom handle, affix Elastoplast to index and middle-finger, and bom-bom, bum-bum off you go."

He returned to Liverpool to take a post as a teacher. He began poetry readings in clubs in Mount Pleasant: Streates and the Phoenix and in 1962 participated in the Merseyside Arts Festival where he teamed up with John Gorman, Mike McCartney and Adrian Henri in an act they called 'The Liverpool One Fat Lady All Electric Show.' They were then offered a seven-week comedy slot in a new television show and turned professional.

Adrian was to leave the outfit and Roger, Mike and John continued as the Scaffold appearing locally at venues such as the Hope Hall, the Blue Angel Club, the Cavern and for the Crosby Division Liberal Association at the Alexandra Hall, Crosby. Mike decided he didn't want to cash in on his brother Paul's fame and now called himself Mike McGear.

In 1964 Paul McCartney produced an album by Mike called 'McGear.' On it, he co-composed the number 'The Casket' with Roger.

In January 1968 Paul McCartney produced an album 'McGough And McGear,' with Roger and Paul's brother Mike McCartney, who was still using the name Mike McGear at the time.

The album was issued in Britain on Friday 17 May 1968 on Parlophone PCS 7047. It was re-released in Britain on Monday 10 April 1989.

The tracks were: Side One: 'So Much', 'Little Bit Of Heaven', 'Basement Flat', (from 'Frink', a book of poems by Roger), 'A Life In The Day Of', 'Summer With Monika', 'Prologue', 'Introducing: Moanin'', 'Anji', 'Epilogue'.

Side Two: 'Come Close And Sleep Now', 'Yellow Book', 'House In My Head', 'Mr Tickle', 'Living Room', 'Do You Remember?', 'Please Don't Run Too Fast' and 'Ex-Art Student.'

In 1969 a Scaffold album 'Lily The Pink' was issued on Parlophone PMC 7077. The group's singles had included '2 Day's Monday', 'Goodbat Nightman', 'Thank You Very Much', 'Do You Remember', 'Lily The Pink' and 'Gin Gan Goolie.'

When the Scaffold disbanded in 1974, Roger contacted Andy Roberts, Neil Innes, Zoot Money, John Gorman and Brian Patten to form Grimms in 1973. The outfit only lasted one year and several other musicians and singers were to join them in performances and the two 1973 albums issued by Island Records: 'Grimms' and 'Rockin' Duck.'

'The Mersey Sound' became one of the most popular poetry books of all time and sold over 1, 000,000 copies. Roger has since written over sixty works, including lots of books for children and his poetry collections include 'Summer With Monika' (1967), 'Out of Sequence (1972), 'Sporting Relations' (1974), 'Defying Gravity' (1993), 'The Way Things Are' (1999) and 'Everyday Elipses' (2002).

In 1978 his book 'Summer with Monika' became a spoken word album issued on Island Records ILPS 9551, with a cover by Peter Blake, the artist who designed the Beatles' Sgt Pepper sleeve.

In 1979 Roger also appeared in the spoof TV documentary, 'All You Need Is Cash' (aka 'The Rutles'). Incidentally, he also contributed to the script of the Beatles' Yellow Submarine film, but was unacknowledged.

Roger, who was awarded a CBE in June 2004, hosts the Radio Four show 'Poetry Please', in addition to travelling throughout the country as a performance poet. He has also been made a Freeman of Liverpool and a Fellow of John Moores University and is a member of the executive council of the Poetry Society, in addition to various other awards and fellowships.

There have been special occasions when the Scaffold has re-formed, mainly for charity events or tributes, such as their concert in memory of Adrian Henri at the Philharmonic Hall, Liverpool in March 2000.

Roger's autobiography 'Said And Done' was published in 2005.

The trio was completed by Brian Patten, who was born in Liverpool on 7 February 1946 at 100 Wavertree Vale and was educated at Lawrence Road Junior School and Sefton Park Secondary Modern School, near Smithdown Road School. He has no recollection of his father, who separated from his mother when he was a child. Brian's memories of childhood recall living in a tiny house with his mother Stella and a crippled grandmother who never spoke to each other and having roguish cousins who were continually in and out of prison.

He began writing poetry the year he left school at the age of fifteen and became a junior reporter at the Bootle Times. He noticed an advert in the Liverpool Echo stating 'Meet Pete The Beat At Streates' (this was probably a friend of mine, Pete McGrath) and he went to the cellar club in Mount Pleasant where he was to meet Adrian Henri and Roger McGough, who he interviewed for his column, giving them some of their earliest publicity.

He began reading his own poetry at Streates and editing and publishing his own poetry magazine Underdog, which contained some of the earliest work of Roger and Adrian.

He left home at the age of seventeen. By that time his mother had re-married and they lived in Underley Street where his mother attempted to commit suicide due to the harsh bullying of her second husband, an alcoholic policeman.

Brian rented an attic flat in Canning Street, began hawking his Underdog newssheet in pubs and clubs and also read poetry at the Cavern, Green Moose and on Monday evenings at Samson & Barlow's in London Road. By 1963 he'd left the Bootle Times and had spent a brief spell in Paris, chalking poems on the pavement.

He returned to Liverpool where the poetry scene had blossomed, moving to different venues and proving host to visitors such as the American poets Allan Ginsberg and Robert Creely. A major turning point came when the Liverpool poets were championed by writer

Edward Lucie-Smith in his book 'Liverpool Scene.' Following that book's publication and shortly prior to the launch of 'The Mersey Sound', Brian had his first collection 'Little Johnny's Confession' published by Allen & Unwin and during that year, 1967, he moved from Merseyside and settled in Winchester.

Later Brian moved London where he lived with sculptor Henry Moore's daughter, Mary, for whom most of his early love poems were written. They parted in 1975 and Brian was to settle in Devon.

Over the years Brian was very active as a performance poet in addition to being a prolific writer. He has written and edited more than 50 books of poetry. His individual works include 'Little Johnny's Confession', 'Vanishing Trick', 'Notes To The Hurrying Man', 'Love Poems', 'Storm Damage' and 'Armada'.

He has edited several collections including 'The Puffin Book of Modern Children's Verse' and has received acclaim for his poetry books aimed at children such as 'Gargling with Jelly', 'Thawing Frozen Frogs' and 'Juggling with Gerbils.'

Brian is a Fellow of the Royal Society of Literature, Liverpool University and John Moores University. He also received the freedom of the City of Liverpool and the Cholmondeley Award for services to poetry.

The anniversary of 'The Mersey Sound' occurred in 2007 when the book was re-published as a Penguin Modern Classic and Brian and Roger set out on an anniversary tour.

'Brian Patten', a critical overview of Brian's work, was penned by Linda Cookson and published by Northcote House in 1997.

In October 2007, on the 40th anniversary of the publication of 'The Mersey Sound', a documentary was broadcast on LWT's 'The South Bank Show.

Roger was to comment: "Living in Liverpool in L8, teaching at the art college; that was good and very buzzy. In a way, everyone had a lot of enthusiasm for things. We had Radio Merseyside beginning in 1967, which was something local and very good, and we were all on the up. It probably wasn't swinging living in Seaforth, if you didn't go to town very much. A lot of people didn't notice what was going on.

"How much swinging Liverpool was to a small group in the centre of town, I don't know."

Recalling the Beatles, he said: "My first wife was at college with John so he used to hang around the flat, as did Paul. They would be at the Kardomah café wearing very expensive suede coats and . . . I was just a teacher.

"They were successful young men on their way to being rich and famous, so we regarded them with a bit of jealousy, really. We were pleased for them because they were putting Liverpool on the map. But they were in a very different world. It was like you admire great footballers. You can't be one and don't want to be one. We were doing something else."

Edward Lucie-Smith, the poet and critic, originally born in Kingston, Jamaica in 1933, who has lived in London since 1951, provided the Mersey poets with their first major recognition in his book 'The Liverpool Scene,' which attracted the attention of Penguin Books, who published a series called 'Modern Poets'.

The series provided collections of the works of three compatible contemporary poets and the 128 page anthology containing works by Adrian, Roger and Brian was published in 1967 as Modern Poets, No.10 under the title 'The Mersey Sound', which was the generic name by which the music of Merseyside had been referred to by the media at the time. There were 30 poems by Adrian, 26 by Brian and 24 by Roger.

Another edition was published in 1983, this time comprising 160 pages with some poems omitted and others, such as Adrian's 'The Entry Of Christ Into Liverpool' included. There was also another book published by Penguin at the same time called 'New Volume.' This collection included the same biographies as 'The Mersey Sound,' but contained all new poems by the trio.

The poet and reviewer S. N. Radhika Lakshmi wrote: "The work of The Liverpool Poets was written to be read aloud in public, and although the poets have now developed separately, their literary outlook is still characterized by their common commitment to reviving poetry as a performance.

"The Liverpool Poets approach to poetry differs from that of other poets in that they consistently give the impression of being real people getting to grips with real and pressing situations. According to Edward Lucie-Smith The Liverpool Poets feel a 'real sympathy for their environment' and are more interested in life than in literature.

"This is the quality that sets them apart from the other post-modern poets. Like the French Symbolists, Baudelaire and Rimbaud, The Liverpool Poets believe that the effect that a poem produces is more important than the poem itself; a poem should be considered as an 'agent' (that conveys the poet's message), rather than as an 'object'."

The publication of 'The Mersey Sound' sparked a revival of interest in poetry in Britain, particularly among the young and led to the intro-duction of many 'performance' poets, including a group calling itself The Medway Poets. It also connected with the contemporary mood with its humour and appeal to the ordinary person. The trio was, in a way, 'people poets.'

As Roger was to comment: "In Liverpool you're a poet one minute, but the next minute you're talking about football, or you're buying bus tickets, or someone's kicking your head in outside a pub. It's all part of living."

One poet of the time has actually continued to make remarkable achievements. Jim Bennett, who was born in Liverpool in 1951, began performing his poetry at O'Connor's Tavern when he was under the legal age to enter a drinking establishment. He began to perform alongside Adrian and Roger in the early Sixties.

In the Seventies he was performing at punk venues in Liverpool and Manchester and began working at Liverpool University.

The Liverpool Daily Post proclaimed Jim Bennett, 'The Best Performance Poet In Liverpool.' Jim grew up in Liverpool during the years of the Mersey Sound and the emergence of the Liverpool poets and is the author of 57 books, including 'Elvis in Liverpool' and 'Made In Liverpool', together with a CD 'Down In Liverpool' a selec-tion of his poetry and music.

Jim has been highly acclaimed by national and international organ-isations for more than thirty-five years and has had numerous awards and accolades. In the 21st century alone he was named Poetry Super Highway Poet of the Year, won the Fante Prize for Literature in New Mexico and was the Sefton Literary Competition Prize Winner.

In 2001 he won the Silver Stake for Performance Poetry at the Manchester Slam. Jim was the Judges Choice and won first prize at the San Francisco Beat Poetry Festival in October 2002 and during the same year was selected to represent Liverpool at the Bristol City of Culture Slam. In October 2003 he opened the National Year of Disability in Sport for the BBC and participated in the DaDaFest Awards, receiving the Individual Performer Award.

He became managing editor of Poetry Kit in 2004 and performed at two book launches with 'Remember The Kop' and 'Everton Eighties' and his poem 'Liverpool Is' was selected to be placed on permanent display at Liverpool FC. Also that year he was asked to read his poetry for the Royal visit of HRH Prince Edward to the headquarters of NWDAF in Liverpool and in December he won the DaDaFest Individual Performer Award for the second year running.

In September 2005 Jim was appointed Birkenhead's Poet in Residence and also took on the post of Poet in Residence for Liverpool's Waterfront and as a visiting poet for New York's Waterfront. In addition, two of his poems were nominated for the leading US poetry Pushcart Awards.

In January 2006 he was voted Poet of the Year 2005 by readers on the New York Western Literary Magazine and in December received two further nominations in the Pushcart awards. In March 2007 he won the European Champions Slam in Brussels.

Jim also runs courses in Creative Writing for the University of Liverpool, Edge Hill University College and the Workers Education Association.

Of course, one famous Liverpudlian has been revealed as a poet only in recent times: Paul McCartney. Paul first began to write poetry whilst at Liverpool Institute. One of his first efforts was called 'The Worm Chain Drags Slowly.'

He was to comment: "When I was a teenager, for some reason I had an overwhelming desire to have a poem published in the school magazine. I wrote something deep and meaningful – which was promptly rejected – and I supposed I have been trying to get my own back ever since."

The person who was a great influence on his reading habits then was his English tutor at Liverpool Institute, Alan Durband.

Paul was to say: "I did A-level English at the Inny, which is my scholastic claim to fame, and we had Alan 'Dusty' Durband, a lovely man, who showed us the dirty bits of Chaucer, you know, the Miller's

Tale, and the Nun's Tale, which were dirtier than anything we were telling each other. He had studied under FR Leavis at Oxford, and he brought a rich pool of information to us guys, and when we would listen, which was occasionally, it was great. He introduced us to Louis MacNeice and Auden, both of whom I liked. It was a great period of my life and I enjoyed it."

He decided to write poetry again when he heard of the death of his childhood friend Ivan Vaughan and said: "After having written so many song lyrics with and without John Lennon, I wrote a poem on hearing of the death of my dear friend Ivan Vaughan," and added, "It seemed to me that a poem, rather than a song, could perhaps best express what I was feeling."

The result was the poem 'Ivan', which inspired Paul to continue writing poetry again. After the publication of his poetry in 'Blackbird Singing,' edited by Adrian Mitchell, Paul began a series of poetry readings insisting that the first one be in Liverpool because it was the city that put the poetry in him.

Commenting on Paul's ability as a poet, Mitchell described him as a popular poet rather than an academic one.

He observed: "A few songwriters, although they know you can get away with banal nothingness in pop lyrics, have a vision and try to convey it to us. A few manage to write truthfully about the world – as Paul does in 'Penny Lane', 'She Came In Through The Bathroom Window' and 'Eleanor Rigby'. Paul takes risks, again and again, in all his work. He's not afraid to take on the art of poetry – which is the art of dancing naked. Paul knows the value of words, how they can help us to enjoy living and loving. He also knows how words can work during the deepest grief – not just as therapy, but as a way of speaking to and for others who have lost their loved ones."

In 2001 Paul said that the favourite poem he had written was 'Her Spirit.'

As a result of the impact of the original trio of Adrian, Roger and Brian, poetry has found root in Liverpool. An example is the Dead Good Poets Society, often referred to as DGPS, which was launched in an upstairs bar at the Pilgrim pub in Liverpool in 1989 when it was initially run by a group called the Pilgrim Poets. They began running events in 1991 under the name the Evil Dead Poets and were later to change to the Dead Good Poets Society, who have moved into several different venues on Merseyside over the years and have their meetings currently at the Everyman Bistro third room in Bold Street.

The aim of the DGPS is to promote poetry through performance and encourage the development of new poets and audiences in Merseyside.

They declare: "Everyone's heard of the Liverpool Poets – and the Beatles – but that was the Sixties. Who has been carrying the poetry torch since then? Well, for starters: Dinesh Allirajah, Mandy Coe, Gladys Mary Coles, Deryn Rees-Jones, Jean Sprackland, Levi Tafari and Glyn Wright.

"All have produced significant work over the last 20 years in Liverpool. For example, Sprackland's 'Hard Water' (Cape, 2004) was short-listed for the 2004 Poetry Whitbread. She and Rees-Jones were lauded as Next Generation poets in 2004 too. Also, deserving mention are some of our own stalwarts: David Bateman, Shehnaz Somjee, Colin Watts, and new voices Clare Kirwan and Cath Nichols.

"We like to think that Liverpool poets and poetry audiences embrace those from further afield. Our regular gigs draw people from Wirral, St Helen's, Wigan, Bolton, Preston and so on. The city has always been a port and people arriving and leaving is a given. Maybe the scene is so vibrant because everybody gets a chance?"

Sarah McLennan of the Dead Good Poets Society tells me that there is, "Some fantastic talent coming up from the grass roots of poetry – the open mics etc. Off the top of my head, more literary poets: Deryn-Rees Jones, Michael Murphy, Matt Simpson, Ade Jackson, Eleanor Rees, Mandy Coe, Michael Cunningham, Gladys Mary Coles, Colin Watts, Rebecca Goss.

"Poets who perform AND sell books: David Bateman, Clare Kirwan, Gerry Potter, Levi Tafari, Janine Pinion, Pat Fearon, Cath Nichols...

"Excellent performance poets (up and coming): Colin Salmon, Peter Crompton, Adam Khan, Alison Down, Curtis Watt, Patrick Graham, Jeffa Kay, John Smith.

"Gosh, I could go on and on! No doubt I'll be poked in the eye for forgetting someone, but at the moment there are more poets performing in Liverpool than you could shake a stick at!"

6. It Started In Toxteth

IT seemed that the black artists on Merseyside travelled a different route than those of the rock and roll kids who created the Mersey Sound. Their influences were different, their style of music different, even the places they performed were different.

Generally, records could be obtained from the Burtonwood base or from black seamen who travelled on routes around the world. Some American influences included doo-wop, singing rather than playing with musical instruments, Jamaican and African inspirations, others were jazz-influenced bands, yet others sang accappella style, all with their core venues being in the Liverpool 8 area.

Having been born in Smithdown General Hospital and reared in Liverpool 8 I found it a place of contrasts. On the one hand you had the Dingle, somewhat of a run-down area with terraced streets, churches and pubs, the home of Gerry & the Pacemakers, Billy Hatton and Brian O' Hara of the Fourmost, Billy Fury and others who were basically working-class musicians.

At the other extreme end you had the two cathedrals, the art college, Liverpool Institute, Liverpool University, the Philharmonic Hall, the creative part with poets, artists, writers.

In the centre of these two sections was the Upper Parliament Street area, part of which had the mansions built on the profits of the slave trade, which now harboured the descendants of that trade, together with the new arrivals from the West Indies.

John Cornelius, an art tutor, was to write a book 'Liverpool 8' about the area, primarily on the cultural aspects while the Real Thing recorded an album 'Liverpool 8', a musical tribute to their part of the area (although the record company refused to allow them to use the name and it became 'Four From Eight'). The black music, which was generally associated with the Mersey Sound, flourished in the clubs, pubs and shebeens around the Upper Parliament Street area.

I remembered a good friend, Wayne Armstrong, who played bass. At one time I'd join him in the room where he rehearsed, while he taught me to sing like the crooners. He also took me along to the club where he played, the Palm Cove. While being interviewed for a documentary about black music called 'Who Put the Beat in Mersey Beat', I was sad to learn that Wayne had passed away. The memory came to me when I saw the list of clubs in the area which Alvin Christie had sent to me.

Alvin commented on what he regarded as just a handful of clubs in the Liverpool 8 area. He wrote: "Stanley House, which sat at the junction of Park Way and Upper Parliament Street was more of a 'Social Centre' than a 'Club' club. Originally it opened in 1944 with the help of the Colonial Office. It consisted of a large hall that could be used to hold dances, along with a gymnasium in the basement (used by world champion boxers Hogan 'Kid' Bassey and Dick Tiger), a library and many small meeting rooms and a Bar on the second floor. It was here that I saw the Chants first public appearance at a Christmas Party for children. It also housed a nursery and Youth club (where I once performed gymnastics for MP Bessie Braddock).

"There was an interesting headline in the Evening Express on 11 Jan 1955 – 'Lord Derby visits the Jungle and feels proud'; the report went on to say 'Lord Derby went into Liverpool's 'Jungle' last night to listen to Negro spirituals and Calypsos and to give his blessing to the work of Stanley House in Upper Parliament St'.

"The West Indian Club was situated on the corner of Grove Street and Parliament Street, which was called Montpelier Terrace at that time, set back from the road in the basement of a large old Victorian house. It was run by Edgar Escofree (who lived at 32 Mulgrave Stewwr.) and George Gardiner. It was mostly a drinking club with music supplied by a Juke box.

"The Palm Cove club opened in 1952 and was situated amongst a row of shops at the top end of Parliament Street, in one of the side streets bounded by Smithdown Lane/Parliament Street and Faulkner Street. Roy and Babs Stevens ran the club (Babs and Roy lived at No1

Eversley Street, L8); it had a dance floor and a jukebox which played Reggae/Calypso/Jazz records. There was a house band with the name The Caribbeans that also played there. The members consisted of: Roy Stevens: Trumpet, Bill Davis: Bongos/Vocal, Owen Stevens (Roy's brother): Tenor Sax, Leslie Stevens: Alto Sax, Wayne Armstrong: Double Bass, Sammy Loggins: Drums, Desmond Henry: Drums.

"It was one of the most popular (if not THE most popular) clubs amongst West Indians and was open every night, I am not sure if the band would play there every night.

"The Pink Flamingo was one of the original 'licensed' clubs in Toxteth (not sure when it opened) and was situated over two floors at the junction of Upper Stanhope Street and Princes Road (next door to the chemist shop with its large display of coloured medicine bottles in its front window) . It had a very grand entrance, from the street there was a half dozen steps up to a portal with two large columns with a balcony on top.

"Dutch Eddie's was situated on the Boulevard in Princes Rd, at the left hand side of the road just where it turns into Princes Avenue.

"Dutch Eddie was from Dutch Guyana and an ex-seaman, and also someone who was known for facilitating loans if you needed one. The club itself was a large affair over two floors with bars and dance floors on each floor. There was live music there featuring such musicians as Trinidadian jazz trumpeter Wilfred 'Pankey' Alleyne, who earlier played with the Caribbean All Star Orchestra founded by Trinidadian born bassist Al Jennings.

"Joe Bygraves was a well known boxer and fought for the European heavyweight championship in 1957. He opened The Beacon Club, just a few doors away from Stanley House on Upper Parliament Street. The house itself was rather grand and featured an imposing central staircase to the first floor.

"There were various voluntary associations based on national or ethnic groupings. Many of these were organised around social clubs.

"This was the case with the Nigerian National Union (Nigerian Social Club, Federal Social Club), the Tho Union (Tho Club), the Merseyside Somali Community Association (Somali Club, Silver Sands), the Ghanaian Union (Ghana Club, TumTum Star), Sierra Leone Union (Sierra Leone Club), the Yoruba Union (Yoruba Club), and the Cross Rivers Associations. These were also affiliated to the Merseyside African Council. But this does not mean that they were not frequented by people only from whatever country the club was named after, on the contrary, drinking sprees would quite often start at one club early in the day, and continue on throughout the rest of the day visiting one club after another."

One of the most colourful characters on the local scene at the time was Harold Phillips, a tall Trinidadian who bestowed himself with the grandiose sobriquet Lord Woodbine.

Woody was a well known character in the Liverpool 8 district where he put his hand to everything from building and decorating to playing in a steel band and acting as barman. He opened his own club, the New Colony Club in Berkley Street, where the Silver Beatles appeared on one or two occasions. He also ran the New Cabaret Artistes Club for Allan Williams, a shebeen where the Silver Beatles backed a stripper known as Janice.

Lord Woodbine also joined Allan Williams, his wife Beryl and her brother Barry Chang in the mini-van with the Beatles on their first trip to Hamburg.

In his later years, Woody had been running a second hand shop and suffered from arthritis. He and his wife Helen died in a house fire on July 5 2000. They were both aged 72 years and were survived by a son and seven daughters.

There were a number of black artists who did participate in the birth of the Mersey Sound, including Derry Wilkie, the Chants, Steve Aldo, Sugar Deen and Colin Areety.

To me, one of the most exciting outfits on the Mersey scene was the Chants. They were a group with immense talent who I desperately wanted to succeed – but unfortunately they didn't, despite the fact that they had a lot going for them: Brian Epstein was their manager at one time, the Beatles backed them at the Cavern, they received a television thumbs up from John Lennon, were virtually 'adopted' by MP Bessie Braddock and enjoyed lots of publicity in Mersey Beat: but all to no avail.

I even took the famous journalist Nancy Spain, (who had a column in the newspaper with the world's biggest circulation at the time – the News of the World), to see them rehearsing in the basement of their

Upper Parliament Street house. Motown hadn't had much success in Britain on the Oriole label, but when EMI took on the Motown account, things started to happen fast. However, I personally felt that the reason why the Chants didn't make it was because the British record buying audience at the time were prepared to buy records by black American artists, but not by black British artists.

This feeling was echoed recently when Steve Aldo, another artist who should have become a star, told me: "When I think back to the 60s the thing that stands out is people in the music scene, especially down south were not interested in black artistes unless they were American or novelty acts."

I was finally delighted and I felt that the Mersey scene was vindicated, when the Real Thing eventually topped the charts with 'You To Me Are Everything.' This was with Eddie Amoo of the Chants leading the group and I was able to write a piece at the time called 'The Fifteen Year Breakthrough', because that's how long it took Eddie to actually find success on record.

Black music in Liverpool existed long before the formation of the Chants, but they proved to be the major black force during the years of the Mersey Sound, so it's worth taking a look at the story of the five-piece vocal harmony group who proved to be Liverpool's most popular black vocal act.

The Chants evolved in the Liverpool 8 district of Liverpool, the Toxteth area, which they felt was totally isolated from the rest of Merseyside, part of it being almost a Liverpool equivalent of Harlem, where the black community had their own cultural influences.

The music the Chants listened to was reflected in their own cultural heritage as they were brought up on what was to become known as R&B, which was introduced to them by the black GIs who came to Liverpool 8 from American bases such as Burtonwood.

This included doo-wop recordings by outfits such as the Del Vikings, along with the music of artists such as Johnny Otis and Little Richard and the Miracles – this was before these artists became mainstream and their music became the embryonic influence of the Shades, their original name.

Joe and Edmund Ankrah's father was a church minister who played organ and he taught his sons how to sing in harmony.

They enlisted a few of their friends to join them in forming a harmony group and rehearsed in the cellar of the Ankrah's house, initially practicing harmony with a version of Paul Anka's 'Don't Gamble With Love.'

Their first approach to the Beatles was reported in an item in Mersey Beat in 1963: "Last year, Joe Ankrah and his brother Eddie joined a vocal group called the Shades, whose only appearances were in Stanley House, Upper Parliament Street. Due to the fact that a rock 'n' roll group in London had the same name. The group decided to call themselves the Chants.

"Joe went along to the Tower Ballroom during an appearance by the Beatles. He had a chat with Paul McCartney, who asked him to bring the group for an audition. The Beatles liked the group so much that they provided backing for them on a number of appearances."

In fact, when they turned up at the Cavern for an audition but didn't have a backing group, the Beatles offered to provide backing for them, but Brian Epstein objected. The Beatles overruled him and the Chants made their Cavern debut on Wednesday, 21 November 1962, with the Beatles providing their backing.

The group's leader, Joe Ankrah, wanted to form an American-style vocal group and the Chants were his third attempt. The other members were Edmund Ankrah, Nat Smeda, Alan Harding and Edmund Amoo.

Joe first met Paul McCartney at the Tower Ballroom, New Brighton on 12 October 1962. He 'blagged' his way into Little Richard's dressing room after the concert and Paul spotted him leaving. Paul wanted to find out who he was and was fascinated when Joe told him about being in an accapella group. He then gave Joe a note, signed by himself, for the Chants to produce at the Cavern when the Beatles returned from Hamburg. They did this, turning up for one of the lunchtime sessions. They waited for the Beatles to come off stage and 'waylaid' them when they left the dressing room as the gig emptied.

Paul introduced them to the rest of the group and then beckoned them onto the stage.

Eddie Amoo recalls, "They went 'apeshit' when we started to sing.

"I can still see George and John racing up to the stage with their mouths stuffed with hot dogs or whatever. The invitation to make our Cavern debut was given as soon as we finished 'A Thousand Stars' for them. They insisted we perform that very night. Everything happened completely spontaneously from that point.

"The Beatles themselves offered to back us when we told them we'd never worked with a band before. We then rehearsed four songs with them and then we ran home to tell all and sundry that we had 'made it'!"

"When Brian Epstein arrived at the Cavern that night he refused to allow the Beatles to back us, but they collectively persuaded him to change his mind – and when he heard us he invited us to appear on many subsequent appearances with them."

On that Cavern debut, the Chants, backed by the Beatles, performed 'Duke Of Earl', 'A Thousand Stars', '16 Candles' and 'Come Go With Me' before an enraptured audience, their set lasting approximately 20 minutes.

Local MP Bessie Braddock took an interest in the group as they were from her Liverpool district, the Exchange ward, and she arranged for them to be the only other Liverpool group present at the Beatles' civic reception at Liverpool Town Hall.

Despite his initial frustration at the Beatles' agreeing to back the Chants against his wishes, Epstein took over the management of the group early in 1963, but only for a short time, and without any formal signing. The group found him ineffectual as a manager and he agreed to release them. They then signed with Manchester agent Ted Ross, who arranged a recording deal with Pye Records. However, they were later to consider they had committed "professional suicide" by signing with Ross, although they were grateful for what he tried to do for them.

On the special all-Beatles edition of the TV show Juke Box Jury, the first record played to them was the Chants' 'I Could Write A Book', which they voted a hit – but it became a miss, despite their positive comments.

The Chants' debut disc, 'I Don't Care', flipside 'Come Go With Me', was released on 17 September 1963. Their second, 'I Could Write A Book', flipside 'A Thousand Stars', was released on 1 January 1964. Their third was 'She's Mine', flipside 'Then I'll Be Home', in June 1964, and their final release for Pye was 'Sweet Was The Wine', flipside 'One Star' on 11 September 1964.

Eddie Amoo wrote 'One Star', credited to Stanley Houseman, as a tribute to Stanley House, where they'd made their first appearance.

Stanley House was a social meeting place in the Toxteth area where young met old and black met white to drink, dance and play football, table tennis, snooker and generally mix together.

Commenting on their period with Pye Records, Eddie comments, "They had no idea what to do with a black doo wop group; they just had no idea."

The group never found record success, despite further releases with Fontana, Page One, Decca and RCA and strong singles such as 'Man Without A Face'.

After they disbanded in 1975, Joey and Edmund Ankrah joined another group and enjoyed a degree of success on the television show 'New Faces'. Eddie Amoo formed a Liverpool soul group, The Real Thing, with his younger brother Chris and finally found UK chart success in June 1976 with 'You To Me Are Everything' which topped the charts, it also reached No. 5 on its re-release in April 1986.

The Real Thing are still active with Eddie commenting: "We have seen our flagship song recorded by Philip Bailey of Earth Wind & Fire and Courtney Pine, one of our leading sax players. 'Can You Feel The Force' was probably our biggest seller in terms of sales and is still being covered and sampled all over the world. We also have two songs in the all-time top 100 of the Guinness Book of Records.

"I had 13 years of struggle and scraping with the Chants – and plenty of fun also – and 23 years of being in a hit band, I think the balance has been more than redressed.

Eddie, who was born in Liverpool on 5 May 1950, when discussing the origins of the Real Thing, recalls: "The Real Thing started with three people, then went to five, then dropped two out and by 1975 they'd become a trio – Ray, Dave and Chris. But by then Chris and I had started to write together. I wrote the first three Real Thing singles.

"I was still with the Chants, but I was writing for the Real Thing, because the Chants were no longer a vehicle for the songs I was writing – the Chants were doing Cabaret, and the Real Thing was able to play these songs live, so I was writing and giving the songs to Chris."

The first formation of the group comprised Eddie's brother Chris Amoo (born 14 October 1952), Dave Smith (born 6 July 1952), Ray

Lake (born 11 February 1946) and Kenny Davis. Eddie attended rehearsals and encouraged them and coached them, recalling that they all grew up together in Liverpool 8, but hung out with some of the street gangs at the time. Eddie was pleased that they became more interested in singing than fighting and says, "I liked the idea because it was something that would keep them off the streets, so I was really up for it."

In 1972 the Real Thing found success on the talent show Opportunity Knocks where they were spotted by Tony Hall, a Radio Luxembourg disc jockey who was later to become their manager.

The vocal group were not initially successful with their records, issuing 'Vicious Circle' on Bell Records, which made no impact.

They next signed to EMI and released 'Plastic Man', a number Eddie had originally penned for the Chants. Although they were able to promote it on Top Of The Pops, it failed to register.

For a time they had had to exist by entering the Cabaret circuit as their EMI releases in 1973 and 1974 failed to make any impact.

Kenny David left the band and Eddie joined in 1975, the year which was their turning point when they signed to Pye Records and also toured with David Essex. They recorded some songs which were written and produced by David Essex, including 'Watch Out Carolina', which also flopped.

Tony Hall was now their manager and in their search for a hit they met with songwriters Ken Gold and Mickey Denne who played them some demo discs of their numbers, which included the song 'You To Me Are Everything,' which the Real Thing recorded and they topped the British charts with it in 1976.

Unfortunately, they couldn't repeat this success in America because the number was immediately covered by Frankie Valli and others.

The group's singles included 'You To Me Are Everything', a No. 1 hit in 1976 and 'Can't Get By Without You' which reached No. 2 the following year. In 1977 'You'll Never Know What You're Missing' reached No. 16 while 'Love's Such A Wonderful Thing', issued the same year, reached No. 33.

Their three singles in 1978 were 'Whenever You Want My Love', which reached No. 18, 'Let's Go Disco', which reached No. 39 and 'Rainin' Through My Sunshine', which reached No. 40.

In 1979 'Can You Feel The Force' reached No. 5 and 'Boogie Down (Get Funky Now)', reached No. 33. 'She's A Groovy Freak' reached No. 52 in 1980 and there was a pause for a number of years until 'You To Me Are Everything (The Decade Re-Mix 76-87)' was issued in 1986 and reached No. 5. The same year there was another remix re-release 'Can't Get By Without You (The Second Decade Re-mix)' which reached No. 6 and a third followed, 'Can You Feel The Force ('86 re-mix)' which reached No. 6. Also that year they released 'Straight To The Heart', which reached No. 71.

In 1997 their 'Hard Times' only managed to attain the No. 90 position and in 2005 they recorded 'So Much Love To Give' with Freeloaders, which reached No. 9.

Their album releases were: 'The Real Thing', 1976; Four From Eight', 1977; 'Step Into Our World, 1979 and 'Can You Feel The Force', 1979.

Incidentally, the Real Thing originally called their second album 'Liverpool 8', but Pye refused to allow them to use that title and it became 'Four From Eight.' Ironically, Ringo Starr's January 2008 album is called 'Liverpool 8.'

In 1998 a live concert album was issued by Waxwork Records called 'Real Thing Live'. A compilation album 'Children of the Ghetto: The Pye Anthology' was issued by Sequel Records in 1999.

The tracks were: Side One: 'You To Me Are Everything'; 'Can't Get By Without You'; 'Watch Out Carolina'; 'I Want You Back'; 'Hallelujah Man'; '(He's Just A) Moneymaker'; 'Young And Foolish'; 'Flash'; 'Keep An Eye (On Your Best Friend)'; 'You'll Never Know What You're Missing'; 'Love Is A Playground'; 'Love's Such A Wonderful Thing'; 'Lovin' You Is Like A Dream'; 'Down To The Way We Feel'; 'Plastic Man'; 'Lightning Strikes Again'; Liverpool Medley: 'Liverpool 8'/'Children Of The Ghetto'/'Stanhope Street'; 'Dance With Me'; 'Whenever You Want My Love.'

Side Two: 'Can You Feel The Force'; 'Rainin' Through My Sunshine'; 'Lady I Love You All The Time'; 'Whatcha Say, Whatcha Do'; 'Give Me The Chance'; '(We Gotta Take It To The) Second Stage'; 'Boogie Down (Get Funky Now)'; 'Saint Or Sinner'; 'The Story Of My Life'; 'You Can't Force The Funk'; 'She's A Groovy Freak'; 'It's The Real Thing'; 'You're My Number One'; 'I Believe In

You'; 'Foot Tappin"; 'Love Takes Tears.' Castle Select issued 'The Very Best Of the Real Thing' in 2002.

The current band is a trio of Eddie, Chris and Dave, who are accompanied by a band of six musicians. They actively tour in 'The Greatest Disco Show' where they only have a 20 minute spot, but in their own concert appearances, such as the Philharmonic Hall show in 2007, they field a 90 minute performance.

Although both the Chants and the Real Thing have been a great credit to Liverpool, they seem generally to have been ignored by Liverpool's powers-that-be.

As Eddie recalled when he was invited to the Albert Dock: "I was invited to an unveiling of a plaque that had been put up for all the number one artists in Liverpool. I went down and I was totally ignored by the Liverpool media; the only people they were interested in were Atomic Kitten and Paul McCartney's brother. I just got up and walked away. That, for me, is typical of Liverpool. I can't think of anywhere else where that would happen."

Unlike other successful outfits from Liverpool who have moved to London, Eddie and the group remain in Liverpool, living only a few miles away from the area where they were brought up. Still remembering being cold-shouldered when he attended the Albert Dock plaque session, he says, "We are a band and we've had about nineteen chart entries and I can't think of one festival or function that we have been invited to do on Merseyside. We do them everywhere else in the country. To me that is totally bizarre."

Derry Wilkie was born Derek Davis in Kent Gardens, Toxteth, Liverpool on 10 January 1941. His first group the Seniors called themselves Derry & the Seniors, then, later, Howie Casey & the Seniors. Derry joined the Pressmen in 1963 but the band split in two and Derry and saxophonist Phil Kenzie formed the basis of Derry Wilkie & the Others, The group toured the U.K. and Germany but disbanded after two years.

Derry was always one of my favourite artists in Liverpool. He was warm-hearted, immensely reliable and friendly – but also tough if trouble waved its head. I remember Derry had the largest hands I had ever seen.

There was the story that a group of thugs were after him and came to the Iron Door club with hatchets, banging on the door to get in. Derry escaped by finding a small way out to the rear.

At one time I was so fascinated by Derry's story and his triumph over hardships, that I began to interview him for a book we were going to write together which I called 'Black Scouse.' Unfortunately, he left Liverpool and we weren't able to finish it. The tapes were lost some years later in London.

Virginia and I met up with Derry again in London and his escapades continued to amuse. I remember at one time he staggered out of the Cromwellian Club, completely tipsy, and didn't have any money to get home, so he stole a bike and wobbled along the road, crashing into the back of a police car which had stopped at some traffic lights!

We lost track of Derry for many years. We heard that he was living in Italy for some time. Then I heard his voice shout to me at Baker Street Station. I was on the up elevator and he was going down on the other side. "I want to form a new group. We've got to get together for a bevvy," he shouted. That was the last time I saw him.

He wrote his own profile for Mersey Beat in 1964:

"As my American friend, Al Aronowitz put it: I'm the first spade singer in town. Four and a half years ago I started singing with a group called The Seniors. Great boys, fab musicians who were very highly rated among groups.

"We were playing for some time; we were popular; we even held our own against The Beatles in those days – we were good friends. We were the first group to go to Germany – Hamburg, you know.

"We didn't know what we were starting – we slept in the gutter to do that. And the Seniors were the first group from Liverpool to make a record. Bit proud of that, even if it didn't get anywhere.

"We got so fed-up of people taking advantage of us that we packed up as the Seniors. It was heartbreaking coming back to town after that.

"You do have your pride, you know what I mean.

"Spent a great six months with a group called The Pressmen because Bill Harry started me singing again. Great group, great sound. History repeated itself, we made more records – none of them got released, they weren't commercial enough, they were rhythm and blues.

"Hit hard times again with the Pressmen – split up again.

"It breaks your heart to do this if you're like me, because I love the people in my groups. And now I've got a new group, the fabulous (that's so true) The Others, and at long last we've found someone who'll be honest with us and will be signing with him in the near future." Sadly, Derry died on 22 December 2001.

Personally, I have confidence in saying the Steve Aldo was the best solo black singer of them all.

Steve was born Edward Alban Jean-Pierre Bedford on 4 October 1945 and tells me: "I was born in Liverpool at the end of WWII the product of a mixed race Liverpool mother and a Jamaican father who met while stationed in Aldershot, she was in the British army and he was in the Canadian army and if my mother had been brave enough to leave Liverpool I would have been Canadian.

"I grew up in a twelve-roomed house in Upper Stanhope Street, L8, so there's no sad tale of living in a slum; in fact I was spoiled rotten, living with my mother, grandad, grandma, and my mother's two sisters.

"As for the music I cannot remember a time when there wasn't music in my life, being born during the Be Bop era and big bands like Basie, Ellington, our house was always filled with rhythm.

"Liverpool 8 was a magnet for black GIs and American seamen before, during and after the war because of the black community living there (later in my life I always thought what an irony it was that these houses that once housed the city's wealthy should be inhabited by the descendents of the people whose blood their wealth came from).

"From a very small child I was singing, in fact my mother told me that at the age of three my favourite song was Nelly Lutcher's, 'Fine Brown Frame', so much so that she took me to see her on the Empire and when she started to play the intro I stood up on my seat and sang out as loud as I could attracting the attention of everyone around us, so you could say my first public performance was at the age of three.

"I once sat and thought about where I lived and realised that in our part of Stanhope Street between Windsor and Berkeley, a space of about 200 yards, there were more than 12 different nationalities and nearly every house played different music, but American black music was the most popular.

"During my childhood there were a lot of house parties in L8 and I would lie in bed listening through my window and always had a gift for learning lyrics and of a weekend when men like Charlie Jenkins Snr or Onie Cole would play in the local pubs I would stand in the doorways with my mates and sing the songs, a few times I was pulled into the bar to sing for the drinkers and I can say in all honesty I loved it, I must have been about 9 or 10, and even better people would press pennies in my hand.

"My first proper performance came at the age of eleven in a talent competition at the Rialto Saturday matinee which I won singing a Sammy Davis Jnr version of 'Because Of You', my prize was a hard-back of Robinson Crusoe and a pen and pencil set. One good thing that came from this was, before I used to be very badly bullied by the poorer kids around where I lived being an only child who had every-thing, so after they all saw me sing so many wanted to be my friend, it was a great defence mechanism. They asked me to teach them songs and some of us formed doo wop groups and would gather in houses and on corners at night singing the latest songs we heard from the GIs.

"My first legitimate stage appearance happened when I was 12 which was a week on the Pavilion in a show called 'The Backyard Kids', which starred Freddy Fowler, who we both know.

"During this show I met someone who was to be my first girlfriend, her name was Iris Caldwell one of the Margaret Cox Dance Troupe and she lived in a really posh area to which she invited me for tea after the show finished.

"It was like going to a new country for me in fact the first time I went there, after I got off the bus and started looking for the house a police car stopped and asked me what I was doing there. I think they were about to take me away, when this tall white guy came running from a nearby house and told them I was a friend, so they let me go with him. He said to me his name was Alan and he was Iris's brother, isn't it strange how some people enter your life, because years after I stopped seeing Iris he came back into my life as Rory Storm, one of the nicest most sincere guys I ever knew.

"In fact the thing with Iris only lasted a few weeks because even though her family were very nice I began to feel very uncomfortable going to where she lived, after being called a selection of names by local boys on the streets while walking to and from the bus, and knew it was only a matter of time before things escalated.

"Up until the age of 13 I sang anywhere people would listen, pubs, parties, the street and after my grandma bought me a record player in my room for hours on end, although I sang lots of popular music of the time, the music I loved with a vengeance was jazz and blues."

It was when he was 14 that Steve first began to sing at Holyoake Hall and on holiday in the Isle of Man he sang with the Ivy Benson Band. He told me, "I went to the Isle of Man with York House Youth Club and stayed there a month. During that time I sang with Ivy Benton and her band at the Villa Marina.

"When I returned home I used to sing certain nights with Howie Casey & the Seniors. I left school and went to Cardiff. I had two jobs there, the main one was at a ladies hairdressers.

"I left Cardiff and went to work in London at Raymonde's – Teasey Weasey's – then I went away to sea for a year. I came home and after about four months I joined the Challengers. I went to Germany with them and stayed to sing with the Dominoes."

The line up of Steve Aldo & the Challengers was Steve, vocals, John Bedson, drums, Robin Gillmore, lead, Ray Pawson, bass and Pete Wilson, guitar.

Steve's first manager was Joe Flannery and when they were discussing a stage name for him, Steve said he liked a name like the film actor Aldo Ray. Joe suggested Aldo Stevens and Joe's partner Kenny then suggested Steve Aldo.

Steve moved to Germany with the Challengers to appear at the Star Club, while there he was asked by Kingsize Taylor to stay and sing with the Dominoes. On his return to Liverpool he joined the Nocturnes for a short time, before becoming a member of the Griff Parry Five in April 1964.

They comprised Steve on lead vocals, Brian Griffiths on lead guitar/vocals, Ron Parry on drums, Vinny Parker on organ and Fran Galloway on bass.

He recalls: "About three weeks after I returned to Liverpool I joined the Nocturnes. I was with them for a couple of weeks until Ron Parry, who I'd met in Germany when he was with Joe Brown, told me about the group he was forming and asked me to join them.

"I was a bit dubious at first as I'd just joined the Nocturnes. He asked me to come along to one of their rehearsals – and when I heard them I just had to join the group."

At the time he was managed by Spencer Lloyd Mason and made his solo recording debut on Decca with 'Can I Get A Witness' c/w 'Baby, What You Want Me To Do' (Decca F 12041) in December 1964. His next release was 'Everybody Has To Cry' c/w 'You're Absolutely Right.' It was issued on Parlophone R5432 in 1966.

The Beatles requested that Steve appear on their last British tour, in 1964, which, with only nine appearances, became their shortest theatre tour of Britain.

Steve became vocalist with the Krew, who also comprised Howie Casey on sax, Eddie Sparrow on drums, Archie Leggatt on bass. Beryl Marsden recommended them to her manager Tony Stratton Smith, but when they arrived in London they were told that they were to become Beryl's backing band. However, that didn't work out and Steve was asked to re-join them.

In 1967 Steve became vocalist with the Fix, a group performing Stax-style music. The other members were Albie Donnelly on sax, Dave Irving on drums, Geoff Workman on organ, Pete Newton on bass, Paul Pilnick on guitar, Mr Zoot on sax and Steve Collins on trumpet.

Other bands he joined were the Fairies and the In Crowd.

When Steve's father died, he decided to return to his home in Liverpool to look after his four younger brothers and sister. For a time he sang at the Wooky Hollow Club, but didn't enjoy it and finally ended up as manager of Casey's, a pub in Casey Street in Liverpool city centre.

Ramon Sugar Dean was born in Canning Street to a Nigerian father and Scottish mother. As a child he was taken to live in Nigeria for four years and on the family's return to Liverpool they were housed in a tenement block off Scotland Road for a period which Sugar describes as 'five years of hell.'

He told Mersey Beat website reporter Rita Martelli that people would kick in their doors, smash their windows, call them names and described that north end area as extremely racist. Eventually they were moved to Chinatown in the Liverpool 1 area.

The music hall maestro and national treasure George Formby – a Lancashire lad, who inspired many post war singer-songwriters including The Beatles

The re-opening of the Cavern Club in 1966, with then Prime Minister Harold Wilson and Liverpool legend Kenneth Arthur Dodd

Billy Fury, a singing Scouser from the Larry Parnes stable of stars, who combined a great voice with good looks and real stage presence

Beryl Marsden — a gutsy singer who was a real rocker of the '60s — pictured here with mods Rod Stewart and Peter Bardens

I read the news today… Gerry Marsden and his Pacemakers check out their local paper to find out about the band's chart-topping success in 1964

Mersey Beat founder Bill Harry presents the Beatles with their first-ever award at the Majestic Ballroom, Birkenhead

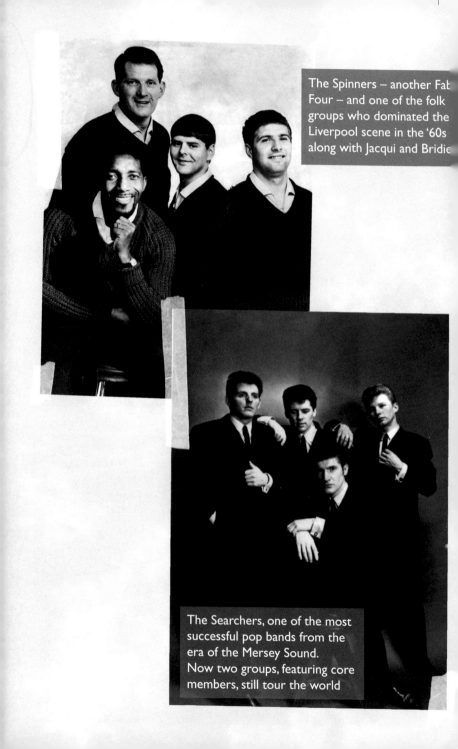

The Spinners – another Fab Four – and one of the folk groups who dominated the Liverpool scene in the '60s along with Jacqui and Bridie

The Searchers, one of the most successful pop bands from the era of the Mersey Sound.
Now two groups, featuring core members, still tour the world

The Mersey Poets meet the Scaffold. Roger McGough, Brian Patten and Adrian Henri with Mike McCartney and John Gorman at a 'creative happening'

Bill and his inspirational wife Virginia in 1963, co-founders of Merseybeat

The Real Thing, from the Toxteth area of Liverpool 8. The band still tour four decades on

From Liverpool to the World, Frankie Goes to Hollywood, who became record breakers with their first three releases all reaching number one

Monocled Mutineers, The Wombats, formed in 2003, are graduates of LIPA – the Liverpool Institute for Performing Arts. Liverpudlians Dan Haggis, Matthew 'Murph' Murphy and Norwegian Tord Overland make up the talented trio

Laura Critchley is the girl from Little Sutton, Wirral, with a big personality and versatility to match. She has made her name at home and abroad

The Zutons, featuring charismatic sax player Abi Harding, were formed in 2001 and released their debut album three years later, the critically acclaimed Who Killed The Zutons?

Hot Club De Paris, featuring Alasdair Smith, Paul Rafferty and Matthew Cameron Smith, were formed in 2004 and released their debut album Drop it Till It Pops in 2006

Sugar came from a very musical family and his mother played the piano and taught her children to harmonise, something which benefitted Sugar in the groups he was to form.

Neighbours would listen to the Dean children singing and were invited to sing at parties, although their mother initially turned down such offers fearing they would be exploitative. She was later, in the Forties and Fifties to accept some invitations although she would accompany her children and see that they were paid one shilling.

As a teenager Sugar met up with Tony Fayle and they decided to form a group, their repertoire influenced by the American doo-wop music of groups such as Frankie Lymon & the Teenagers.

However, despite their aspirations to make a mark with their music, black youths had prejudice to face. Rita Martelli reported for the Mersey Beat site: "Sugar, and the other prospective musicians in the city, did not just get together for the sake of music. In many cases, it was also for social reasons. They saw this as a way out of the prejudice and harassment they were subjected to. For example, he recalls that, if three-four black lads were standing on a corner talking, they would automatically be arrested, because Liverpool was permanently patrolled by police cars at that time. They would be loaded into police vans and taken to 'Cheapside', the lock-up, where they would be given a choice of offences, - drunk and disorderly, loitering with intent or urinating in the street. Most would choose drunk and disorderly, even though this was untrue.

"The black lads also had to face trouble if they 'dared' to go to venues for a night out, which would invariably end up with a fight – for which they would get the blame, true or not! So, for Sugar and others like him, getting a group together was their way of getting out of the forced gang culture they were becoming involved in, through no fault of their own."

Sugar even remembered one gig when the MC announced his group with the words: "Ladies and Gents, there are four blacks coming on stage now. I don't like them, you might, here they are." As the MC left the stage the audience booed him.

There were only a handful of black vocal groups at the time. Like black American artists they were basically vocal groups who didn't play instruments.

Sugar was in several vocal groups, initially performing in the Toxteth area in venues such as Stanley House and the Rialto. In 1960 Sugar was a member of a vocal group the Earls, who comprised himself, Joey Grant, Tony Fayal, Lawrence Areety and Okin Eyo.

Other bands included the Conquests and the Ramons and for a short time he joined the Washington Soul Band. Another outfit was the Valentinos who initially comprised Eddie Williams, Lawrence Areety, Tony Fayle and Chris Smith. Sugar joined them when Smith left.

At one point they travelled down to London for one of their gigs and made the acquaintance of Gene Latter, who had musical contacts which led them to making a record for EMI, 'It Takes A Fool Like Me.' However, the record didn't receive adequate distribution and after some time, Sugar managed to order the record from NEMS, although the entire box was discovered to be faulty.

Tony left the group and they changed their name to the Harlems and added backing musicians. Their line up was Sugar, Lawrence Areety, Vinnie Ishmael and Barry Philbin and they managed to appear on Opportunity Knocks.

They were then approached by Mickey Hayes who became their manager. He'd originally intended managing the Buzz Brothers, but claimed he found them unmanageable. Hayes then got them a record deal with DJN (the record label set up by the Beatles music publisher Dick James). They managed to record five numbers for an album which was never completed. Although a single was released the number also suffered from lack of adequate promotion.

Over the years Sugar, at one time an Equity committee member, has been promoting equal rights for black actors and musicians. He also helps young people entering the music business and in recognition of his achievements over such a long period of time in October 2001 he was one of the Liverpool recipients of the Men Of Merit Award, which recognises the achievements made to the black community.

Sugar also appeared as Marzo in the 2006 film Dead Man's Cards.

Incidentally, Lawrence Areety, who was in various groups with Sugar, had a very talented brother Colin.

In 1965 Colin joined the Dennisons when Eddie Parry left and the group then became a soul band, although they never found success and disbanded in 1967. Colin continued as a solo singer and recording artist, his single 'Holy Cow' was issued on Deram. Sadly, he has since passed away

Another important black contribution to Mersey music in the early Sixties was that of the brothers Bernie, Willy and Bobby Wenton, who were born and bred in Toxteth, the sons of a musician. They originally began performing their vocal act locally and were backed by a number of outfits, including the Shuffler Sound. They then changed their name to the Buzz Brothers and were a particularly exciting song and dance act that attracted large crowds wherever they appeared in the clubs on Merseyside.

The act initially comprised Willie Wenton, vocals; Bobby Wenton, vocals, Silver Chantre guitar; Mick Kearns, sax (he passed away in 1992), Bill Good, bass, Alan Sef, drums and Ivor Ali on organ. At one time Tony Goldby, provided the bass sounds.

At one time the Buzz Brothers were managed by London impresario Don Arden. As Bernie's Buzz Band they recorded two singles in 1968: 'When Something's Wrong With My Baby' c/w 'Don't Knock It' on Deram (DM 181) and 'The House That Jack Built' on Decca (F22829).

The brothers split to become members of other bands or turn solo, for instance at one time Bernie played with a band called Just Us while Bernie sang with Bernie's Buzz Band.

Bernie performed with several other Liverpool artists during the 1960's and in the Seventies he and his brother Willy toured as backing vocalists to Chris Rea.

But it was in 1991 that he found fame when he won ITV's Stars In Their Eyes talent show, performing as Nat King Cole. After winning his heat he went on to win the Grand Finale, watched by an audience of more than ten million. He appeared on several television shows including This Morning, The Time & the Place, The Late Late Show Sky TV, GMTV and Pebble Mill. His numerous cabaret appearances took him to London's Hackney Empire and the Hamilton Palace Hotel, the Gleneagles Hotel, Scotland, the Moat House Hotel, Liverpool, the Floral Pavilion, New Brighton and the Butlins and Pontins holiday camp circuit. Bernie died at his home in Toxteth in April 2006 after a long battle with cancer. He was 59 years old and was survived by his second wife Trisha and his four children.

More information on the music in Toxteth was provided to me by Alvin Christie, who presents these sober thoughts: "The endemic racism that existed in Liverpool at that time, served only to 'corral' black people into the district of Toxteth.

"The valiant efforts of bands like the Chants to break down the barriers succeeded only to the extent that they were extremely popular on a 'local' level but not nationwide like some of the other exponents of the Mersey Sound. This in part was due to the fact that record labels had no idea how to handle black groups and fed them sanitized versions of American music to record, backed by white musicians.

If they had been allowed to record in the styles they wished to, perhaps they may well have been more successful. Then as now, with every new musical form put forward by black musicians, it is assimilated into the mainstream and eventually in the words of Steve Aldo becomes "the property of no one".

"From the time in 1831 that popular circus clown Dan Rice blackened his face to perform 'negro songs' for a variety show in New York's Bowery district, black music has illustrated its depth of 'innovation and has been copied, pastiched, simulated and assimilated into the mainstream of popular music. But, and most importantly, it has not always been credited, as was the case in Liverpool in the late 50s to mid 60s. We were there and took part, but we were invisible."

Alvin St Joseph Christie was born at Sefton General Hospital on 12 December 1949 and lived in Selbourne Street. His father Alvin St Joseph Christie Snr originally hailed from Jamaica and his mother Ivy Christie, nee Hampson, was a Liverpudlian. His detailed memories of his musical career provide an interesting insight into the life of a musician growing up in the Toxteth area and eventually finding success in London.

He recalls: "Selbourne St, in the early Sixties, was a very lively street. Eddie Williams of the Valentinos used to be a good friend of my brother Myron and often used to hang out on our front steps along with other local guys such as Alan Harding of the Chants.

"It was also Alan Harding who taught me how to play my first three chords on the guitar; I sat for ages playing 'Michael Row The Boat Ashore'!... but I was on my way towards being musical.

"It was in 1963 I think, that I and my brother Colin plus two friends

Alan Courtney and Derek Woo decided we should form a group together, but the problem was that we had no money to buy instruments. We found a way around this by making whatever we could. I made a makeshift bass by stretching some piano strings over a biscuit tin that I had cut away the top from so it was open, and covered it with a wet chamois leather so that when it dried it was quite taught, this made a kind of dull sound but it was ok and was played by Alan.

"As the drummer, I used an old washtub donated by my mother, which I kicked with my foot (not having a bass drum pedal!!) at first, but this was a bit unwieldy so I eventually made my own construction which worked up to a point.

"Derek, as I recall, had the brilliant idea of calling someone at the Liverpool Echo to see if they were interested in doing an interview, and to our surprise they were! So, we were photographed in my white-washed backyard doing our thing, and the next day there appeared an article in the Echo with a large picture stating "Liverpool's newest and youngest band the Casuals" (we had to drop the name because there was already a Casuals band that we didn't know at the time), and went on to say that "screaming fans lined the backyard walls as the group bashed out its music." It wasn't true of course, but that article made me, and the rest of the guys, very happy, and not least a little well known in Toxteth for a few weeks.

"The day after our picture was in the Echo my uncle Les came to tell us that he could get us a 'gig' at the David Lewis centre. Wow, were we impressed, and somewhat apprehensive at the thought of facing an audience! We were to go on in between the dance bands sets, so we duly carried out all our stuff onto the stage, set it up and did our 'noise'. We were well received, and I remember my uncle Les was behind the curtains saying "smile boys, smile..."

"At the end of our performance Les told us to walk through the audience carrying the washtub bass drum between two of us so that people could place money in it. I can't remember how much was in it by the time we reached the other side, but at least it was our first (and last) paid gig.

"The next day we were in the Echo again with a short report that we had played our first gig. All this would have happened around 1962/63, after this in 1964 I joined the Royal Navy and went away to sea for the next five years, leaving the navy in 1969. That for me was a wondrous year, I was 20-years-old and for the first time in my life I was able to feel that the world was my oyster, but having spent so much time in the navy it was difficult to know how to handle civilian life. It wasn't structured like in the navy!

"I didn't have to do things like clockwork (and didn't), I lived off the State for a while trying to find my feet. I and two friends used to hang out together, go to places like the Cavern, but by then the Beatles didn't play there any more. It was 'Sweet Soul Music' that ruled, Otis Reading, Arthur Conley, Temptations, Four Tops, Marvin Gaye these were the gods that drove us into the night. We learned to sing from them, we learned to dance by watching them, we dressed like them. It was cool.

"Along with my two friends Benny Brown and Paul Barber we formed a vocal group by the name of Soul Motion. We started off by mimicking American doo wop such as Anthony and The Imperials, Shep and The Limeliters, The Impressions, The Drifters, The Marcels etc. We would rehearse in the kitchen at my home in Selbourne Street and in Paul's little room (in a house just up the street from me), Benny would sing lead and Paul and I would sing the harmonies.

"We only ever did one gig, which was at the A&B club in Devonshire Road. We appeared on the same night as another group by the name of the Guess Who, who had just had a hit with 'These Eyes'.

"I believe we did 'Sweet Was the Wine' by The Marcels and 'People Get Ready' by Curtis Mayfield. We went down well, and were offered another gig in some club in Chester, but, subsequent events prevented us from fulfilling that opportunity. Not long after our one and only gig Benny went into the Army and Paul went off to be in the musical Hair.

"By 1969 the whole Mersey scene had quietened down and everyone on the streets in Toxteth was into 'Accapella'. So if more than two or three guys were together we would sing in harmony, we sang wherever we went, in shops, parks, pubs, clubs anywhere they would give us a free drink. But I wanted more, I wanted to move. I went to London in 1972.

"I arrived from Liverpool with an acoustic guitar and a suitcase full of dreams, hopes, and enthusiasm, and not much else. I didn't have a clue what was happening, I stayed with Paul in Earls Court Road, which in itself was an eye opener. Paul by then was an established actor and was in the stage show Jesus Christ Superstar. I used to just hang out in the theatre with him at rehearsals and the like, but just to be back stage all the time was great, actors have so much fun!

"I had met a guy from Canada and together we would go busking in the streets with our guitars. Our favourite place to busk was Trafalgar Square, in the underground. It was always warm and we could earn about £5 a day each that was enough to keep mind and soul together.

"After a while I managed to get a job as a roadie with a band named Everyone Involved, run by a South African by the name of Michael Klein. They used to rehearse in a basement of a clothes shop just of Piccadilly Circus. I didn't really know anything about setting up equipment like amps and PA equipment, not having had any in Liverpool.

"Luckily for me at the first gig the drummer never turned up and I ended up on the drums, while not knowing any of the songs I think I did alright. I must have gotten something right for they asked me to join them.

"The conga player was Richard Lanchester, son of the man who designed Lanchester cars, the drum kit was also his. I was not too popular with him because I kept breaking the skins on the Tom Toms because I used to have them at such an acute angle. We would play two shows at a small theatre in The Haymarket every Monday night, between the shows I would go out to the edge of the stage with my acoustic guitar and sing some Neil Young songs - 'Needle and The Damage Done' etc. We also did some open air shows in and around London, and several free shows at Windsor. Eventually after about 3 years, my lack of owning my own kit led to me being asked to leave the band.

"In 1977 I was living in a flat in West Hampstead with Paul and it was during this time that I met an African guy who I was to form a new band with. Gus Anyia was from Nigeria and played lead guitar. I went to his place later that day and we had a jam together, it was good, we seemed to compliment each other well, me being a rhythm guitar player. Our fate for the next three years was sealed on that day!

"We played together a few times after that, and things just got better. We found that it was easy to write together, he was into jazz –

Miles Davis, Donald Bird etc. I was into pop – Beatles, Neil Young (Crazy Horse) etc. and the two styles just seemed to fit together well.

"But soon after that he decided to go to Nigeria for a few months.

"Gus came back from Nigeria all fired up and raring to go. The band we formed was called Dambala and we toured Europe twice, once in 1978: Holland, West Germany, Belgium etc, and again in 1979 topping the bill this time was unlike anything I've ever experienced.

"When our first single 'Zimbabwe' reached No. 4 in the Black Echoes and Jazz Review magazine, we started to get quite a lot of recognition, and were invited to write the theme music for a Channel 4 show about black people in England called 'Black On Black', and appeared during the opening credits.

"We had also been voted Best British Newcomers in the same magazine. Soon after this, during another tour of Holland, we started to have problems of the 'musical differences' type. Not long after our return from the tour the band split up."

7. The Nashville of the North

LIVERPOOL had the biggest country music scene in Europe which, unfortunately, tended to be overshadowed by the success of the Beatles and the Mersey Sound.

As one Mersey musician pointed out: "Before rock 'n' roll I'd been into Country and Western music. Actually, in Liverpool everybody used to play Country and Western: anything with some real lyrics about a bit of trouble, or a bit of heartache."

Hank Walters, leader of Hank Walters & the Dusty Road Ramblers points to the huge number of groups registered with the North West Country Music Association and says that he had a list of 127 Liverpool country bands.

In addition to the Association, the Country scene had its own version of the Grand Ole' Opry, held annually at the Philharmonic Hall.

There were Country clubs such as the Black Cat Club and Wells Fargo and Country bands such as Phil Brady & the Ranchers, the Miller Brothers, the Texans, the Saddlers, the Alaskans, the Blue Mountain Boys, the Westerners, the Drifting Cowboys, Cyl Con & the Westernaires, the Kentuckians and others who performed on the numerous social clubs throughout the area.

The most successful of the bands was the Hillsiders, which originated with Kenny Johnson. Kenny, like a lot of Liverpool youngsters, loved both music and football. He was a talented soccer player and was in the Liverpool Schoolboys team, but his love for music took precedence and he began singing at the age of 16 during the skiffle craze.

He recalled: "I started playing Spanish guitar, but I just wasn't good enough, so I started singing. Together with a group of young lads I played in pubs and youth clubs for six months – we didn't have a name for the group during that time.

"When the skiffle craze died down, I formed a CW group called the Country Four and played mostly at the Black Cat Club and in working men's clubs. I think Clubland people appreciate country music more than the younger set."

The origin of the group stretches back to 1958 when Kenny and Joe Butler formed a band in Liverpool called Sonny Webb and the Country Two, which then became Sonny Webb and the Country Four.

Kenny had chosen the name Sonny Webb because it referred to his heroes at the time – Sonny James and Webb Pierce.

After about 18 months, Kenny left to join the Wild Cats and the Country Four found another lead singer in Brian Ewan. Several months later Kenny asked Joe to join him in the group as their bass guitarist had left them. Joe was playing lead guitar at the time but decided to change to bass and joined them and they had now changed their name from the Wild Cats to Sonny Webb & the Cascades.

Apart from Kenny and Joe, the other members were John State on lead guitar, formerly with the Connaughts and drummer Roger Wilcox who was previously with the Gerry Owen Four.

There was a completely different line-up when the group became the Hillsiders in 1964.

The original group members were now Joe Butler, bass guitar/vocals; Brian Hilton, lead guitar/harmonica/vocals; Frankie Wan, steel guitar; Brian 'Noddy' Redman, drums and Kenny Johnson, lead vocals. They initially played in the style of country artists such as George Jones and Buck Owens' Buckaroos.

Among their repertoire at the time were Buddy Knox songs such as 'I Think I'm Gonna Kill Myself', 'Party Doll' and 'The Girl With The Golden Hair', Del Shannon's 'Runaway', Carl Perkins 'Pink Pedal Pushers', 'Sure To Fall' and some Chuck Berry numbers.

1964 was also the year when Decca released their debut album 'Hillsiders Play The Country Hits' and they also toured Germany with Red Sovine (he was No.1 with the record 'Giddy Up Go' at the time) and then with Molly Bee.

Among the other country acts which the Hillsiders opened for during their career were Marty Robbins, Glen Campbell, Jerry Lee Lewis and Gene Watson.

It was Joe who approached Spencer Lloyd Mason, their manager at the time, saying he'd discovered a fantastic number which they wanted to record as a single. It was called 'Release Me.' 'Spen' approached their Decca A&R man Noel Walker who agreed that they should record it as their next single and also arranged for them to be backed with an orchestra. Immediately prior to their session Walker then told them that he had decided that they couldn't record it as he wanted to use the number they'd found with another artist – Engelbert Humperdinck!

This betrayal obviously soured their relationship with Decca and they signed with the Lucky label, Britain's first Country Music label and issued their second album 'It Takes A Lot Of Money' in 1965.

The Hillsiders then toured Germany with Country star Bobby Bare and in 1966 travelled to Nashville where they recorded 'The English Country Side (Bobby Bare from Nashville and the Hillsiders from Liverpool)', produced by Chet Atkins and issued on RCA Victor in 1967. The record climbed into the Top 20 of the American Country Music album chart. 1968 saw them not only issuing the album 'The Leaving of Liverpool', but appearing in a BBC TV series with George Hamilton IV.

Another member later on was Ronnie Bennett on steel guitar and they eventually evolved into a line up with Dave Rowlands, steel guitar/Dobro; Brian Hilton, lead guitar/harmonica/vocals; Brian Redman, drums; Kevin McGarry, lead vocals/guitar and Mick Kinney, bass guitar/vocals.

In 1971 they became part of RCA's Country Caravan tour of Scandinavia and won their first 'Group Of The Year' award from the CMA (GB) – the British Country Music Association.

They changed labels and released 'The Hillsiders By Request' in 1972 and 'Our Country' in 1973, which included 11 original songs, both albums on the Polydor label.

Kenny Johnson left the group at the end of 1974, due more to do with conflict with the group's manager than anything else and early in 1975 he was replaced by Kevin McGarry, a former member of the Westerners.

That year they released 'To Please You' on Sire Records and in 1976 they organised the 'Goodbye Scottie Road' album with other Merseyside bands. That year they also signed with the agency Live Promotions. In 1978 their next album 'On The Road' was issued on the LP label and the same year they were featured on an in-concert programme on BBC 2 which was recorded from Snape Maltings.

In 1979 Ronnie Bennett left the group to start a steel guitar business and they were joined by Dave Rowland.

In 1981 they recorded a BBC TV special with Billie Jo Spears and also recorded for Dutch Television. In 1982 they flew to the Falklands to entertain the troops.

The group recorded their 13th album 'Only One You' on the Suitbag label in 1984 and in 1986 released their next album 'If That's The Way You Feel' to tie in with their tour with Slim Whitman.

In 1989 they celebrated their 25th anniversary with the release of their '15-25' album, which also included Kenny Johnson and Ronnie Bennett. During that year they received the BCMA Committee Award.

When Kenny left the Hillsiders he then formed his own outfit Kenny Johnson & Northwind, which eventually disbanded in 2002. Kenny now has his own country music programme on Radio Merseyside.

Joe Butler left to work with the group's booking agents Ricky McCabe Entertainments and was replaced by Mike Kinney. The group then appeared on a live radio broadcast for the BBC which was transmitted live by satellite to over 200 million homes in America and Canada. At the 1997 British Country Music Awards they received the Ambassador Award.

Sadly, Joe contracted pancreatic cancer and died in May 2007.

Hank Walters was one of the legendary Liverpool Country Music founders who established country music in Britain, which led to Liverpool having the largest Country Music scene outside America and worthy of the accolade 'the Nashville of the North.'

He was born William Ralph Walters in Liverpool on 2 August 1933.

Hank is a great Cajun accordion player and traces his love of Cajun music to his Grandfather who sailed from Liverpool on the Alice Aleigh. He jumped ship in Louisiana and survived in the Everglades, catching frogs to sell to restaurants in New Orleans.

During his performances, Hank would reminisce about his grandfather, with humorous tales of his adventures.

His grandfather had gathered a collection of Jimmy Rodgers records which he'd brought home from his shipping trips and these became Hank's first major influence.

At the age of 11, when he was at the Venice Street School in Anfield, he formed Spike Walters & the Hillbillies for a Christmas concert at the school and decided to keep the group on.

They then began to play in local pubs, at weddings and then in dancehalls. His epiphany came in 1949 when, at the age of 16, he heard Hank Williams' 'Lovesick Blues' on the jukebox of the Blue Bell Café in Aintree.

He was to tell writer Kevin McManus: "When I heard 'Lovesick Blues' I went bananas. That's the way it hit everyone who ever heard it. I went mad on it; so they got the record out and took the number off it for me. I went to a place in Robson Street and gave them the number. I got one of the first pressings of the record. The girl in the shop started getting me catalogues. I couldn't wait for Saturdays so I could go to the record shop and spend my one and nine on a record. I bought every single Hank Williams record."

During his National Service, Hank was sent to the Middle East where he formed Hank Walters & His Dusty Road Ramblers. He completed his army service in 1953 and began working on the docks for the Mersey Dock & Harbour Board Company.

In 1955 he gave his first radio show in the UK and by 1957 was appearing at the Cavern club and during the same year began his own weekly Country Music club.

Hank and the band began to appear regularly at a Country Music venue called The Black Cat Club above Samson & Barlow's Restaurant in London Road, which opened on 12 February 1957. By this time Country bands had begun to appear all over Merseyside and the establishment of The Black Cat Club saw bands appear such as the Miller Brothers, the Kentuckians, the Blue Mountain Boys and others.

Also, a huge boost to the development of Liverpool's unique Country scene was Merseyside's 'Clubland' and there were over 300 clubs affiliated to the Merseyside Clubs Association. These ranged from venues for unions such as the National Union of Railwaymen to factories such as Crawford's Biscuit Factor, many of them eager to book the burgeoning Country Music acts.

Walton Lane Social Club, more popularly referred to as 'Ossie Wade's' provided the showcase. Club secretaries used to frequent the club on Sundays to watch the acts audition and would then ply them with bookings.

Another of the Liverpool country clubs was called Wells Fargo.

Hank is also a song writer and many of his compositions reflect his love of Liverpool, such as the first song he ever wrote, 'Sweet Liverpool', which was based on Jimmie Rodger's song 'Mississippi Delta River.'

Hank Walters & the Dusty Road Ramblers was resident band at the Black Cat Club for 12 years and were sacked from the club when they took the night off to support Bill Monroe & His Bluegrass Boys at the Philharmonic Hall. In 1991 Hank created Hank Walters & the Arcadian Ladies, a four piece outfit in which he was joined by his three daughters Pauline, Claire and Lorna Gail.

In 1998 they participated in an album project 'City With A Heart' to celebrate Liverpool's Country and Folk Music talent.

Phil Brady & the Ranchers were led by Phil Brady on vocals and rhythm guitar. There were various personnel changes in his band who included Frank Peters on steel guitar, Ray Owen on lead, Tommy Bownett on bass and Eddie Watt on drums. Other line-ups included Ritchie Galvin on drums, Ritchie Mitchell on bass and John State on lead.

The group recorded their debut record 'An American Sailor At The Cavern' for the new Cavern record label. It was penned by Tim McCoy, a former seaman who used to be our handyman at Mersey Beat, building counters and fixing shelves. The flipside was 'Sidetracked', penned by Cavern disc jockey Bob Wooler. 2,500 copies were pressed and issued on Cavern Sound IMSTL 2 in March 1965. However, the official receiver seized most of the copies when the Cavern went into liquidation.

The group's second release was 'Little Roza' c/w 'Just One More Time' issued on Rex R 11011 in September 1965. Their final release was 'Please come Back' c/w 'Lonesome for Me', issued on Go AJ 11406, also in 1965.

Jim Clarke was born in Wavertree on 9 December 1940 and recalls: "My brother Norman was in the army and he had an American friend who was based at Burtonwood Airbase just outside Liverpool (I would be about 11 then) and our Norman would bring him back to our house every Saturday night and he would stay over and he used to bring his Country Music LPs with him, (we would listen to them all Sunday until he went back to camp) so that's how I was introduced to country music.

"My first major inspiration was without doubt Webb Pierce, followed by Slim Whitman, (I developed my falsetto voice and learned to yodel listening to him)."

Jim joined a skiffle group, and then a band called JC & the Strollers, who changed their name to the Four Dimensions in 1963. They were joined by Irene Green, who sang under the name Tiffany and became Tiffany's Dimensions and were to record songs such as 'Tears On My Pillow' with George Martin. When the group split up, Jim teamed up with another member as the two Dimensions.

He says: "In 1980 my wife Dorothea and I formed a duo called James and Dodie White and worked for the next ten years, working home and abroad. After ten years on the road she had had enough and wanted to retire from performing on stage, I carried on using the name Clarke James (as some one else was using the name James Clarke), I was singing a lot of Neil Sedaka songs, Bee Gees, Elton John and Soul Music."

Jim then decided to go on the Country Music circuit as Country was his first love and he currently performs the songs of Hank Williams, Webb Pierce, Hank Locklin, Vince Gill, Brooks and Dunn, Kenny Chesney and Tracy Byrd.

He entered the Country Music field performing in Britain's first country and western talent contest in Blackpool, won the first prize of £1,000 and was crowned Britain's 'King of Country Music.'

One of Britain's leading Country performers is Charlie Landsborough.

Charles, like so many children of Merseyside families, was shuttled off to Wales during the war when Liverpool was to suffer heavy bombing raids. He was born Charles Alexander Landsborough in Wrexham, Wales on 26 October, 1941, son of Charles and Aggie

Landsborough and Charlie's siblings were: Harry, Derek, Arthur, Jack, Dot, Sylvia, Doreen and Joyce.

Soon after Charlie was born, the family moved back to Merseyside as the bombing had stopped and Charlie was raised in Birkenhead.

He recalls: "I was reared in the dockland area of Birkenhead and the view from our front window was a mixture of docks, dumps, railway lines, oil factories and the coal wharf. It sounds grim, but my childhood was far from that. I was surrounded by a loving family; animals, and of course music, my early years were extremely happy."

Regarding the mention of animals, Charlie comments: "Our house was always full of animals and apart from dogs and cats we also kept chickens in the back and at one time a duck. There were also birds – budgies, canaries and finches and a very special gift of a monkey smuggled in by my brother Harry. This little delight with the unimaginative name of Jacko made me very popular with school friends."

However, it was the influence of music which was to have a profound influence on his life. He says: "My brothers were all sailors and apart from the guitars and all the music, they brought home gifts from all around the world. I remember sitting enchanted by the scent of the wood in a guitar brought from Spain, my imagination afire at the sight of a small canoe carved by natives of West Africa, pistols with real revolving chambers from the US and getting my first pair of dungarees from Canada. Small wonder I so eagerly awaited the return of each brother from another trip."

From the age of three Charlie's mother used to sing him to sleep and his father was a ballad singer, known locally as 'the silver voiced tenor.'

After leaving school (where his headmaster had remarked that Charlie had a good academic future ahead of him "until he discovered that damn banjo!"), he worked on various jobs on the railways, in flour mills, as a postman – and then signed up to join the army for four years, hoping to be sent to Hong Kong. Instead he was sent to Germany. This was in the early Sixties and he joined a group called the Chicago Sect in Dortmund, Germany. He then married his childhood sweetheart Thelma and returned to Merseyside, appeared with some local bands, had a number of jobs and then became a teacher.

In fact, it was while he was working as a teacher that he began to write songs in his spare time and also performed as a semi-professional musician.

Then, in 1994 came the big breakthrough when his song 'What Colour Is The Wind' topped the Irish charts. He then followed with a chart album in Ireland and began appearing on television shows in Britain such as Pebble Mill and GMTV.

Charlie had been introduced to Ireland by Tony Allen, who loved the song 'What Colour Is The Wind', which told of a young blind child's attempt to envision the world. Initially Gerry Anderson began playing the track in Northern Ireland and the song then came to the attention of Pat Kenny, who hosted a chat show in Dublin, and invited Charlie to appear on the popular Kenny Show Live. The following week the album 'What Colour Is The Wind' topped the Irish album charts.

Charlie then, over a period of time, recorded a further ten albums and had two more No. 1 records in Ireland. Most of his albums have topped the British Country Music charts.

He tours extensively with his five piece band, who comprise Pete Brazil, lead guitar, accordion, harmonica, vocals; Pete Ariss, bass guitar, double bass, vocals; Bob Wallis, keyboards; Gary Freeman, drums.

In 1999 he recorded his album 'Still Can't Say Goodbye' in Nashville and won the BCMA Best Male vocalist (2000) for the third year in succession. While in Nashville he made three appearances on the Grand Ole Opry.

He toured Australia and New Zealand in 2001 and returned for another Australian tour in 2008 which was a busy year for him with appearances at the Summer Pops in Liverpool and the television series Songs Of Praise. He also appeared at the Philharmonic Hall on 5 November promoting his latest album 'Under Blue Skies' and his DVD 'A Special Performance.'

A major international country star, he was nominated as the Best Global Country Artist at the Country Music Awards in Nashville and has been voted Best Male Vocalist three times at the British Country Music Awards.

Charlie's album releases are: 'Under Blue Skies'; 'The Storyteller'; 'Heart & Soul'; 'My Heart Would Know'; 'The Lighter Side'; 'Reflections'; 'Smile'; 'Movin' On'; 'Once In a While'.

His singles include: 'Half The Ghost Of a Chance'; 'Saviour's Song'; 'My Most Wonderful Time'; 'I'm A Lucky Man'; 'I Don't Know'; 'Who Is This Man'; 'It's About Loving You'; 'Song For The Dragonfly'; 'Twenty Four Hours Times Two'; 'My Heart Would Know'; 'I Am Red'; 'I Know What It Is To Be Loved'; 'The Closest Thing To My Heart'; 'Going My Own Sweet Way'; 'Moate'; 'He Still Holds You'; 'Nothing Will Ever Be The Same Again'; 'Like A Stone'; 'I'll Be Missing You'.

Apart from his popularity as a singer, Charlie has also found success as a songwriter, with his numbers being recorded by a number of Country Artists including Jack Jones, Pat Boone, Foster and Allen, George Hamilton IV and Daniel O'Donnell.

In his personal life, Charlie reverted to Catholicism and says: "I'm a believer. I truly do believe in God, in an afterlife. I wouldn't hide that from anyone. At the same time I'm no saint! I have my failings – many of them – and that includes enjoying a drink."

Here is just a selection of the many awards which Charlie has received:

In 1990 Charlie won the British Country Music Awards with 'How Do You Do These Things' voted as the Single of the Year. He also won the 'Record Of the Week' award on Radio 2 for 'Heaven Knows'.

1992 saw him win the Country Music Award as 'Top Solo Performer Of The Year.'

In 1994 he won 'North Country Music Song of the Year' from BBC East Midlands for 'What Colour Is The Wind', while the album of the same title won 'Favourite Album' in the Country Music Round Up International Awards and Charlie was voted 'Most Popular Male Vocalist' at the Country Music Round Up International Awards.

In 1995 'What Colour Is The Wind' became 'Best Album by A British Act' in the UK Country Awards and the awards also pronounced the number the 'Best Single' and also 'Best Song By A British Songwriter.'

In 1996 he received The Great British Country Music Award as 'Best British Male Vocalist' and the UK Country Radio Award for 'Best Single' with 'Further Down The Road' and the UK Country Radio Award for 'Most Nominations' plus The Irish Record Music Association Award for International Country Music Album of the Year with 'With You In Mind' and the UK Country Radio Award for 'Best Single' with 'Forever Friend' and the Scottish Country Music Award as Most Popular Male Artist, the Scottish Country Music Award for Most Popular British Album for 'What Colour Is The Wind' and the Scottish Country Music Award for Most Popular British Song with 'Forever Friend'.

In 1997 the Great British Country Music Awards once again proclaimed him Best British Male vocalist.

The 1998 awards began with BBC Radio Scousology Award for Best Music and Best Personality and he won the Best British Male Vocalist awards again at the Great British Music Awards and also won 'Best Single' at the UK Country Radio Awards with 'Further Down The Road' and again he received the UK Country Radio Award for 'Most Nominations.

2000 brought Charlie Best British Male Vocalist at the Great British Country Music Awards plus Best British Album at the same awards for 'Still Can't Say Goodbye' and the UK Country Radio Award for Best Album for 'Still Can't Say Goodbye.'

Of course, Liverpool's former premier position as one of the world's major ports led to the area becoming a huge cosmopolitan centre in which the Irish contingent (half a million Irish people moved to Liverpool early in the last century), in particular, brought in several musical genres.

As researcher John Kerrigan points out: "The Irish folk music which had been exported to the United States by the brothers, sisters and cousins of the Liverpool settlers transformed into one strand of American country music, was electrified into Country & Western, and subsequently re-imported into Irish communities throughout Britain over a hundred years later. If you went into any Liverpool Irish pub in the late 50s, the songs of Hank Williams and Patsy Cline were being performed alongside the traditional jigs and reels."

An example of the link between Liverpool, Irish roots and Country Music is to be found in Michael Snow who has moved from the World Capitol of Pop (Liverpool) to the World Capitol of Country Music (Nashville).

Michael, the son of Irish immigrants, was born and raised in Liverpool. During the era of the Mersey Sound he joined the group

The Barons in 1962 and the group were to record their single 'A Love She Can Count On' c/w 'Foolin' in 1964 for the Parlophone label. Michael played piano, guitar and sang harmony vocal on the record.

(This track is now part of 'The Mersey Sound', a 30-track CD I compiled which was issued by EMI Gold in February 2008.)

In 1964 he moved to London and joined a band called West Five, who had a hit with the Jagger/Richards composition 'Congratulations.'

After that single and two subsequent ones failed to chart the group disbanded and he next spent six months with the Blue Aces, a show-band from Waterford, Ireland.

While in London Michael became a freelance pianist/musical director with visiting American artists such as Edwin Starr, Ben E. King, Doris Troy and the Checkmates.

He became a full member of the Checkmates in 1966, aiding the band's transition from R&B to mainstream rock, with the band changing their name to Ferris Wheel.

Michael was also enjoying success as a songwriter and composed Marmalade's first hit 'Can't Stop Now.'

He left Ferris Wheel in 1969 to concentrate on studio session work and song writing and among the works he contributed to as a session musician were those by artists Dusty Springfield, Badfinger, Lulu and PJ Proby. He was even one of the 45 voices on John Lennon's 'Power to the People.'

Michael also teamed up with Billy Kinsley, former member of the Merseybeats and the Merseys and Jimmy Campbell, former member of the Kirkby's, in Rockin' Horse, who released their album 'Yes It Is' in 1970. The band didn't enjoy success on record and Michael then composed the international hit 'Rosetta.'

The number topped the chart in nine countries, was recorded by Georgie Fame and Alan Price and won the Ivor Novello Award in 1971. That year and the following year saw Michael as pianist with Chuck Berry on a 60-date concert tour, followed by Colin Blunstone's first solo tour.

He moved to Nashville, Tennessee in 1973, becoming songwriter, music publisher and recording executive, with his songs recorded by Earl Scruggs, Julie Andrews and Ray Stevens.

In 1986 Michael began his collaboration with Dennis Locorriere, lead singer and songwriter with Dr Hook, also opening his own recording studio and publishing company.

Michael decided to return to his Liverpool-Irish roots in music and collaborated with the Brady Family in the studio and on concert.

He also produced Elizabeth Reed, the Celtic band Ceolta Nua and other Celtic/American musicians in Nashville.

He was able to add a Celtic flavour by his expertise on bodhran, accordion, tenor banjo and vocals on recordings by a variety of artists including Robert Earl Keene, Gloria Loring, Adie Grey and Cathryn Craig.

In 2000 Michael formed his own record label Irish Eye Records and began to record a trilogy which expressed his Liverpool-Irish roots. Using a term for Liverpool/Irish – 'Skelly', he began the trilogy with 'Here Comes The Skelly,' originally recorded during a six week period in 1998 and reflecting on his childhood in Liverpool.

The following year saw the release of the second volume 'The Rats and the Rosary' and the final chapter 'Never Say No To A Jar' was issued in 2003.

In 2004 Michael took part in the second Nashville Beatlefest 'The Beatles – The Nashville Connection', participating in a panel discussion with former Beatles publicist Tony Barrow, George Harrison's sister Louise, Chris Huston, former member of the Undertakers and Joey Molland of Badfinger.

Michael also joined Al Kooper, Mark Hudson and Henry Gross to perform 'Being For the Benefit of Mr Kite.'

Unfortunately, Michael was incapacitated after a fall at Lime Street Station in Liverpool in 2007.

He suffered compound fractures of the ulna and radius of his left forearm, which required surgery at Royal Liverpool University Hospital, four visits to the OR and a week of in-patient care. On his return to America be began undergoing rehabilitation therapy at St Thomas Hospital in Nashville.

As there was some nerve and tissue damage, the restoration of full playing capability in his left hand is going to take some time and a lot of effort.

Irish music and the Irish community are well served in Liverpool with an annual 'Liverpool Irish Festival' taking place annually.

The 2008 event, for example took place between 17 October and 2 November and numerous venues around the city, including St Michael's Irish Centre, the Silvestrian Centre, the Picket, St George's Hall Concert Room, the Arts Centre, the Casa, the Playhouse, the Royal Court, the Beatles Story, Philharmonic Hall and the Bluecoat.

8. Folk's Fab Four

THE Spinners, often referred to as 'the other fab four', were Britain's leading folk music outfit for decades.

They were occasionally called the Liverpool Spinners due to the fact that there was an American band called the Spinners, while the American band, in Britain, was known either as the Motown Spinners or the Detroit Spinners.

When they originally formed in the autumn of 1958 they comprised Cliff Hall, Tony Davis, Hughie Jones, Mick Groves, Jacquie MacDonald, Stan Francis plus Tony's wife Beryl and his sister Joan.

The Spinners were initially a skiffle group. But when a seaman called Redd Sullivan suggested that they include sea shanties in their repertoire, they changed direction musically, and also began to include English folk songs into the act.

As a folk act, based on Merseyside, they became a quartet, with Hughie Jones (guitar, harmonica, banjo), who was born in Liverpool.

Cliff Hall (guitar, harmonica), was born in Orient Province, Cuba of Jamaican parents. When his mother died he returned to Jamaica with his father who worked in the plantations. There wasn't enough money to provide Cliff with further education and as a teenager he worked moulding breezeblocks and milking cows.

When RAF personnel came to Jamaica on a recruiting drive, Cliff claimed he was older than he was, signed up and came to Britain in November 1942 and was stationed in Worcestershire. He married a Scottish girl Janet Massie in 1947 and the couple had three children.

By 1953 he was working as an electrician in Leeds and when he was sent to work in Capenhurst in Cheshire he met Tony Davis and was invited to join the Spinners. Mick Groves (guitar), born in Salford was to say: "I think our strong Liverpool identity is actually a great tribute to the city. They call it a melting pot and we all melted together greatly."

Tony Davis (banjo, tin whistle, guitar, kazoo), was born in Blackburn, but moved to Merseyside at the age of 14. The Spinners had founded a folk club in Liverpool in October 1958 which they called the Triton Club and their live performances formed the basis of their debut album 'Songs Spun In Liverpool' in 1962. The Spinners ran the club for 25 years and it continues with new regulars under the name Triton Folk.

The group signed with Philips Records in 1963 and recorded eight albums on the label before signing with EMI Records in the early Seventies.

Apart from performing vintage folk numbers, they also included original folk songs penned by Hughie in their repertoire, including 'The Ellen Vanin Tragedy' and the 'Marco Polo.' One highlight of their act was a tribute to their native Liverpool with a song originally written by Peter McGovern in 1962, 'In My Liverpool Home,' while Cliff included some traditional Jamaican songs into their repertoire.

One of the original songs on the debut album, 'Quayside Songs Old And New' included the song 'Liverpool Girls,' which was penned by Cliff and was his comment on British cooking. He said: "My first wife couldn't cook the dishes I liked at first, but I called the song 'Liverpool Girls' so as not to offend her."

Oddly, the record company were uncomfortable about promoting a multi-racial group and placed a cartoon on the cover in which all the members appeared to be white!

The group recorded over forty albums prior to their retirement in 1988, thirty years after their original formation, having achieved considerable fame in Britain via their many concert and television appearances. They even had their own television show on BBC 1 in 1970 which ran for seven years and another of their own series was aired on BBC Radio 2.

They officially retired following a concert at the Philharmonic Hall after a 120 date farewell tour. A year after their retirement as a group they gathered together to lead the community singing at the 1989 FA

Cup final and also performed some Christmas shows in1992,1993 and 1994. There was also a reunion performance at the Everyman Theatre in 2004.

During the last 17 years of their career, John McCormick acted as their double bassist and musical director. When the Spinners decided to retire, he said that the Spinners had become an institution and "who wants to end their days in an institution."

Following their retirement, Cliff moved to Australia with his third wife Dottie (he had been widowed twice) but passed away on 26 June 2008 at the age of 82.

Tony continued performing and Mick became Chair of Education at Wirral Borough Council and later moved to Devon.

Hughie Jones has also continued to perform and had has three albums released, including 'Liverpool Connexions' issued on the Fellside label on 14 November 2005. It contained the tracks: 'Mist Over The Mersey'; 'Moles Of Edge Hill'; 'Down By The Dockyard Wall'; 'Blue And Red; Betsy Of New York'; 'Rent Collecting In Speke'; 'Here's To Cheshire'; 'Unmooring'; 'Cape Horner'; 'Liverpool Lullaby'; 'Derbyshire'; 'Seth Davey'; 'Shanghai Brown'; 'Dirty Old Town'; 'Safe In Snug Harbour'; 'King Of Edge Hill'; 'Alexander Selkirk Is My Name'; 'Daughter Of Water Street'.

The Spinners 1994 CD compilation 'The Spinners' contains the tracks: 'Lord of the Dance', 'All Day Singing', 'Blaydon Races', 'Last Thing On My Mind', 'Amazing Grace', 'We Shall Not Be Moved', 'Guantanamera', 'Jamaica Farewell', 'To Be A Farmers Boy', 'The Foggy Dew', 'Greensleeves / Lovely Joan', 'North Country Maid', 'Liverpool Hornpipe', 'The Colliers Rant', 'Dance The Flora', 'Banks of the Ohio', 'The Shepherd Lad', 'Waters of the Tyne', 'Lamorna', 'Bucket of the Mountain Dew', 'When I First Came To This Land', 'So Long It's Been Good To Know You'. It was reissued on 13 January 2008.

Their discography, together with year of release, includes: 1962 'Quayside Songs Old And New' (EMI CLP 1500 (Mono); 1963 'The Spinners' (Fontana TL 5201); 1964 'Folk at the Phil!' (Fontana STL5219); 1965 'More Folk at the Phil' (Fontana STL 5234); 1966 'Another LP By The Spinners' (Fontana STL5431); 1966 'The Family Of Man' (Phillips TL 5361); 1967 'The Spinners Live Performance'

(Contour 6870-502); 1967 'Another Spinner from The Spinners' (Fontana 6857006); 1967 '16 Startracks' (Philips LP 6308-064); 1967 'The Singing City' (Philips 6382 002); 1969 'The Spinners Clockwork' Storybook (Fontana SFL 13191)(Later re - issued as 'Stop, Look, Listen'); 1969 'The Spinners' (Contour CN 2026); 1969 'Stop, Look, Listen' (Contour 6870 529); 1969 'Spotlight On The Spinners' (Philips 6625 014); 1969 'Not Quite Folk' (Fontana STL 5495).

1970 'The Spinners Are In Town' (Fontana 6309 014); 1970 'The Spinners Collection' (Contour PDA 026); 1970 '10 Of The Best' (Fontana SPXL51); 1971 'Spinners Vol. 1-3' (Phillips 6382 046/7/8); 1972 'An Evening With' (Contour, LP 6870 588); 1972 'Love Is Teasing' (Columbia SCX 6493); 1973 'The Liverpool Spinners' (EMI ST6406); 1974 'The Spinners At The London Palladium' (EMI YAX 4832); 1975 'Sing Out, Shout With Joy' (EMI SCX6526); 1976 'Liverpool to Coney Island' (Philips SON Q08); 1976 'The Spinners English Collection' (EMI OU 2120); 1977 'All Day Singing' (EMI, LP EMC 3167); 1978 'The Spinners Sing Songs of the Tall Ships' (EMI NTS 154B1979); '20 Golden Folk Songs' (EMI NTS 193); 1979 '18 Golden Favourites'; 1979 'By Arrangement' (EMI, TCEMC 3009), re-released as 'Everybody Loves Saturday Night' (MFP 50339).

1980 'Blaydon Races' (Ideal TCIDL 7); 1981 'Around The World And Back Again' (Dingle's LP DID 712); 1981 'Carribean Sunshine Hits' (One-up, LP OU 2235); 1982 'Here's To You From The Spinners' (PRT N145); 1983 'Here's To The Spinners' (TC-MFP 41 1038 9); 1983 'In Our Liverpool Home' (PRT SPN1); 'The Best of The Spinners' (DTO 10068); 1984 'Last Night We Had A Do' (PRT N6553); 1985 'Your 20 Favourite Christmas Carols' (Capitol, LP ED 2607471); 1986 'Spun Gold' (PRT, PYC 12, LP N 6560); 1986 'The Spinners In Concert' (MFP, CC 212); 1987 'The Spinners Christmas Cassette' (RTS 1679); 1988 'The Spinners Final Fling' (EMI EN5007).

1991 'The Best Of The Spinners' (Pickwick PWK 103); 1992 'The Best Of The Spinners' (Castle MATCD 228).

Other compilations include: 'Meet the Spinners' (Warwick WW 5058); 'This Is The Spinners' (EMI THIS 7); 'The Spinners' (EMI

Ideal TC IDL 7); 1994 'The Spinners' (EMI 724383018925).

Their EPs include: 'Songs Spun in Liverpool' (Topic TOP 69); 'The Singing City'; 'The City Sings Back'; 'Flowers of Manchester'.

Their singles include: 'Maggie May/ Linstead Market' (Fontana TF 450); 'Shine Eye Gal/ Amen'; 'Dirty Old Town/ Philimiooriay' (Fontana TF494); 'The Old Dun Cow/ Hold Him Joe'; 'Family of Man/ Shortness of Sight'; 'Funeral in Berlin/ Diamonds and Pearls'; 'Orange and the Green/Mrs. Hooligan's Christmas Cake'; 'Seth Davey/ All For Me Grog'; 'I've Been on the Road/ Bluenose'; 'Uncle Sigmund's Clockwork Storybook//Mechanical Blackbird'; 'Black and White/Strangest Dream'; 'Malaika/ Wing Like A Dove'; 'Here's To The Couple/ Deep Blue Sea'; 'Castles In The Air/ Lamorna'; 'Last Thing On My Mind/ We Shall Not Be Moved'; 'The Wind Is Blowing/The Wren Boys Song' (PRT 7P316).

Jacqueline Macdonald first began performing with the Spinners on Merseyside in the late Fifties, but left the group after three years and founded a folk club in Liverpool in 1961 (she still runs the club after all these years which now takes place at Sefton Park Cricket Club on the third Thursday of each month).

She was a teacher and met up with another teacher Bridie Gallagher to form a folk duo, turning professional in 1964, becoming the first full time British female folk-song duo.

Initially they called themselves Jackie & Bridie, but this was changed to Jacqui and Bridie. The duo was to spend 28 years singing full time together appearing in Britain, Europe and North America.

In fact, they made annual tours of North American for many years and the two also had a weekly two-hour Radio Merseyside show for seven years.

When Bridie died from cancer, Jacqui originally decided to retire from active performing, but then continued as a solo artist from 1992 and has recorded 14 albums.

Jacqui had also written a book 'Of These Years I Sing' which describes the life on the road of Jacqui and Bridie, through the songs they have written, with words and illustrations.

Jacqui now lives in the Lake District but continues to perform and sometimes teams up with Hughie Jones, former member of the Spinners.

Jacqui and Bridie's first EP together contained the tracks: 'To Hear the Nightingale Sing'; 'Love Is Teasing'; 'Pop Goes The Folk Song'; 'Michael Flynn'.

Their singles included: 'We Only Needed Time' c/w 'Come Me Little Son'; 'Cathedral In Our Time' c/w 'Lord Of The Dance'; 'I Was A Maid' c/w 'Scarborough Fair'.

Their albums were: 'Jackie & Bridie On Stage'; 'The Folk World Of Jackie & Bridie'; 'Jackie & Bridie Live at The Liverpool Philharmonic'; '10th Anniversary Of The Folk House Folk Club'; 'A Place In The Choir'; 'How Can You Keep From Singing'; 'Next Time Around'; 'Our Language'; 'The Perfect Round'; 'Hold Back The Dawn'; 'Here's To You'; 'Tour Of Scotland'; 'Tis A Gift to Be Simple'; 'Hello Friend'; 'International Garden Festival', 'Liverpool '84'.

Jacqui's CD album releases include: 'Jacqui's Best Loved Songs Vol.1'; 'Jacqui's Best Loved Songs Vol 2', 'Jacqueline Of All Trades'; 'Lady Of The Sounds', 'Herself'; 'Well Met'; 'Tools Of The Trade'; 'Liverpool Spinners Live.'

The duo's recording of 'Liverpool's Favourite Folk Songs' contains the tracks: 'Ferry To New Brighton'; 'Mist Over The Mersey'; 'What Was The Colour'; 'Paddy's Market'; 'On The Rope'; 'Knowsley Zoo'; 'Minstrel of Hoylake'; 'Johnny Todd'; 'The Leaving Of Liverpool'; 'The Pegue'; 'Back Buchanan Street'; 'Liverpool Lullaby'; 'Wallasey Centipede'; 'Liverpool Lou'; 'One O' Clock Gun'; 'Double Thick Marmalade'; 'Seth Davey'; 'Liverpool Medley', including 'Liverpool Home' and 'Maggie May'.

In his book 'Liverpool: Wondrous Place', Liverpool author Paul Du Noyer asks: "Why did the art school R&B bands of South-east England become the new aristocracy, while the Liverpool boys (the Beatles, as usual excepted) got consigned to cabaret or civvy street?"

In the same book another writer says: "the blues passed Liverpool by."

Yet musician Mal Jefferson of the Mastersounds says: "Liverpool was full of good blues bands, my own band specialising in it, and we played alongside Alexis and the early Korner bands. How about Supercharge?"

In August 1963 Alexis Korner told Mersey Beat: "The only place in

England that a blues guitarist would be able to find recognition is Liverpool".

Blues and Rhythm & Blues had been popular in Liverpool for some time and American blues artists such as Sonny Terry & Brownie McGhee, Muddy Waters and John Lee Hooker were to be found appearing at Liverpool clubs, ranging from the Cavern to the Mardi Gras.

In fact, one Mersey Beat Cavern advert features a great Blues bill: John Lee Hooker, The John Mayall Bluesbreakers, The Roadrunners, the Clayton Squares, the Cordes, the Hideaways and the St Louis Checks, while another features news of an "R&B Marathon when eight groups are featured from 4 – 11.30pm." They were: Alexis Korner, The Clayton Squares, Victor Brox Blues Giants, The Hideaways, The Georgians, The Feelgoods, Derry & the Others and The Tabs.

Liverpool also had its own virtuoso guitar legends such as Brian 'Griff' Griffiths and Colin Manley. Yet another point, mentioned before, is that on hearing from George Harrison that the Rolling Stones were "almost as good as our own Roadrunners," London A&R man Dick Rowe then rushed down to sign the Rolling Stones, but had no interest in the Roadrunners, who George Harrison considered were a better band.

The reason is simply that the Roadrunners were a Liverpool outfit and London didn't want to know any more bands from Merseyside and were particularly looking for a London rival to the Beatles.

The blues artists in Liverpool never had the opportunity to make their mark due to the fact that Britain's musical capitol at that time was London and it was bands from the south who were to receive the promotion from the musical powerbase, while Liverpool had become a 'no go' area for A&R men, despite it still remaining a hotbed of talent.

Yet, despite all this, music from Merseyside continued to thrive, arguably returning to the state during the early days of the Mersey Sound when it was nurtured in isolation, receiving relatively little or no attention from the media. The Cavern died, but Eric's rose like a phoenix in its place.

Groups such as Liverpool Express appeared now and then to top the

British charts – and despite the power of the London scene, eventually Liverpool won out when the Guinness Book of Records and a nationwide poll declared Liverpool as Britain's number one music city!

A final word on Merseyside and the Blues comes from Al Willard, former member of the Almost Blues, who runs Groovin' Records 'The Merseyside Home of the Blues', who told me recently: "I remember going for a meal with Roger Eagle and Alexis Korner at Reno's Taverna after he had played Adams Club in Seel St in the 1980's.

"As far as the Blues is concerned in relation to the Liverpool music scene it has always been there but more in a background capacity.

"To me when asked about the lack of Blues in the city I always refer to Liverpool's preference of popular music and on many occasions when playing live have been asked to bring a more varied style to my live performances by pub landlords and promoters.

"I think that there is a general fear about the term Blues Music as that of a genre that is laden with sadness and pathos and not conducive to a 'happy clappy' night out. To me Blues is a wonderful medium that portrays the truth about life in all its glory and remains the most potent vehicle for political protest. 'Working Class Hero' by Lennon in my opinion is one of the most poignant Folk Blues songs ever written!

"Blues or should I say Folk Blues survived throughout the 1960s to today in the Folk Clubs and on many occasions I would go to see The Spinners because of Hughie Jones's performance and appreciation of the Blues.

"Blues also survived in its heavier format on the Pub Rock circuit at the Moonstone and Liverpool Stadium in the 1970s.

"But it is the 'Music Men' the likes of the late Roger Eagle and Zane Branson who have always been in favour of adding the Blues to their promotions - men who are not afraid to buck the trend putting on people like Sonny Boy Edwards, Homesick James, Brownie McGhee & Sonny Terry, Snooks Eaglin, Blind Boys of Alabama etc.

"Buddy Guy has recently played the Philharmonic the very place that I saw Muddy Waters who signed my programme with a MW in the early 1960s.

"Many Jazz Clubs did pay homage to the Blues promoting the likes of Big Bill Broonzy, Josh White and Brownie & Sonny etc and in particular the Cavern that saw the likes of Sonny Boy Williamson and John Lee Hooker backed by John Mayall.

"I think you probably know the story about Bob Wooler getting in touch with me saying that 'there is someone you'd love to meet at the Cavern this afternoon' so I sagged off from Liverpool Junior Art School to meet a well oiled Sonny Boy Williamson. I just didn't know what to say to the man on this occasion but what a charismatic harmonica player! In 1999 I visited his resting place in Tutweiller Mississippi.

"At the time of the 'Almost' Blues there were quite a few Blues based bands spurned from the Art College fraternity like the Roadrunners and another Hope Hall favourite the St Louis Checks.

"The 'Almost' Blues supported Alexis at Hope Hall on one of their earlier gigs and as usually the case were persuaded by EMI to move away from their original Blues format into a more soulful outfit that put paid to my vocal input with me transferring to trumpet. I have now reverted back after all these years.

"So you can see external as well as internal influences working against the Blues. Having said that there is now a proliferation of 'Jam Nights' that often produce a lot of Blues Players and venues that have Blues Nights throughout the city.

"There are many fine Blues Players around Liverpool like Raphael Callaghan & Christine Purnell of Blue C, Joey Sheils and the Wheels, Xander Brothers, Neil Partington's Forty Four etc

"Another point of interest is that when American Blues Artists arrived in this country they always had British musicians backing them either from London or Manchester never from Liverpool.

"This once again shows the position of the Blues in the popular culture of these major cities with Manchester and London producing the more sought after session musicians. What a great pity that Liverpool has not nurtured the same respect for this most influential of music forms that so inspired the early Beatles."

Among the Mersey Blues records available from Groovin' Records are: 'Rockin' Rhythm & Blues – Lawnmower R 'n' B' (Groove 01); 'The Lawnmower Man - A Dozen Choice Cuts' - 'Lawnmower Classics – The Cat', 'Lawnmower Man, Messin' with the Blues', plus an Anti-War Blues Trilogy dedicated to John Lennon (Groove 02); Willard & The Poor Boys - 'Five 'Live' Deep Blues Classics' (Groove 03); 'The 'Almost' Blues - Abbey Road Sessions' (Groove 04); 'The Mount Street Tapes – The Opposition' (Groove 05); 'The Canon Tapes' – 29th & Dearborn EP (Groove 06); 'No More War Blues' – The Bluesman – CD Single (Groove 07); 'Liverpool Blues' – AL Willard Peterson's CD.

Among Merseyside's R&B/Blues bands were The Roadrunners, who originally formed in Birkenhead in 1961 under the name the Tenabeats. At the time they comprised Dave Percy, the assistant manager of the Hope Hall, on lead guitar, Mike Hart on guitar and vocals, Dave Boyce on drums, John Peacock on piano and Pete Mackey on bass guitar.

The group was admired by the Beatles and had a following among Liverpool's bohemian student set, performing music popularised by artists such as Muddy Waters, Little Walter, John Lee Hooker and Howling Wolf, and were soon engaged in 'happenings' with noted Liverpool poet Adrian Henri.

By 1964, in addition to Hart, Boyce, Mackey and Peacock, they were augmented by Nick La Grec on sax (like a name out of a movie!), Bob Harris on trumpet and Johnny Philips on sax. Johnny was an American who had travelled to Liverpool to become part of the music scene. Their music had now changed to an urban style of contemporary blues, inspired by artists such as Bobby Bland, Ray Charles and James Brown.

The group appeared frequently in Germany where they made most of their recordings – and their only British solo recording seemed to be an EP they made for the Liverpool University rag charities, called 'Pantomania.'

In a 1 September 1964 piece about R&B music in the Star Club News, part of it read: "The Roadrunners are the only one of the bands mentioned above who came from Liverpool. They were chosen at last year's Star Club Band Competition from about twenty bands as the only sensational one.

"Regretfully, bandleader Michael Hart still studies architecture and thus the band can only perform here for a month during the semester break. In December 1963, during the last guest appearance of the

Roadrunners only one hour before the band left for England again a live LP recording was done at the Star-Club, that was released only last month. (Ariola 71224-JT). Although in the past live recordings were of rather low quality due to technical problems, this record is of excellent quality. Every lover of R&B music should have heard this recording. There will be few to leave the record store without having bought this record.

"The Star Club has often featured unknown bands, which later on became famous. We never dared to predict any of this. Now we want to break this rule and are ready to claim that the Roadrunners are one of the bands to whom the future belongs. We will hear quite a bit from them."

On 28 February 1964 they appeared at a prestigious R&B festival concert at Birmingham Town Hall on a bill with Sonny Boy Williamson, the Yardbirds, Long John Baldry & the Hoochie Coochie Men, the Spencer Davis Rhythm and Blues Quartet. The event was recorded by the legendary entrepreneur Giorgio Gomelsky.

By July 1965 they had reverted to a quintet with Peacock now on keyboards, Mackey on bass, Terry McCusker on drums and Mike Kontzle on guitar. Hart, who was to join the Liverpool Scene and also recorded his own solo album (produced by John Peel), had been replaced by Mike Byrne on vocals and guitar while Johnny Philips had decided to remain in Hamburg following one of their Star Club seasons and their second recording there, and later joined the Eyes.

In 1966, an affluent young man phoned the Cavern to ask if they could arrange for a Liverpool band to play at his 21st birthday party in Switzerland. The group selected was the Roadrunners and they had such an enjoyable time they remained there for a month. On their return to Liverpool they disbanded.

During their career the Roadrunners performed regularly at the Cavern club, many times on bills with the Beatles and were also performing on the last Beatles appearance at the club, in addition to being the first group to record for the Radio Luxembourg series 'Sunday Night At The Cavern.'

However, if there was a venue which could be described as 'home of the Roadrunners', it was the Hope Hall in Hope Street, which later became the Everyman Theatre, which attracted a different audience from that of the Cavern, including lots of university and art college students. Despite their lack of recordings in Britain, their Star Club albums are available from Big Bear Records in Germany. Here are the details of their recording product:

Their first album for the Star Club label was 'Twist Time In Star Club 4.' The tracks were: 'Rip It Up', 'You Can Make It If You Try', 'Little Ruby', 'Baby You Don't Have to Go', 'Slow Down', 'That's Alright', 'Beautiful Delilah', 'Long Tall Sally', 'Hoochie Coochie Man', 'You'd Better Move On', 'Roadrunner'.

The group wasn't happy with this recording because it took place in the Star Club at 3 o' clock in the morning shortly after the group had arrived back in Hamburg from playing in Kiel. They weren't happy with the set and decided to repeat it despite their tiredness – but they felt that the second set was much better. Then they discovered that the sound engineer had packed up all his gear following the first gig and had left with the master tapes.

On their second Star Club album they shared the vinyl with a Newcastle group called Shorty & Them and therefore only had six tracks on the album: 'Mary Ann', 'Have You Ever Had The Blues', 'My Baby Left Me', 'Hitchhike' and 'Got My Mojo Working'.

Their EP for Panto Day, 'Pantomania' featured four tracks: 'Cry, Cry, Cry', 'Fun at Twenty-One' and 'The Leaving Of Liverpool' by the Roadrunners and 'If You Want to Know the Time' a comedy number performed by students.

As mentioned, a highlight in Britain was their appearance at an R&B festival at Birmingham Town Hall. The event was recorded and issued as an album 'The Steampacket/the First R&B Festival.' The Roadrunners are featured on two of the tracks 'Mary Ann' and 'Bright Lights, Big City,' although they are billed as the Liverpool Roadrunners (to prevent confusion, because it was a popular name for groups). There was also an introduction by Cavern compere Bob Wooler. The recording was later re-released as a CD 'The First British R&B Festival' with two Roadrunner tracks: 'You Can Make It If You Really Try' and 'Mary Ann,'

Another band, the Georgians emerged in 1963 when three students from Quarry Bank High School decided to form a band. They comprised Laurence (Lol) Ashley, lead/vocals, Geoff Jones, bass/vocals and Tim Dugdill, rhythm/harmonica/vocals. They needed a drummer and recruited Mike Sloan, brother of Frank Sloan, the original drummer with the Mersey Beats.

Tim and Lol were taking their A' level exams; Mike was a butcher and Geoff an insurance clerk.

Initially they played at youth clubs and schools (particularly Quarry Bank) and their favourite venue was St. Barnabus Hall in Allerton, which was nicknamed 'Barnies.' Their equipment in those days was entirely 30 watt.

The group's early influences were Muddy Waters, Howlin' Wolf, Buddy Guy, Sonny Boy Williamson and Chuck Berry, all of whom they were to play with as support bands later on.

They weren't even billed on their first Cavern gig and recalled that if Bob Wooler liked you, you could play for expenses, about ten shillings in the old money. Geoff arrived with all the equipment in a Triumph Herald driven by his mother while the rest of the group travelled by bus carrying Mike's drum kit.

Tim recalls: "In the Cavern I remember hovering in the band room, especially when the Beatles were on, and feeling privileged if John chose to stub his ciggy out on my head. Pete Best and George Harrison were lovely guys and would acknowledge me, or anyone, in the band room. John would give a grunt if in the mood, but Paul was usually rather aloof, possibly because he was nervous. Of the four, I always thought that Paul was the most nervous and worried before a gig. He regularly had to go to the loo just before their act and invariably forgot to button his fly before going on stage. That gave the reputation of him doing it on purpose for the ladies, and maybe it was, but I believe it was accidental.

"Being a support act in those days was pretty disconcerting. The girls in front always had their hair in curlers, doing their knitting, while we were on and, about ten minutes before we finished our first set and the class act was to come on, they would start removing their curlers and combing up the beehive hairdos. When the class act had performed and we came back on, they went home! Boy, did we feel important!"

Tim also recalls: "I remember being there the night after Pete Best had been sacked from the Beatles and Pete's mates, possibly without his knowledge, came to seek retribution from the rest of the Beatles.

"George got a hiding, but John gave some of it back and then Paddy and the rest of the bouncers sorted it out."

Due to the fact that the band played mainly R&B, they began to perform alongside the Roadrunners at the Hope Hall, situated in the basement of the Everyman Theatre in Hope Street. Regulars at the gig were Adrian Henri, Mike McCartney, Roger McGough, Brian Patten and John Gorman while Adrian used to stage his 'Happenings' there.

After the Beatles had become an international name, major acts began to appear in Liverpool, particularly the British and American R&B artists, including Alexis Korner's Blues Inc (including Graham Bond, Ginger Baker and Jack Bruce). London bands such as the Yardbirds (including Eric Clapton) and John Mayall's Bluesbreakers.

Geoff Jones left the band to join the Clayton Squares, and the Georgians then recruited Lewis Collins. Lew had recently returned from Hamburg having played with the Eyes (Gibson Kemp, Paddy Chambers etc) and was looking for local Merseyside work.

Mike Sloan also left and Roger Bioletti, a former friend from Quarry Bank took the drum seat (his grandfather's barber shop, Bioletti's, was the one featured in 'Penny Lane' by the Beatles)

The line-up was completed by a tenor and alto sax. The alto player didn't last long, but the tenor sax, Roger Lewis, staying with the Georgians until they disbanded.

Lewis Collins received an offer to join the Mojos, a move promoted by his dad, Bill Collins, his biggest fan and manager. This was an offer he couldn't refuse as the Mojos were already a big name with a recording contract.

The Georgians decided not to look for a new bass player, they simply got Lol to change from lead to bass, but began to turn from R&B to 'Soul' and appeared more regularly at the Mardi Gras, in addition to gigs at Universities.

The Georgians disbanded in December 1964.

Tim then took up an offer to join the Kinsleys, a new outfit formed by Billy Kinsley, although Billy then left to join the Merseys. The other members were Dave Preston, George Peckham and Tommy Murray. Just before they left for Hamburg to appear at the Star Club, Peckham left, to be replaced on bass by Mike Pemberton. They had to recruit two sax players for the Hamburg season, but the sax players left and due to the fact that they had no brass section, the group missed out on Hamburg but were sent to Frankfurt, Stuttgart and Offenbach.

On their way back home the group's van broke down and as they had no money to repair it, under German law their equipment was sold to pay the debt and the Kinsleys then had to disband, with Tim then playing for several years in a semi-pro band called Familiarity Breeds.

In recent years he re-formed the Georgians and they now play occasionally in Liverpool and have revived live music at the Hope Hall.

An example of a Liverpool blues band who were encouraged to steer away from blues music was the Clayton Squares, who formed late in 1963.

The Clayton Squares originally comprised Brook Williams, guitar/vocals; Mike Evans, alto sax; Bobby Scott, drums; Pete Dunn, lead; Geoff Jones, bass and Terry Hines, vocals. They were initially managed by George Roberts and the group practiced in his cellar in a house in Huskisson Street, L8.

The group's first appearance was at the Blue Angel where they were spotted by Bob Wooler, who agreed to co-manage them with Roberts. They became one of the first group's to be represented by the Cavern Club's Agency, Cavern Artistes, which also meant that they received a string of Cavern gigs.

Although the Clayton Squares were a blues group, Bob Wooler encouraged them to change their musical direction into what was described as 'soul beat.' This resulted in personnel changes and the lead singer was replaced by Denny Alexander and they also found a new bass guitarist, Geoff Jones and Les Smith became a second sax player.

They were spotted by London impresario Don Arden at the Cavern, which resulted in them obtaining a recording contract. Rolling Stones manager Andrew Oldham produced the record, but it wasn't released. They then recorded with A&R man Ian Samwell and their single 'Come And Get It' was issued on the Decca label on 8 October 1964. The band penned the flipside 'Tears Fell.'

The group then played the Star Club, Hamburg and the Storyville Club in Frankfurt, but on their return they discovered there had been a dispute between Wooler and Arden. By that time Pete Dunn had been replaced by Barry Womersley

Although Wooler had predicted: "If any new wave Merseyside group is likely to put Liverpool back on the pop map I predict it will be the Clayton Squares."

The group never found major success and disbanded in August 1966.

9. Music is a Religion

THE genre of Christian Rock is considered to be that of music by bands whose members are Christians who perform numbers expressing their faith.

Although Christian music was to become particularly popular in the United States in the late Sixties, one pioneering outpost of Christian Rock music prior to that was Merseyside.

Although the first rock band to play in a church in America was said to be Mind Garage in 1967 and the first Christian music festival in America took place in 1970, Merseyside was ahead of the game.

Christian music was alive and well and flourishing on the banks of the Mersey at the same time as the Mersey Sound at the end of the Fifties and beginning of the Sixties. Numerous churches, both Catholic and Protestant, were providing an outlet for the Christian bands at the scores of church halls around Merseyside.

Merseyside Christian groups of the Sixties included the Concords, the Vigils, The Warriors, the Beacons, the Crofters, the Gospel Rhythms, His Servants, The Gospel Messengers, The Informers, the Ambassadors, the Sowers, Time Ltd, The Heralds (a Salvation Army group), the Te Deum 5 (from St Catherine's Parish in Birkenhead), the Witnesses (from Richmond Baptist in Liverpool) and the Travellers (from Dovecot City Mission in Liverpool). Christian music on Merseyside continued throughout the Seventies with outfits such as the Informers, Trinity Folk, The Believers and Millstone. More Christian groups flourished and a number are still active today.

Typical examples include The Protests, a Catholic Christian group who began performing in church halls. In February 1964, Harry Phillips, a salesman from Everton and a parishioner of St. Francis

Xavier's, took over management of the band. The group comprised Bob Smith on drums who attended West Derby Tech, Joe Cooke who went to St Augustine's, Carl Crane and Phil Nealan who were former pupils of Sacred Heart and Cardinal Godfrey Technical School and Tony Cottrell who was at Highfield School and then John Hamilton Tech. The group also played at the re-opening of the Church of England St John's, Tuebrook, Youth Club.

In addition to Catholic Youth clubs they turned down paid bookings in order to help the Freedom From Hunger campaign and also took part in a Mersey ferry cruise on behalf of St Nicholas' parish.

The Sowers were a group who formed in Chester at the beginning of the Sixties. They attended Kingsway Chapel in Chester and decided to begin Sunday night sessions in the Kingsway Church building. The original line-up was Stan Sheward on organ, Stuart Millar on guitar and Ernest McQuoid on guitar/vocals. They soon decided to change to electric guitars and drums and then comprised Stuart Millar, lead guitar; Brian Fawkes, drums; Ernest McQuoid, vocals and Jim Porter, rhythm guitar. The group performed their Christian music at churches, schools, colleges, coffee bars and halls throughout the north of England.

They supported the evangelist Dick Saunders at Chester Town Hall, appeared on the Gordon Hall Youth Rallies in Liverpool and also appeared in Northern Ireland, the Isle of Man and Wales.

Toward the end of the Sixties there were some minor line-up changes and the group eventually disbanded in the early Seventies.

The Sowers had a repertoire of 150 numbers which comprised old hymns which they had set to a modern beat, pop songs which they had adapted to a Christian message and original songs penned by themselves. Numbers in their repertoire included 'Batman', 'I'm In Love With Jesus', 'It's No Secret', 'Oh Mr Singer' and 'When Will You?'

The Witnesses toured with the Fourmost and issued their album 'Why' on Herald1070 in 1966. The tracks were: 'Why', 'Everything Will Be Alright'; 'Another Day', 'The Winning Side.' The Liverpool band comprised Phil Jones on lead vocal, Jimmy Nunnen on bass, Chris Keenan on rhythm guitar and Norman Smith on drums.

The group were managed by Dave Eastwood, who was also a disc jockey, and he ran the Christian Endeavour Cruises.

The Vigils were a group who were inspired to form after seeing the Crossbeats at Cheadle Youth Club in February 1964. They comprised Paul De Barr on lead guitar; Chris Mosley on bass guitar; Pete Rose on rhythm; Phil Watson on drums; Graham Nicholson on keyboards and John Campbell on lead vocals.

The Crossbeats were arguably the best British Christian group of the Sixties and Merseyside was the major centre for Christian music at the same time that the Mersey Sound was flourishing.

The Crossbeats, who formed in Bootle, were originally known as 'The Seekers' and formed in the summer of 1962 with four founder members. Eddie Boyes was the original rhythm guitarist who then switched to bass from October 1966 and became lead vocalist from 1975 until the group disbanded. John Boyes on lead guitar was a member from the beginning to the end. Tony Mathias on lead vocals was with the band from the start until 1975. Eric Knowles on drums was a founder member and continued until May 1968.

John Millington joined very early on, and played bass. On his marriage and move to Wigan in 1966 he was replaced by Sam Pennington; Sam played rhythm while Eddie shifted to bass. When Eric Knowles left the group in 1968, he was replaced by Joe Roberts on drums, and Joe remained with the group until they split.

They were managed for a time by the Rev. John Banner, curate of St. Leonard's Church, Bootle and who worked specifically in St Mary's Bootle as part of the Team Ministry.

The group made their debut at St John & St James in Bootle on Sunday 29 January 1963, and during their career appeared on more than 700 gigs, including numerous performances throughout Merseyside.

These were scores of venues around Merseyside where the Christian groups played, almost an underground scene completely unknown to the main purveyors of the Mersey Sound. The Crossbeats also played regularly at Walton Prison and Central Hall, Liverpool.

There were numerous Christian coffee bars which sprang up, particularly between 1964 and 1970; one of the earliest was at St Mary's, Cheadle in November 1964. Others were run by churches but held in more secular venues; some even ran seven days a week, manned by volunteers from the churches.

The group spent much of their career performing throughout the Merseyside area – Liverpool, Birkenhead, Southport, St Helens (the most Christian town in Britain), Wigan, Formby and all the areas around, but they also travelled widely, with several appearances in the Isle of Man, a tour of the south of England, in addition to appearances in cities throughout the UK. Apart from their regular performances at Walton Prison, they also appeared for the inmates of Strangeways in Manchester.

On Saturday 8 October 1966 the group travelled to London and performed an open-air concert in Trafalgar Square for the 'Feed The Minds' campaign. They played on the Royal Albert Hall twice. They were also offered an American tour in 1967.

In 1970 they embarked on a two-week American tour appearing in Michigan, Ohio, Virginia and Niagara Falls.

Their final appearance was at St Paul's Church, Warrington in November 1975.

During their career, the Crossbeats also performed at traditional Liverpool rock venues such as the Cavern, the Peppermint Lounge and Litherland Town Hall.

Unlike most of the Mersey groups of the time, who performed covers of American numbers, the Crossbeats wrote their own material and by 1965 were performing fourteen of their own numbers during their shows and eventually penned 70 original numbers. They were all Christian songs, inspired by Jesus – and in some ways, it must be admitted that the Crossbeats and other Mersey Christian groups were virtually the world pioneers of Christian Rock Music, which now has such a vast audience throughout the world.

They went to Hollick and Taylor Recording Studios in Handsworth Wood Birmingham in September and November 1965 and recorded six self-penned songs, including 'If Only', 'He Wants To Know', 'I Know' and 'He Waits'.

These recordings were issued on the Pilgrim label and released in late 1965 and in early 1966. Their first release was 'I Know' c/w 'He Waits' on PSR 7002 and their second 'If Only' c/w 'He Wants To Know' on PSR 7001.

For their debut album, they recorded at CBS Studios in New Bond Street, London on 7 and 8 April 1967. Entitled 'Crazy Mixed-Up

Generation', the ten track album was issued in September 1967. The tracks were:

Side One: 'Busy Man', 'Do Not Disturb, 'Are You Afraid', 'Back Where You Belong,' 'Snow Covered Mountains.' Side Two: 'Change', 'Tears', 'Time', 'Crazy Mixed-Up Generation', 'Do You Remember.'

In December 1967 the Christian magazine Buzz reported: "One of the best Christian music albums of the Sixties hit the shops this month: 'Crazy Mixed-Up Generation' by the Crossbeats. Five young men from Bootle in the heart of Liverpool's dockland immediately became the CCM equivalent of the Beatles and instant role models for Christian bands all over the UK."

These recordings are now eagerly sought after by collectors.

Where are the members now in 2009? Eddie Boyes is living in Huyton, and is part of St Bartholomew's Church, Roby. He works at the University of Liverpool. John Boyes is retired from the University of Liverpool. He lives in Orrell Park, and is still part of the fellowship at St Leonard's Church in Bootle.

Tony Matthias is also retired, after working for many years in Church House Liverpool, and then for the RNLI. He lives in Formby and attends Holy Trinity, Formby. Eric Knowles works for Merseyside Waste Disposal Authority, and lives in Aughton and he attends Aughton Parish Church. John Millington is living somewhere in or near the Lake District. Joe Roberts is believed to be living in Australia.

When the Crossbeats disbanded two of the members Eddie Boyes and Sam Pennington continued playing as a duo and were then joined by other Christian musicians to form the band Crimson Connection. They comprised Eddie Boyes, lead vocals, rhythm and bass; Sam Pennington, rhythm and bass; Paul Lalgee, congas, bongos and other percussion; Pete Davies, lead guitar; Steve Bray, rhythm and bass.

They also made a number of recordings of songs written by the band in the late Eighties which were transferred to CD and a number of them are now available to download on MP3.

Among their Merseyside appearances were the Richmond Baptist Church, Liverpool; Barnstondale Camp, Wirral; Gordon Hall, Liverpool; Mitchell Memorial Mission, Muirhead Avenue, Liverpool; Wood Street Mission, Hoylake; Holy Trinity, Formby; Bank Hall

Mission Church, Bootle; West Derby Chapel; Trinity Evangelical Church, Rainhill; New Brighton Baptist Church; Vale Park, New Brighton; Mabel Fletcher College, Liverpool; St Gabriel's, Toxteth; Stockton Heath, Warrington and Ebeneezer Chapel, Queen's Drive, Liverpool in addition to gigs in various places ranging from Stoke-on-Trent to Blackpool.

In addition to the numerous church and church hall venues (also appearances at both Liverpool Cathedrals), Merseyside Christian groups appeared at prestigious venues such as the Philharmonic Hall, St. George's Hall, Central Hall, on Royal Iris cruises and cruises to the Isle of Man.

Some examples include the three Christian Grand Endeavour Cruises from Liverpool to the Isle of Man, 70 miles away, each time with an audience of 2,000 aboard. The cruise on Monday 3 August 1964 featured the Heralds and the Seekers. There was also a 100-strong Merseyside Youth For Christ Choir.

The next Grand Endeavour Cruise to the Isle of Man took place on Monday 30 August 1965 and the 2,000 people aboard were entertained on the trip by Liverpool bands the Crossbeats, the Witnesses, the Heralds and Manchester's the Gospel Four.

The final cruise on Monday 29 August 1966 featured the Crossbeats and the Heralds.

Central Hall, Renshaw Street, Liverpool was also a popular venue for Christian events and in June 1963 alone, for instance, there were Christian rallies at the hall on June 8, 15, 22, and 29.

Saturday 16 Jan 1965 saw another Christian Rock event at the Hall and other events included the Gospel Rhythm Festival, 'the first major event of its kind in the north' which took place on Saturday 20 February 1965. Hosted by Dave Eastwood it featured Liverpool's Salvation Army group The Heralds, Birkenhead's the Te Deum 5; Dave Cowley and his guitar; Liverpool's the Witnesses, the Travellers and the Crossbeats; Oldhams's the Gospel Folk Four; Preston's the Cobblers, Ben Smith on the piano and Mike Bews on the piano, accompanied by the Crossbeats.

Another major venue for Christian Rock events was the Philharmonic Hall in Hope Street (an appropriately name for a street with a Cathedral at each end!), Liverpool.

Beat Capital '68 for example, took place at the Philharmonic Hall on Saturday 4 May 1968. Saturday 28 March 1965 saw a concert at the Philharmonic Hall featuring the Seekers and the 100 strong Merseyside Youth Voice Choir.

The Philharmonic Hall also hosted a Hallelujah Beat Concert on Saturday, 30 April 1966. This was in aid of the Feed The Mind Campaign (a Bible charity). Artists featured were the Crossbeats, the Witnesses, the Newsham Five and Tom Cooper.

Beat Capital '70 at the Philharmonic Hall on Saturday 17 January 1970 was subtitled 'Gospel Pop at the Phil' and featured the Crossbeats, the Informers, Time Ltd and Trinity Folk.

St George's Hall, William Brown Street presented a Merseyside Youth for Christ event on Saturday 1 June 1963 featuring the Seekers.

A Christian cruise on the Royal Iris took place on Tuesday 6 July 1965. The ballroom programme was compered by Dave Eastwood and began at 7.30 with "Light entertainment with the Witnesses Rhythm Group, plus a local minister's account of his most embarrassing ten moments." Then from 9 it was "A programme of Gospel songs, spirituals and rhythm with the Crossbeats and the Merseyside Youth for Christ Choir, plus a short epilogue. No collection!" Soft drinks and fish and chips were available as the Christian events did not sell alcohol.

Christian rock music is still alive and well and flourishing on Merseyside. One of the leading Liverpool Christian bands in recent years has been Supervision, who comprised James Harding, bass guitar, known as 'the Beat', Mark Doohan, vocals/guitar, known as 'the Doog', James Burch, drums, known as 'Burchy' and Ian Finch, guitar, known as 'Finchie'.

In May 2003 the group originally won the Ultimate Events National Battle of the Bands at Alton Towers and signed a recording deal with Elevation. During that year they recorded three tracks for the album 'This Way Up', which spotlighted new groups. The tracks were 'How Long', 'Here I Am', and 'Back Up.'

A month after their recording they were awarded UCAM Best New Band at the UK CMA's which were held at the Garage in London in December 2003. The group had made several independent records previously, including their EP '12 Hours', named after the fact that it took 12 hours to record. Their 'Son Of A King' was on 1999's

'Dayglo', 'Pretty People' was on the 'Shining Star' EP in 2000 and 'She Stares In The Mirror' was included on the 2002 compilation 'Bring You Up To Speed.'

2004 began with a 36 date British tour and the release of the 'This Way Up' album.

They appeared at several festivals including Spring Harvest and Greenbelt before taking time off to write material for their debut album 'Day Of Small Beginnings', which was issued in March 2005.

They then headlined a tour in April and May, appearing once again at the Spring Harvest and performing before 10,000 fans at Alton Towers at the end of the tour.

They were to continue appearing at various festivals including Greenbelt once again and also performed before an audience of 30,000 at Merseyfest. Merseyfest was a project formed in 2002 by churches and Christian organisations on Merseyside to change their communities and help the neediest parts of the region with practical demonstrations of kindness. The musical side of Merseyfest took place in Sefton in 2004 with Supervision, Yfriday and bandwithnoname headlining.

Despite their success Supervision decided to disband in the summer of 2006. They were to say: "We have not fallen out, there aren't any 'musical differences', there are no egos at play and there is no hidden agenda! – it's just four people feeling that at this point in our lives that we can no longer continue touring or making music together as well as balancing family life, personal calling in addition to full time careers."

James completed his PHD and then left England with his wife Kate to teach at Bible College in Bangkok. Mark has become director of an architect firm while James Burch, now works for a software company. Ian Finch continues as a musician and now leads a new band, Finchley.

Ian Yates, who attends and leads worship at Bootle Elim Church is another example of a current Liverpool Christian Rock artist.

He has received NCM Awards in 2007 and 2008 as Contemporary Christian Artist of the Year and had led worship at various events throughout the country during the past nine years. His 2008 album 'Desperate To See Your Glory' contains 12 passionate worship songs, including 'King Of Kings.' Ian told me: "Musically I was inspired by Guns and Roses, mainly Slash, and then around the age of 15/16 I heard a Christian band called Delirious? and they really inspired me.

"I started out writing when I was 17/18 and started a band called Seraphim with the aim really to say to people that Christian music isn't boring, it's not about singing kumbaya and that Christianity and Christian music could be relevant. That lasted about seven years with various line ups. We played quite a lot of gigs and recorded a few times.

"That time was a learning experience and we got some great opportunities. Then about three or four years ago I started writing songs for church. I love to write, it's how I express myself, and I am always writing down thoughts and ideas. I've recorded an EP and an album.

"Recently two songs were recorded on Soul Survivor's People's Album 3 and I have just recorded a single with Survivor Records.

"I mainly lead corporate worship at church events, conferences and Youth events, I think Christian music has a real stigma to it, hopefully my songs can break down the barriers, with regards to whether Christian music can break into the mainstream, I think the quality of Christian music is getting a lot better, especially in the States. A lot of songs are being recorded in top studios with well known producers."

10. The Liver Birds

FOR some reason there is a perception that the original Mersey scene was a completely male-dominated one with little presence from females. This is arguably because only two girl singers from the era of the Mersey Sound have received prominent publicity: Cilla Black and to a lesser extent, Beryl Marsden.

In fact, Liverpool must take some pride in one aspect of the history of chart-topping records in Britain. When the charts were first launched in 1952, the first artist in the No. 1 spot was Al Martino with 'Here In My Heart', followed by Jo Stafford, Kay Starr, Eddie Fisher, Perry Como. A completely American-dominated list until the seventh No. 1 was British vocal group the Stargazers with 'Broken Wings'. Then, the first British solo artist ever to top the British charts became Liverpool's Lita Roza with '(How Much Is) That Doggie In The Window', a song which, incidentally, she hated. Nevertheless, Liverpool could lay claim to the first solo No. 1 by a British artist.

Lita was born Lilian Patricia Lita Roza at 13 Upper Pitt Street, Liverpool on 14 March 1926, one of seven children (Henry Francis, Lita, Alma Elizabeth, Malverna Anne, Ernest Vincent, Madeleine Christine, Maureen Marguerite) to Elizabeth Ann and Francis Vincent Roza. Her father, who was Spanish, was originally a Marine Engineer and also played accordion and worked as a pianist at several Liverpool night clubs.

At the age of three Lita attended St Michael's School and at the age of eight moved to Granby Street Council School. When she was 12 she spotted an advert in the local paper for 'juveniles for Pantomime' and passed the audition.

Together with other successful candidates she was sent to the Ken Moore School of Dancing in London and then appeared in the pantomime Babes In The Wood in Norwich. Various Pantomime engagements lasted until she was 15 and she also appeared in the review 'Black Velvet' with Liverpool comedian Ted Ray.

When Lita told her mother that she wanted to go on the stage, her mother answered, "What? The landing stage?'

When Lita was 16 she answered another newspaper advertisement. This was for the job of resident singer at the New Yorker club in Southport, which she successfully passed, receiving £5 per week.

She saved up her money and then received permission from her mother to try her luck as a singer in London. Within two weeks she secured a job with the Harry Roy Orchestra and remained with them for a year until the band set off for Egypt to entertain troops. As she was only 17, she wasn't allowed to go and began to appear in London clubs with the Art Thompson Band, working simultaneously at the Embassy Club in Bond Street and the Albany in Saville Row.

In 1944 she married an American officer and the following year, with the end of the war, moved to Miami with him. However, she felt the need to continue singing and the marriage ended after five years.

Lita returned to England in 1950, basically for a six month stay. She'd sent a demo tape to bandleader Ted Heath, auditioned for him and then became lead female singer with the Ted Heath Band.

In 1956 she turned solo, appearing on variety bills, television shows and cabaret. The same year she married trumpet player Ronnie Harris. Her agent was Joe Collins, father of Joan and Jackie.

Lita was voted Top British Female Singer in the New Musical Express consecutively from 1951 – 1956 and was also voted Top Female Singer in the Melody Maker in 1951 and 1952. She was presented with a statuette by the Daily Mirror which was an 'Award of Merit' for her services to the music industry.

Each year the British Academy of Composers & Songwriters, in association with The MCPS–PRS Alliance celebrates those who have served the creative community with distinction through the Gold Badge Awards. Both Lita and I were presented with the Gold Badge award at the same event at the Savoy Hotel in London.

In 1960 she toured Australia and the following year was appearing at the famous Flamingo in Las Vegas. Over the years Lita continued to tour internationally – New Zealand, Australia, South Africa, Cyprus, Singapore, Spain and the Middle East and from 1982 was asked to appear in a series of Ted Heath Orchestra concerts with Denis Lotus. These lasted until the year 2000.

The following year, on her birthday, she was invited to open the 'Wall of Fame' in Mathew Street, Liverpool, a tribute to the many Liverpool artists who topped the British charts, making Liverpool 'the capital city of music.' On 28 November of that year she was asked to perform at the Empire Theatre, Liverpool for the anniversary of Radio Merseyside's first broadcast and that was her last ever performance. Lita decided that after the appearance she would retire from a musical career which had spanned decades.

Sadly, Lita passed away on 14 August 2008.

The other major Merseyside female presence which had its origin in the Fifties was the Vernons Girls.

The Liverpool football coupons firm Vernons Pools launched the Vernons Girls as a singing choir in the 1950s, made up of employees, mainly the girls who checked the pools coupons. Initially they were a 70-strong choir and made charity appearances and entertained at old folk's homes, but they became so popular that Vernons realised the commercial potential for them promoting the Vernons name and funded the choir, which became professional when slimmed down to only 16 girls.

Vernons also decided to hire some 'outsiders' and ambitious young girl singers in Liverpool sometimes joined the pools firm specifically hoping to become members of the singing troupe.

In 1958 16 of the girls moved to London where they were spotted by television producer Jack Good who signed them up for regular appearances on the BBC show 6.5 Special. When Good moved to ITV to produce the shows Oh Boy! and Boy Meets Girl, he also booked the Vernons Girls as regulars on the programmes as the female element seemed popular in shows which featured such up-and-coming names as Cliff Richard, Marty Wilde and Joe Brown. The girls also began to appear on concert bills, made records in their own right and acted as session singers for numerous artists.

The original sixteen also had a couple of other girls as back-up singers and the Vernons Girls at the time included: Barbara Mitchell, Maggie Stredder, Betty Prescott, Maureen Kennedy, Margot Quantrell, Francis Lee, Jean Owens, Vicki Haseman, Jean Ryder, Vera Brooks, Lynn Cornell, Ann Simmons, Mary Redmond, Ann O'Brien, Joyce Baker, Carmel French, Helen Taylor, Rae Parker, Dilys Jones, Sally Sallies, Gill Graham, Eleanor Russell, Joyce Smith and Sheila Prytherch.

In 1962 due to marriages and various singing combinations, the girls split into several groups, although Maureen Kennedy, Francis Lee and Jean Owen continued to perform as the Vernons Girls. They signed to Decca Records as The Vernons Girls Featuring Maureen and reached No. 16 in the charts with 'Lover Please.'

It was this trio who featured with the Beatles on the TV show Thank Your Lucky Stars on Saturday April 20 1963. Later that year they also appeared on the first all-Merseyside edition of Thank Your Lucky Stars on June 20. The Vernons Girls was part of the Beatles' autumn tour of Britain between November 1 and December 23 1963 and were included on the Pops Alive! show at the Prince of Wales Theatre in London when the Beatles topped the bill on Sunday May 31 1964.

The trio was also booked to appear on the Beatles Associated Rediffusion Television show Around The Beatles, first transmitted on Wednesday May 6 1964.

Maggie Stredder, Marian Davies and Gloria George became a trio called the Ladybirds and appeared regularly on television on Top Of The Pops and The Benny Hill Show. At one time Penny Lister became a member.

Joyce Baker left to marry Marty Wilde and joined her husband and Justin Hayward in the trio, the Wilde Three. Joyce was to give birth to Ricky and Kim and her daughter Kim was to become a chart artist in the 1980s. Mary Redmond and Ann O'Brien became the Redmond Twins.

Lynn Cornell and Ann Simmons became the Pearls. The blonde-haired Lynn was a member of the Vernons Girls when they recorded the single 'We Love the Beatles', although the novelty record failed to reach the charts. She did have some success as a solo singer with the record 'Never On Sunday.' She later joined a group called the Carefrees with another ex-Vernons Girl, Betty Prescott. The group recorded 'We Love You Beatles', which was issued in the U.S.A. on London International 10614 and reached No. 19 in the Billboard charts, with a chart life of five weeks, making it the most successful Beatles novelty single ever recorded.

As a solo singer Lynn was booked to appear on the special all-British edition of the U.S. TV series Shindig on which the Beatles appeared. Lynn had lived quite close to Paul McCartney in Liverpool and during rehearsals at the Granville Theatre, Fulham, she was able to talk over old times with Paul. She was also married to Andy White drummer on the recording sessions for the Beatles' 'Love Me Do' and 'P.S. I Love You.'

Maggie Stredder and Jean Ryder became the DeLaine Sisters.

Betty Prescott, Margot Quantrell and Vicki Haseman became the Breakaways, who signed to Pye Records in 1962 and issued the single 'He's A Rebel'. Margot Quantrell married Tony Newman, drummer with Sounds Incorporated. After 12 months Betty left to appear in a summer season and Vicki left due to some personal problems.

Margot was left to perform on her own until Vicki returned and they were then joined by Jean Ryder and recorded 'That Boy Of Mine' in 1963.

The Breakaways appeared with the Beatles on the Little Richard Show at the Empire Theatre, Liverpool on Sunday October 28 1962.

They also backed various artists on numerous hits including, in 1964 alone: Lulu on 'Shout', Cilla Black on 'Anyone Who Had a Heart' and 'You're My World', Dusty Springfield on 'Stay Awhile' and Petula Clark on 'Downtown'

Vicki, real name Victoria Mary Haseman was the eldest of three children and born in Liverpool on August 23 1940. As a teenager she was a member of the Liverpool Philharmonic Choir. She was to marry Joe Brown in 1963 and the couple had a daughter Samantha born on October 7 1964 who was to become a hit singer in her own right as Sam Brown. They also had a son Peter, who is now a record producer.

The Breakaways became the resident singers on Ready, Steady, Go! Jean left for a short period and another former Vernons Girl, Anne Simmons, deputised for her. They continued to record and appear as session singers and also backed Clodagh Rodgers when she performed 'Jack In The Box' in the 1971 Eurovision Song Contest. The group eventually split up in the 1970s and continued with solo careers. Sadly, Vicki contracted cancer and died in Henley on Thames on June 16 1991.

Eleanor Russell, the daughter of a well-known Liverpool industrialist was one of the original Vernons Girls who left the group to join the Fordettes, who travelled the country with Emile Ford. She then began to run her own quintet and in 1963 married Barry Kingston of HMV Records.

Maggie Stredder joined the Vernons Girls in 1957. That was the year when Jack Good asked Maggie not to remove her glasses when she appeared on his television shows, which became something of a trademark look for her. She left the sixteen strong group to form the vocal group the Two Tones and in 1963 they added a third voice when they became the trio the Ladybirds, who were extremely popular on television variety shows, appearing on most of the major series of the Sixties – Les Dawson, the Two Ronnies, Morecambe & Wise, Little & Large, Tommy Cooper, Shirley Bassey, Benny Hill and Mike Yarwood.

The other two girls were Marion Davies and Gloria George. They re-formed as the Vernons Girls when they were asked to appear on Cliff Richard's 30th Anniversary concert at Wembley Arena.

In 1990, Maggie decided to re-form the Vernons Girls as a trio, with Sheila Bruce and Penny Lister. Maggie was born in Birkenhead on 9 January 1936 and has published her autobiography 'The Girl With The Glasses.' Sheila had originally been one of Paul McCartney's earliest girlfriends – and he'd broken her nose by throwing a ball in her face. At one time she was married to Tommy Bruce, the gravel voiced singer noted for his hit recording of 'Ain't Misbehavin'. She also had a solo career and won the ITV New Faces show. The trio continues to perform today.

Another singer was red haired Samantha Jones, born Jean Owen in Walton on 17 November 1943, who joined the Vernons Girls in 1961 when she was 17. Her parents divorced and her mother was blind.

Samantha recalls: "I have looked after myself since I was seven. I literally went three miles into town to buy my clothes and then went home to tell my mother all about it."

She used to go to Paddy's Market in Liverpool to buy her coats and says: "I used to bargain with the stallholders and they used to cost just one or two shillings.'

When she'd only been a member of the group for three months, it was decided to whittle down the 16 girl outfit to three and the three girls who signed with Decca Records as the Vernons Girls were Jean, Maureen Kennedy and Frances Lee.

Among the singles she recorded with them were 'Lover Please', 'Only You Can Do It' (on which Sam performed the lead vocal), another hit single was 'You Know What I Mean' and the tribute song 'We Love The Beatles', which was appropriate because, as a member of the group, she appeared on several shows with the Beatles, including their special 'Around The Beatles.'

On the 'Around the Beatles' show, Samantha was given her own spot when she sang a duet with Long John Baldry after Cilla Black had refused to do it.

Samantha remembers the first time she met the Beatles. It was at a party at Bruce Welsh's house. She says: "John Lennon came up to us and said 'You're the Vernons Girls, aren't you?' I have got a song for you if you are interested.' But Maureen wasn't impressed and turned him down.

"It was some time later when we were with the Beatles again. Maureen said to John, 'Anyway, what was that song you were going to give us?' 'Forget it' he said, 'You blanked us last time.'"

The trio toured with the Beatles, Cliff Richard, Marty Wilde, Joe Brown, Eddie Cochran and Del Shannon and appeared on various television shows such as Oh Boy, Boy Meets Girl, Six-Five Special and Thank Your Lucky Stars. They also appeared on four Royal Variety Shows at the London Palladium and on the Albert Hall with the Rolling Stones.

The trio split in 1964 when Maureen married Mike Keen of the comedy duo Hope & Keen. Sadly, she died in a motorway car crash in 1969.

Jean signed with United Artists in 1964 as a solo artist and the record label gave her the name Samantha Jones. They'd originally considered calling her Roberta King, but the label's president Mike Stewart thought it sounded "too black."

Sadly the several singles she released with them, such as 'Surrounded By A Ray of Sunshine' failed to chart and she only had one album release with the label, 'Call It Samantha' which was issued in America only in 1968. Interestingly enough, 'Surrounded By A Ray of Sunshine' has become something of a cult Northern Soul song.

As mentioned previously, during the days of the Mersey Sound only two female singers were prominent, the most famous being Cilla Black.

She was born Priscilla Maria Veronica White at Stanley Hospital on 27 May 1943 and reared at 380 Scotland Road. But how did she get the name Cilla Black? That's my fault, I'm afraid.

Cilla was a friend of Virginia and me and when I launched Mersey Beat I was keen to promote my personal friends such as the Beatles, Cass & the Cassanovas, Rory Storm & the Hurricanes and Cilla so I asked Cilla to write a fashion column for me.

While I was preparing the first issue I decided to feature an article called 'Swinging Cilla.' One evening Virginia and I dropped by the Cassanova Club in the State Ballroom, Dale Street where Cass & the Cassanovas were performing. Cilla was there with her best mate Pat Davies and gave me the fashion column she'd written.

In the early hours of that morning I began to put together articles for the first issue and began to write one I headed 'Swinging Cilla.'

However, when I came to write her full name, I forgot her surname. I knew it was a colour, but couldn't figure out which one. I'd been writing so much in the early hours of the morning my mind had gone blank.

I recalled that her surname was a colour and decided to opt for Black and wrote: "Cilla Black is a Liverpool girl who is starting out on the road to fame...."

When the issue was published, Cilla came round to the office to tell me that I'd got her surname wrong, but said she preferred it and had decided to keep it as her stage name.

I continued to promote Cilla in the paper and she often dropped into the Mersey Beat office suggesting that I become her manager, but I was too occupied with producing the newspaper. During one of her visits I took her to the nearby coffee bar, the Coffee Pot, opposite Central Hall, where she described the career she had in mind.

Peggy Lee was her idol and she wanted to become a jazz singer. She asked me if I could arrange for her to have a jazz trio backing her.

This situation lasted for some time, until one evening in 1963 at the Blue Angel Club. I noticed Brian Epstein huddled in conversation with Rolling Stone manager Andrew Loog Oldham near the basement bar.

Cilla was there with her friend Pat and I thought this was an ideal moment to try something out. I asked Cilla if she would sing a number with the band and then I went up to Brian and asked him if he'd do me a favour and listen to a girl sing. He agreed. Then I asked the band on stage, the Masterminds, who were currently the resident group, if they would back Cilla on 'Boys'. They said 'yes.'

When Cilla finished singing I took her over to Brian, introduced her and left them to it. She came over to me later, delighted, and said that Brian had asked her to come to his office the next morning. She was to phone me the next day and said that Brian was signing her up.

When Cilla's biography was published some decades later, I was surprised to see that her version of what had happened was a complete distortion. She said that she was singing 'Bye Bye Blackbird' with a jazz group when Brian spotted her at the Angel.

I then got onto a member of the Masterminds who e-mailed me to confirm that I had requested that they back Cilla on 'Boys' that night.

I then contacted Andrew Loog Oldham, now living in South America, and he confirmed it. In addition he said that while Brian went on to sign Cilla, he went on to record the Masterminds with the Dylan number 'She Belongs To Me.'

Cilla was working as a Dictaphone typist at BICC, the Cable Company, when she first started singing with local groups. It all began when she went to the Iron Door club with her friend Pauline Behan, who was going steady with George Harrison at the time and was later to marry Gerry Marsden of Gerry & the Pacemakers.

The group on stage was Rory Storm & the Hurricanes and Pauline asked them if Cilla could get up with them and sing 'Fever'. As a result she made several further appearances with the band.

Rory's drummer was Ritchie Starkey, who Rory had dubbed Ringo Starr. Rory had also given him his own five-minute spot in the show called 'Starrtime' and he generally sang one song per performance.

'Boys', the song popularised by the Shirelles, was the number he usually performed, but when Cilla began to sing with the band it was also the number that she preferred. There was a bit of a dispute about this, which was resolved when they performed it as a duet.

Commenting on the compromise, Cilla said: "We did it as a duet, and even then he didn't concede anything. He had a microphone over the drums and I used to have to sing it bent over his kit."

Ringo also took to calling her 'Swinging Cyril.'

While still working as a secretary, Cilla began to sing with the Big Three at the Zodiac Club – and was paid for it! She also sang with Kingsize Taylor & the Dominoes, the group led by Ted Taylor, but had to leave the group when they set off for a season in Hamburg.

The numbers in her small repertoire at the time were 'Fever', 'Always', 'Boys' and 'Summertime'.

Her debut single, 'Love Of The Loved', despite being a Paul McCartney composition, didn't prove to be the right song for her and was only a minor hit, reaching No. 35 in the British charts following its release on 27 September 1963.

Initial 1963 publicity described her as 'The Gal with the Bright Red Hair and the Jet Black Voice' and she made her concert debut at the Odeon, Southport, in a show with the Beatles in 30 August.

She then appeared with the Beatles on the all-Merseyside edition of the Thank Your Lucky Stars TV show and was booked for the Beatles Christmas Show at the Finsbury Park Astoria in north London from 24 December.

Her career changed direction with a number Epstein picked for her, 'Anyone Who Had A Heart', which had been a big hit for Dionne Warwick in America. He heard the number while on a trip to the States and brought the record back with him, taking it to George Martin as a song for Cilla to record. George said it would be perfect for another of his artists, Shirley Bassey, and told Epstein that Cilla couldn't cope with such a song and wouldn't have a chance with it.

Sticking to his guns, Epstein insisted and Cilla's version of the song topped the British charts.

Brian was delighted at the opportunity of moulding a female artist and was able to continue placing her in concerts and TV shows with his other acts.

She toured with Gerry & the Pacemakers and Billy J. Kramer, appeared on Around The Beatles and The Music of Lennon and McCartney TV specials and featured in the Gerry and the Pacemakers' film Ferry 'Cross The Mersey.

By 1965, using his prestige and contacts, Epstein attempted to break the 22-year-old Cilla in America. She made her debut on the Ed Sullivan Show on 4 April and her American cabaret debut at the Persian Room in the Plaza Hotel, New York from 26 July.

However, American success was to elude her and her sole chart entry there was 'You're My World', which reached No. 26 in the Billboard charts in July 1964.

Success on record in Britain continued throughout the decade.

Incidentally, George Harrison once wrote a song specifically for Cilla called 'I'll Still Love You'. Arrangements were made for her to record it during a hectic summer season at Blackpool and she travelled to London on a Sunday to do so, with George producing and Ringo playing drums. Unfortunately, Cilla had toothache and a swollen mouth at the time and the session didn't work. Cilla was awarded an OBE in 1997.

Beryl Marsden was the other girl singer I wanted to build up via Mersey Beat and Virginia actually created an award for her as Best Female vocalist at the Mersey Beat Awards.

We were also party to her changing her stage name. Her real name was Beryl Hogg and one night Virginia and I were in the office of Bill Marsden, manager of the Majestic Ballroom, Birkenhead, along with Beryl and her then manager Joe Flannery.

We were discussing how she should adopt a new surname and inspired by Bill's presence, suggested that it be Marsden. So she became Beryl Marsden – although we didn't realise at the time that people would associate her with Gerry Marsden and think she was his sister!

As with Cilla, I was also thinking of ways I could help boost her career. One night John Lennon and I were having a drink in the downstairs bar of the Blue Angel. Suddenly, I had an inspiration. "Have you got a number to give to Beryl Marsden?"

John told me that he had a number which he thought was ideal for her, a number called 'Love of the Loved.' (This was actually mainly penned by Paul). When we next had a drink he was very apologetic and told me that Brian Epstein had said that as the manager it was he who would decide who would record their numbers (which meant his own stable of artists). Brian later used it as Cilla Black's debut disc.

Beryl's family had moved to Wavertree when she was seven and she attended Earle Road Secondary Modern School, but left at the age of 15, with no levels.

Beryl made her stage debut at the Orrell Park Ballroom. Chris Huston of the Undertakers was to recall: "We first saw Beryl at the OPB. She was at the front of the crowd that surrounded the stage.

"They were inebriated, or as we Scouse would say, sloshed and she was being 'egged' on by several other girls to get up and sing.

"After a bit of backward and forward chat we hauled her up onto the stage. The first song that she ever sang with us (and most probably the first she ever sang in public) was Wanda Jackson's 'Let's Have a Party'. She was an instant hit with the crowd.

"It wasn't the alcohol that gave her courage, we soon found out, she really had a great voice and an equally great personality. Next time we played at the OPB she was there and she got up with us again. After a couple of weeks, she started coming to gigs with us, in the van.

"She would usually meet us at our first gig, remember we had to come over from Wallasey, and then go with us to our other shows. Pretty soon we had a good half dozen songs that we could do with her. Brenda Lee was really popular at the time, so her records were a natural for Beryl to learn."

Recalling the time, Beryl says: "I sang with them for a dare and they asked me to stay. I was earning one pound a night – good money at the time. They went to Germany after six months but I was too young to go with them. So I went to work at Woolworth's, but I couldn't stick it."

When I was chatting to her recently she revealed to me that Brian Epstein had gone to see her parents and said that he'd like to manage her. Beryl turned him down.

Cavern compere Bob Wooler was to say: "I preferred her to Cilla.

"If Brian had taken Beryl she would have been a big seller." She was managed by various other Liverpool personalities including Joe Flannery, Spencer Lloyd Mason and Jim Turner.

She was sixteen when her debut disc 'I Know (You Don't Love Me No More)' was released by Decca in August 1963, a number originally recorded in America by Barbara George. The song was in the Marsden style local audiences were used to. This wasn't the case with her second release 'When The Love Light Starts Shining Through His Eyes', released in January 1964. This was a cover of a Supremes number and it was the Supremes, not Beryl, who reached the charts with the single.

Both her records were unsuccessful and at the age of seventeen she began appearing at the Star Club in Hamburg.

Beryl was also booked to appear with the Beatles on their last tour of Britain from 3 – 12 December 1964. Perhaps for the sake of nostalgia, the Beatles also had other Liverpool acts on that tour such as the Koobas and Steve Aldo.

She recalled: "As soon as the curtain went up, there was all this screaming, manic screaming. By then they had had enough. If there was no one listening, what was the point in playing?"

Her next manager was Tony Stratton Smith, who almost succeeded in establishing her name nationally. She had two more singles released, this time on the Columbia label: 'Who You Gonna Hurt?' in October 1965 and 'Music Talk' in December 1965.

In March 1966 Rik and John Gunnell were putting together a group, Shotgun Express and Beryl joined the outfit, sharing vocal duties with Rod Stewart. Another member of the group was guitarist Peter Green and he and Beryl had a romantic affair.

Shotgun Express made their recording debut with 'I Could Feel The Whole World Turn Round/Curtains' released on the Columbia label on 21 October 1966.

After Shotgun Express disbanded Beryl joined She Trinity, initially a North American female trio.

Beryl also sang on John Lennon's 'Instant Karma' single. She was at the Speakeasy Club at the time and was asked with some friends to come down to the studio and sing backing vocals.

Some time later she returned to Liverpool and the 1970s she resumed her career as a vocalist and formed a group called Sin-bad with Paddy Chambers.

Beryl then moved permanently to London, at one time appearing with her group, the Gamblers and also doing a lot of session work. She then appeared as a member of Martha & the Vandellas.

Currently she leads her own Beryl Marsden Band and is quite popular in Germany.

However, while it has been suggested that the Mersey scene at the time was mainly a male-dominated one, it turns out that, on the contrary, female artists flowered.

Solo singers included Irene Brown, Irene Green, Christine Ching (a 12-year-old who had her first single 'Winter's Here Again' released in November 1964), Irene Carroll, Vicki Cheetham (a 14-year-old who sang with groups such as Ian & the Zodiacs at the Orrell Park Ballroom), Kim Cross, Susan O'Doherty, Barbara Dee (sang with a number of groups, including the Mersey Monsters, had a Saturday residency at the Majestic Ballroom, Birkenhead, backed by the Detours and toured Top Rank ballrooms), Beverley Fraser, Myra Grayson, Barbara Grounds (who sang with several bands, including the Black Cats, Faron's Flamingos and Billy Kramer & the Coasters), Rita Hughes, Joan Malloy, Karina (who sang with Earl Preston & the T.T.'s), Lilli Leyton, Jackie Martin, Jill Martin (she sang with the Darktown Skiffle Group and the Merseysippi Jazz Band), Maura Meadows, Bernadette O'Toole, Rita Rogers, Beryl Ward and Lorraine White (she used the stage name Polly Pepper and aimed for 1920s nostalgia in a Roaring Twenties style act. Her father Billy White was bandleader of the Royal Iris and her grandfather constructed a violin from 5,600 matches – and Yehudi Menuin played it when he appeared at the Empire, Liverpool).

Vocal groups included the Breakaways, the Poppies, the Mystics, Collage (a female vocal group from Chester comprising Joan Webster, Carole Bait and Chris Williams), the Charmers (who had a single 'Are You Sure', backed by the Nocturnes), the Rontons (Marilyn Dease, Susan McKevitt, Ann Brown, Carole Sayle) and the Three Bells (They comprised the twins Carol and Sue Bell, together with their elder sister Jean. When the twins were 11 they entered a singing competition in Blackpool with their sister and were signed up to do a season on the Central Pier, they recorded two discs for Pye, 'Steady Date' in 1960 and 'You' in 1961 and went to Hamburg, then to Turkey, returning to Liverpool in 1964).

Girls with groups included Beryl & the Centremen, Carol & the Memories, Carole & the Corvettes (the group also had a female rhythm guitarist), Christine & the Rondels, Four Hits & A Miss, The Galaxies With Doreen (they comprised Doreen Savage on vocals, Dave Kent on lead, Bob Hewlett on bass, Dave Walker on rhythm/vocals, Jim Stead on piano/clavioline and Rob Allin on drums), Irene & the Sante Fe's (a country music group), Irene & the Tallboys, Jeannie & the Big Guys, Jenny & the Tallboys, Joan & the Demons (Joan on lead vocals, Geoffrey Jones on lead, Paul Liddy on drums, Dave Rushton on rhythm, Michael Daly on bass. They occasionally backed Chester opera singer Lee Vaughan), Linda & the Beautniks, Lottie & the Weimars, The Q Cats with Wilma York, Rita & the Renegades, the Rontons, the Squad With Rita, Tiffany's Dimensions, Vikki Lane & the Moonlighters. Christine & the Wranglers and Tiffany's Thoughts.

All girl rock groups included the Squaws, the Liverbirds, the Fast Cats, the Tomboys (Carol Morris, Chris McCloud, Helen Clinch), the Kandies and the Demoiselles (Sheila McGlory on lead, Susan Henderson on bass, Linda Turner on drums and Sheila Lewis on rhythm), the Blue Notes (Pauline Burke, Sheila Fenton, Christine McCloud) while duos included Babs & Joan and Jackie & Bridie (two Liverpool schoolteachers Jacqueline McDonald, Bridie O' Donnell, who recorded singles such as 'Roses' on Fontana and an album 'Hold Back The Dawn').

There were also numerous girls who joined the bands as singers specifically for tours of U.S. bases in France. In 1962 I began reporting the upsurge in Liverpool bands seeking a girl singer to accompany them to foreign parts. This was as a result of an agent advertising in Mersey Beat for bands to work in the U.S. bases.

Many groups took on the gigs and thoroughly enjoyed them. Others regarded them as something akin to slave labour – long hours, not much money (although such a regimen on their first trip to Hamburg helped to forge the Beatles).

Despite that, Liverpool groups poured over to France to play in the bases in a sort of mini-boom similar to the initial rush of Mersey groups to Germany.

Some groups already had female singers, others took pot luck by taking along girl friends and secretaries. Carol Lane, a vocalist from Birkenhead, travelled with Wayne Calvert & the Cimmarons, Norma Maynard joined the Travellers, Nicolette Moran accompanied the Cruisers while the Hi Cats already had Barbara Harrison in their line-up. Pam Connelly took time off work as a secretary to join Faron's Flamingos and the Remo Four and the Hurricanes were among other bands who took girl singers with them to France.

Several of the girls made records, ranging from Tiffany to Christine Ching, from Cindy Cole to Greta-Ann.

With female artist Lita Roza being the very first Liverpool singer to top the British charts, a trio of females, Atomic Kitten became the most recent in line to reach the No 1 position – not once, but three times with 'Whole Again', 'Eternal Flame' and 'The Tide Is High.'

Merseyside singers with major girl groups include Melanie Chisholm who rose to fame as 'Sporty Spice' in the Spice Girls and then went on to a successful solo career, with No. 1 hits such as 'Things Will Never Be The Same Again' and 'I Turn To You.'

There is also Heidi Range, voted one of the most beautiful women in the world, who was an original member of Atomic Kitten and is now a member of Sugarbabes and there is also Nicola Roberts a member of Girls Aloud. Huyton born Carol Decker was lead singer with T-Pau while Jacquie Abbott from Whiston sang on hits such as 'Rotterdam', 'Perfect 10', 'Don't Marry Her' and 'Dream A Little Dream' with the Beautiful South, a band led by Birkenhead-born Paul Heaton.

Over the years the styles of music by Merseyside girls has ranged from the post-punk, techno and new wave of Jane Casey and Margie Clarke as Margox to the horror rock of Zombina & the Skeletones and goth rock with Megan Burns singing as Betty Curse.

Every musical genre has been explored by Liverbirds – from the pure pop of the Reynolds Girls to the blues of Connie Lush, a singer who has been voted 'Best Female Blues singer' on three occasions.

Along the way there have been female vocalists from Merseyside in every decade from the Fifties to the present, with current singers such as Laura Critchley who was nominated as Newcomer of the Year in the Merseyside Women of the Year awards and recently sang the title song for a Hollywood movie; Candie Payne who is now produced by

Mark Ronson who launched Lily Allen and Amy Winehouse, and Kathryn Williams the singer/songwriter who has released five albums.

In fact, there has been an almost unbroken chain of female singers on Merseyside over the decades, who performed in all styles of music – pop, country, jazz, blues and so on.

From the era of Eric's, the legendary club on the Eighties, we had singers such as Jane Casey and Margi Clarke, also vocalists Arlene Smith and Shirley Alston with the Love Pastels, Sue James bass guitarist with Dead or Alive, Lori Larty with Lori and the Chameleons, Betty Bright with Deaf School and Julia Kneale with the Id.

A short-lived purely pop duo was the two Liverpool sisters who comprised the Reynolds Girls: Linda, born in 1971 and Aisling, born in 1973, come from a large family of three brothers and six sisters.

In 1988, when the two girls decided they wanted a career in music Linda was 18 and Aisling 16. They approached Pete Waterman when he was in Liverpool recording his weekly radio show and he agreed to listen to their demo tape. As a result he decided he liked their voices and invited them down to record at the PWL Studios in London.

Linda gave up her job in a hairdressing salon and Aisling dropped out of her A levels to team up as the Reynolds Sisters.

They recorded a Stock, Aitken and Waterman number 'I'd Rather Jack', which is said to have arisen from a chance remark made by Matt Aitken. They were discussing Fleetwood Mac and Matt said: "Hmmm….I'd rather Jack."

They made a video on the streets of Liverpool, against the background of familiar sites such as the Liver Buildings, the Anglican Cathedral and a Mersey Ferry, dressed in striped leggings and red tops (with their family members popping up at the end of the clip) and the record appealed to teens and reached No. 8 in the British chart in March 1989, with a chart life of twelve weeks.

That same year the girls appeared on 'The Hitman Roadshow' along with Big Fun, Halo James and Shooting Party. They had first night nerves, but said: "It really is a good atmosphere. All the bands are equally brilliant."

Unfortunately they parted the way with the Stock, Aitken and Waterman team. This was said to have come about just as they were due to enter the studio and record their first album. Waterman was to say that they had refused to cancel a pre-booked holiday in order to record and promote their second single and he decided they were 'getting too big for their boots' and dropped them

The girls then recorded a follow up record, 'Get Real', on their own label Renotone, later that year, which received hardly any air play and failed to make any impact on the charts, turning them into 'one hit wonders.'

When the record flopped so dramatically, Linda moved to Ireland and received an offer to join a seven-piece band called HYPE as their lead singer. HYPE toured the UK and cut an album, with Linda being acknowledged as a soulful singer and the band supported Take That twice on tour and also toured with artists such as Two Unlimited, Sonia, Oceanic and Alison Limerick. The band generated interest from record companies, but split up before they completed a record deal and Linda returned to Ireland

One female singer who has settled abroad who enjoyed international success – and has a famous name - is Ruth McCartney. She was born Ruth Williams in Liverpool on 24 November 1959; began studying singing and dancing at the age of four, began learning the piano at the age of seven and the guitar at the age of 12.

Her widowed mother, 34-year old Angela Williams, married Paul McCartney's father, 62-year-old Jim McCartney in November 1964.

The two had been introduced on the steps of Jim's house that August by Angela's friend Betty Robins, who was Jim's niece.

Ruth was five years old at the time, was given the McCartney surname when she was officially adopted by Jim and went to live at the McCartney home in the Wirral, Cheshire.

Paul McCartney had always had an affinity with children and bought her a pet dog, which she called Hamish, when she suffered a broken leg. She also grazed her knees so often that Paul referred to her as 'Scabby.'

She was educated at West Kirby County Grammar For Girls and in school one day she got hit on the head with two Bibles by a girl called Linda Bailey, who was a Rolling Stones fan who hated the Beatles!

She was to recall: "I may have only been a child, but with the 20-20 vision of hindsight I can safely say that even though I suffered the rigours of having my hair chopped off by teenage souvenir seekers as a tot; going to the school cloakroom and finding my raincoat and wellies missing because they had the name McCartney embossed inside them; being told never to give my name or phone number to any strangers in case they were kidnappers, or worse - JOURNALISTS; growing up never knowing if my friends wanted to play with me for me or if they had the ulterior 'meet a Beatle' motive....but I wouldn't have missed it for the world!

"I would never have had the memory of John and Paul arguing out a song together in the attic at Cavendish Avenue: the honour of having 'Blackbird' written for my maternal grandmother Edie, the photos of four-year-old me with Paul in the Bahamas on the location of 'Help!'; the recollection of a 'blind without glasses' John wakening up at Rembrandt to be told by mother Angie that they were number one in the charts – again; the birth of all my nieces and nephews; the look on Jim's face when he heard Paul had recorded his one and only musical composition (Walking In The Park With Eloise) with Chet Atkins and Floyd Cramer, and a jillion other pick-me-ups too numerous to mention.

"The reason I'm most grateful to have been there is, still to this day, that Jim chose to give me his name. It's a responsibility I take very seriously. McCartney is a fairly common name, as is Lennon, and if you look in any telephone book in most major cities in the world, you'll find a slew of them.

"I remember Jim's words 'toler and moder' ...toleration and moderation, and try to live by them. (except when it comes to buying shoes!)

"I clean my teeth, say my prayers, don't do drugs, don't smoke, TRY to pay my bills on time and completely believe in Karma. The significance of being there through the 'Beatle Years' is only just now beginning to dawn on me. Having finally realized the value and responsibility of 'the name' I must say, it's certainly a helluva perk to be related to Paul. But it's a helluva privilege to be related to Jim.

"Why? Coz there's no hairs on a seagull's chest!"

When Ruth was nine years old she was playing the piano one day, but her effort to perform the traditional hymn 'Golden Slumbers' wasn't going well and she asked Paul if he could read music. Paul couldn't, but he was intrigued by the number and composed his own lyrics to one of the verses. As a result he recorded the number and it appeared on the 'Abbey Road' album.

Ruth spent 12 years with the McCartney family, but the situation changed when Jim McCartney died.

She attempted a career in show business and attended the North West Stage School and the Royal Ballet, then led a dance trio called Talent, but they were unsuccessful and in 1981 she moved to King's Lynn with her mother and worked as a salesgirl in Debenham's store.

As a talented and determined young lady, Ruth went on to become a highly successful singer, songwriter and businesswoman.

As a singer she toured Russia nine times, with over a million people buying tickets for her concerts, although she donated most of the proceeds to a fund for Armenian refugees. Her East European appearances took in Russia, Lithuania, Armenia, Uzbekistan, Turkmenistan and Siberia. Ruth has lived in Sydney, London, Liverpool, Munich, Moscow, Hollywood, Nashville and Los Angeles.

While in Australia in 1982 she met David Skinner and they penned a single for Tina Cross called 'New Blood' which reached No. 11 in the Australian charts.

She relocated to Los Angeles in 1983 and formed a writing partnership with Barry Cotting and they have penned numbers for several feature films, including 'Mystic Pizza', 'Midnight Crossing', 'Police Academy', 'Party Line', 'Deadly Intentions' and 'The Girl Gets Moe.' They also wrote 'Cigarette In The Rain' for Randy Crawford's album 'Rich and Poor', which became the third single from the album, reaching No. 32 in the Billboard R&B chart and selling 600,000 copies

In 1989, she returned to Moscow to shoot a music video for the self-penned 'Russian Nights', which was nominated for Russian MTV's 'Video Of The Year.'

Ruth married Dieter Bockmeier in Germany in 1990 and based herself there, writing songs for her Jupiter/BMG Records debut album 'I Will Always Remember You', released in 1992. While in Germany she teamed up with Grammy Award winner Harold Faltermayer to pen 'Forever Human', the theme tune for the 1992 Barcelona Olympics, commissioned by the German TV network ZSF.

In Germany Ruth also met and fell in love with Martin Nethercutt, who became her second husband. In 1995 she issued a cassette, 'Ruth McCartney In Russia' featuring ten songs, most of them co-written by Ruth and musicians from Nashville. They included numbers such as 'Kidnap Your Heart', 'Russian Nights', 'Swimming Pool Music' and 'Overnight Success.' One of the numbers on the cassette was 'The Casket', penned by Mike McCartney and Roger McGough and featured on Mike's 1973 album 'McGear'.

On her last tour of Russia, she was the subject of a Russian documentary 'Picture Of Ruth' which was screened on Russian National Television in January 1998.

She is a highly successful businesswoman in America and Artist Relations Advisor and CEO of McCartney Music & Media Inc, founded in Nashville in 1995, and now based in Los Angeles. Ruth also coordinates the online presence of many clients including country legend Clint Black, LeAnn Rimes, REO and Speedwagon and her company's technology iFanz babysits the databases of stars from Paula Abdul to Fleetwood Mac.

Of the female vocalists currently on Merseyside also worth a mention is Candie Payne, a singer/songwriter, born in Liverpool in 1982.

When she was four years old, Candie's family moved to New York. She recalls: "We were always in Queens, just different areas of it, Jackson Heights mostly."

From the age of five she became passionate about art and in the different schools she attended, she was always progressing her artistic talent and comments: "I wouldn't say I was shy, but I was very sensitive and quiet, so I just used to absorb myself in my pictures and the other kids would come over to see what I was drawing, and get me to draw things for them. That's how I would make friends."

Her interest in music was sparked off by her parent's record collection. "My Mum and Dad have always had fantastic records: Artie Shaw, Billie Holiday, Frank Sinatra, any of the greats you could name, and they were always on."

Candie became an art student and had ambitions of becoming a designer. She continued her artistic dreams when the family returned to Liverpool in the early nineties when she was ten years old.

Back in Liverpool she intended to continue her passion for art, particularly in the field of design and had often designed and made clothes for herself and friends. However, by the time she was seventeen she became disillusioned by a foundation course at college so much that she abandoned the idea of an artistic career.

Initially, because he brothers were involved in music, she'd decided she wouldn't follow in their footsteps, although abandoning her dreams of becoming a designer had left her without any focus for the future.

She says: "I was totally directionless, I knew I wanted to do something creative, I just didn't know what, so I made a conscious decision to be open to any opportunities that came my way. And these proved to be many, due to a plum job landed in the trendy vintage clothes shop Resurrection in the centre of Liverpool, with all the bands, DJs, photographers, movers and shakers passing through for jeans and stopping for coffee to exchange records or gossip.

Her boyfriend was in a local group called Tramp Attack and he asked her to join the group to sing 'Jolene.' Then she was approached by Edgar Jones, former leader of the Stairs, who wanted her to become part of his new outfit Edgar Jones & the Joneses. She was in the band for almost a year, but decided to opt out when they changed their musical direction and for a short time she joined a local jazz group.

Fortune arrived when a friend Gary Bandit of Bandwaggon introduced her to Liverpool producer Simon Dine, who teamed up with Candie to write songs which resulted in her critically acclaimed album 'I Wish I Could Have Loved You More,' released on the Liverpool label Deltasonic.

In 2006, after five years writing, recording and singing, she was still unable to find a manager to direct her career. She says: "No one was interested because it was still all about finding the new Arctic Monkeys."

Music runs in the family and Candie's brother Howie Payne was formerly lead singer with the Stands while her brother Sean is the drummer with the Zutons.

Her music has been labelled 'pop noir' and her personal style reflects her love of music by singers such as Roberta Flack, Minnie Ripperton and Ella Fitzgerald and she is a singer who eschews backing singers in her performances or recordings.

In the field of blues there is Connie Lush. Liverpool-born Connie has been voted 'Best Female Blues Singer' three times.

Connie has her own band Blues Shouter, formed in 1993 who comprise Connie's husband Terry Harris on bass and John Lewis on guitar. Carl Woodward on drums joined the band in 1997. Blues Shouter formed in their native Liverpool; where they all still live and their base is Parr Street Studios.

John first began playing the guitar at the age of 15, appearing on all-night sessions at the Cavern Club while doing his O' levels. During the Seventies and Eighties he performed with several Liverpool bands, including China Crisis and then became a member of the Liverpool R&B orchestra Supercharge who toured Europe backing artists such as B. B. King, Fats Domino, Chuck Berry, Buddy Guy and Albert King.

Connie, who has also been voted 'European Blues Vocalist of the Year' in 2002, 2003, 2004 and 2005 and 'Blues Personality of the Year' in the Digital Blues Awards in 2006 has also been voted the UK's No. 1 Female Blues Vocalist by BluePrint magazine and 'Best UK Female vocalist' by readers of Blues In Britain in five separate years. Together with her band she toured with BB King in 1998, culminating in a concert at the Royal Albert Hall, which was recorded live. King was to say: "That woman makes my heart sing."

She has also recorded in Hollywood and Memphis. In Memphis she recorded with the Memphis Horns and Al Green's backing group the Hodges Brothers. She also gigged in clubs on Beale Street, including BB King's Club. While in New York she performed in Greenwich Village and was recorded live on Hollywood Boulevard in Los Angeles.

So far she has recorded five albums, 'Live at The Cavern Club', 'Unfaithfully Yours', 'Live At The Albert Hall', 'Connie Lush And Blues Shouter' and 'Blues Shouter'.

Another singer worth a mention is Laura Critchley, born in Little Sutton, the Wirral, on 27 March 1984, who first took to the stage at the age of six when she was to sing before an audience of 1000 at Merseyside's Floral Pavilion – unfortunately, she got stage fright, burst into tears and ran off the stage. However, from the age of seven she continued singing and by the age of ten she was back on stage performing. Laura joined the Jigsaw Music and Drama School, singing and dancing before large audiences in Liverpool and remained with the group for seven years until she was 16. At that age she penned her first song 'Changes', which was played on Radio Merseyside

She then entered Fame Academy in 2001 and out of 36,000 entrants she was selected to be in the final 50, although she failed to reach the final ten.

For a while she took a job in a bank while continuing to compose songs. At the age of 22 she moved to London in 2006 and was asked to perform at the 10th anniversary party for Big Print Records by its founder Andrew Gemmell. This resulted in her recording contract, with a fellow Merseysider, Liverpudlian Steve Power, Robbie Williams' recording manager, producing her records.

This originally came about because of MySpace, the internet showcase for artists (she has 10,000 friends on her page) and resulted in her being signed to Big Print Records, in addition to securing a management contract with Jeremy Marsh, manager of acts such as Take That and Annie Lennox.

Discussing the networking website, Laura says: "MySpace is brilliant. I was invited to play at the gig where I was signed through MySpace, so I really owe it everything. I'm definitely a MySpace case."

In March 2007 she toured with Sugababes and also joined a tour with Ray Quinn in October of that year. One of the gigs with fellow Scouser Ray, who came to fame through The X Factor, was in Rhyl and Laura recalled: "I used to do pub gigs singing and stuff in Rhyl. I went to my first ever concert in the Rhyl Pavilion – Peter Andre!"

In fact, it was at Rhyl that Laura realised that her voice, which had been causing her problems, was back to normal. She had been suffering from severe acid reflux, which had burnt her vocal chords.

Laura first encountered her vocal difficulties during her tour with Sugababes at Wembley Arena in April 2007. As she was about to sing she found she had lost her voice which had been reduced to a harsh whisper and she then had to mime to five songs and recalled: "I felt a total fraud – I'd always hated other artists who mimed, and here I was in front of 10,000 fans doing exactly that."

Eventually advisors, including a clinical vocal consultant and a

Harley street specialist discovered the problem. It occurred when Laura slept and her larynx became bathed in corrosive acid, which could damage the cartilage in her larynx.

Medication and a change of lifestyle were recommended: reducing fatty foods, not eating late at night, cutting down on alcohol and cigarettes – and no more curries!

What is so remarkable about this young artist is that even before she has achieved any chart success, she has received incredible acknowledgements from celebrities and music industry figures. Terry Wogan advises his listeners to look out for Laura.

Hollywood star Jamie Foxx, on hearing her record 'Sometimes I' says: "You gotta check out this girl. You gotta buy this record."

Robbie Williams says: "I Love 'Sometimes I'." In fact, Robbie was so impressed with Laura's voice that he invited her to record in Los Angeles and she recorded three songs with him on his album.

Ronan Keating says: "'What Do We Do' is a huge song." Jeremy Marsh says: "She's the most natural talent I've heard since getting Natalie Imbruglia's demo of 'Torn.'"

Jeff Archer, the Oscar-nominated screenwriter of 'Sleepless In Seattle' comments: "If you take Sheryl Crow and Natalie Imbruglia and send them back to Liverpool, Laura Critchley is what you get.

"This is another British Invasion and it's just about to happen."

Laura has also been selected as the 'face' of Fly Pink, a new airline flying from John Lennon Airport in Liverpool which is aimed specifically at female fliers. Laura's face is featured on the side of the plane.

An interesting young star is Megan Burns who was born in Liverpool on 25 June 1986. When she was three years old, her father deserted her mother and herself. In some ways during her formative years, Megan was something of a recluse and found it hard to make friends, even at school.

When she was 11, her grandmother sent her to a drama class and her initial career as an actress began.

In her film debut as Teresa Sullivan in the art film 'Liam', she was awarded the Marcello Mastroianni Award at the Venice Film Festival in 2000. This brought her to the attention of director Danny Boyle, who cast her as Hannah in '28 Days Later.'

She says: "I can't believe how lucky I've been. So many people try their hardest for it and I've never really fought for it. I think it comes more naturally if it's just a passion within you rather than an inspiration."

Megan was more interested in music and created her alter-ego, a character within her, struggling to get out. The result was Betty Curse.

Megan was to say that the name came from her love of Betty Page and Betty Boop and, as the Damned were one of her favourite bands, she chose the surname Curse, leading her to form a Goth-style band, with herself on vocals, Rich Curse on guitar, Alex Curse on guitar, Olly Curse on bass and Dominic Curse on drums.

She said that she decided to pursue her musical ambitions rather than an acting career because music has always been her main interest from the time as a seven year old when she used to watch 'Top Of The Pops' and was frustrated that she wasn't performing music herself and she recalls that the first song she really connected with was Nick Cave and Kylie Minogue's 'Where The Wild Roses Grow.'

Initially, she chose acting because she felt she couldn't sing, dance or play an instrument – and she didn't want to perform pop music.

She'd joined a band while at college but when it came to their first rehearsal she couldn't sing, she froze and was too nervous to return.

At the age of 15 she was obsessed with the Finnish rock band HIM and had the band's logo tattooed on her back, something she now regrets – it's an inverted pentagram with a heart shape.

She also has a tattoo that says 'cursed' with a little bat above it on her wrist and on her fingers she'd had a teardrop tattooed.

However, the career of Betty Curse began at an 80s Matchbox B-Line Disaster gig. Songwriter Steve Ludwin, former member of Little Hell, who had decided he was to old to continue to front a rock group, spotted her and sent his girlfriend over to ask her if she could sing.

She liked the ideas he had in mind for her and the fact that he would give her total input in the lyrics.

Steve was to recall: "I was talking about how I needed to find someone different and I turned around and said she needed to look like that" and pointed at Megan with her jet black hair and gothic appearance.

As Betty Curse she signed with Island Records and her first single was the double A sided 'Met On The Internet' and 'Excuse All The

Blood', which was released on 29 May 2006. Her debut album 'Here Lies' was released on Halloween, 31 October 2006 on iTunes and the CD version 'Here Lies Betty Curse' was issued in April 2007.

'God This Hurts', her second single from the album, was issued on 28 August 2006 and in November 2006 'The Girl With Yellow Hair' was the third single issued from her album and she performed the number on The Slammer, a CBBC children's TV show.

Although Betty was named 'Emerging Artist of the Month' by Yahoo, Island Records dropped her in April 2007 when her single 'Do You Mind (If I Cry)' was released. However, her recording career continued with Universal.

Of course, the Goth/Halloween image brings with it bizarre features and Betty admits to being fascinated by death. The girl with the Vivienne Westwood skull necklace says that her obsession with death, since she does not know what happens afterwards, has rid her of the fear of death itself.

Betty is continually touring, making videos to promote her records, such as 'Do You Mind If I Cry.' However, Megan Burns has not been completely submerged within Betty Curse, she is still something of a recluse. She loves touring and being on the road because the option is to sit inside her house all day watching videos and listening to music.

Over the years there have been scores of other female artists, both singers and musicians, who have been part of the Mersey scene. Here are just some of them:

Natalie Reeves in the electro latin pop band Chione; Tina Labrinski and Sarah Lamarra, the vocal duo the Creamy Whirls; Kathy Freeman of the Accelerators; Lisa Florek of the Adams Family; Kate Finlay of Ad Lib; Paula Molyneux of Alien Heat; Genevieve Mort of Amsterdam; Norma Lies of a.P.A.t.T.; Sue McCormack of Big Game; Brenda Kenny in Da Books and Naafi Sandwich; Carolyn Stewart in Death Kit; Diane Rowland in the Debonaires; Karen Jones in the Decemberists; Mandy Morgan in Decomposed; Joanne Ellis in Eat At Joe's; Melanie & Katrina Michael in Experimental Gardens; Judith Laity in Ex Post Facto and Goat People; Babs Norris in Fag Ash Lil; Sarah Parry in Fallen People; Barbara Donovan of Glass Torpedoes; Elizabeth Kay of Goat People and Marshmallow Overcoat.

Jane Alexander of White Russians and Gone to Earth; Amanda Todd in Heaven Tonight, Mandarin Orange, Topsy Turvey and Zale Out; Kathy Marsha Morrison in Hey Marsha!; Mandy Shaw of Iconoclasts; Julia Kneale of the Id; Jacquie & Jeanette, a duo; Carol Bushell of Jegsy Dodd & the Original Sinners; Emma Longworth and Sarah Bloor of Jessica's Ghost; Marie Woods of Jigger; Samantha Kearney; Shirley Alston of Love Pastels; Rosie Hamlin of Love Pastels; Arlene Smith of Love Pastels; Joanna Harrison of Made for Jane; Nina Guido of the Mogadons; Curly Sue Donaldson of Neon Hearts; Donna Lowe of Neuklon and Lloyd Collection; Sue Forshaw of Numbers 48 and Big Game; Helen Stringer of 051; Siobhan Mahler of Passion Polka, Persuaders, River City People and Peep Show.

Tina Lee of Sister Moon; Susan Elenni of 16 Tambourines; Babs Norris of Thin End of the Wedge; Elaine Harris of Third Man; Marie Matazz of the Unhealthy; Sue James of the Upsets, Dead Or Alive and Stopouts; Lisa Baron of US Companion; Jacqui Lancaster of the Vow; Cheryl Leigh of When It Rains and Word for Word; Linda Wright of Zoots Navarro;Laura Caseberry of Perfect Virus; Tracy Smith of Acacia Gum; Kathy Freeman of the Accelerators and Kathy-X; Anna Jenkins of Amsterdam; Jennifer John of Black & Blue; Alexandra Vienskavitch of Blue Vein; Carolyn Stewart of Death Kit; Diane Rowland of the Debonaires; Kate Milner of Divine Thunderbolt;

Debbie Rimmer of Fag Ash Lil; Sarah Parry of Fallen People; Jacqui Mercer of Fantasia; Diane Love of Fashion Play and Orchid Falls; Rose Goodwin of Fiascos; Paula Staunton of Fifth Column; Muriel Box and Sue Greenough of Flambe Flabs; Louise Hanman and Karen Timms of Flamingo 50; Denise D'Arcy of Fragile Friends; Kate Gill of Glass Torpedoes; Julia Kneale of the Id; Ruth Evison of Islands of Dance; Jo Bywater.

Michelle Brown of Kit; Tracey Smith of Luminescence; Maxine Dunn of Mahalia, Steal and CD Drift; Rachel, Chloe, Claire and Clare of Marlowe; Heidi Cure of the Moderates; Sophia Churney of Ooberman; Katie Evans of Pincushion; Sheila Norris of Restless; Christine Levine of Richville; Jayne of Savoire Fayre and Roulade; Diane Rowland of Six; Susan Ellenie of 16 Tambourines; Lisa Barton of US Companion; Jacqui Lancaster of the Vow; Cheryl Leigh of Word For Word, Young World and When It Rains; Linda Wright.

11. The Hosts with the Most

WITH so many venues there were obviously lots of comperes who introduced the shows.

They included Allan Ross; Jeff Martin; Derek Jeffrey; Ron Appleby; Pete Stephens, compere at the Jive Hive, Crosby and numerous others at the various ballrooms and clubs.

I even had my own stints: Jazzshows hired me to be one of the comperes on their 'Mersey Beat' boat to the Isle of Man, although I was seasick for most of the trip. Then Gordon Knowles of the Locarno insisted that I become disc jockey once a week at the Locarno, playing all the releases by the Mersey artists and Allan Williams also asked me to host a 'Bill Harry Night' at his Maggie May club where I introduced new bands.

Allan Ross had entered a talent competition at the Floral Hall Pavilion, New Brighton in 1959 and was placed second. He then turned semi-professional, working in clubs on Merseyside and Manchester and his first professional engagement was at the Odeon, Manchester where he appeared in The Marty Wilde Show. He then appeared in cabaret in London at the Club Condor, Club Panama, Club Bagatelle, Whiskey A Gogo, Trocadero and the Ranch House. He occasionally returned to Liverpool to host shows.

Jeff Martin, who lived with his parents on the Wirral near Birkenhead was called up for National Service in 1956 and stationed in Germany where he began to work for the British Forces Network as a disc jockey.

On his return to Merseyside he became DJ at the Majestic Ballroom, Birkenhead and recalled: "All the top groups played there nightly, including the Beatles who made their debut performance of

'Love Me Do' before it entered the charts. They used to relax at the Conway Arms pub opposite the Majestic. The Beatles were just beginning to hand out autographed photos. They gave me one which, regrettably, I gave away a little later (today it's worth a fortune).

"I was a DJ at other halls on Merseyside. Famous in Chester was the Riverpark Ballroom, whose manager was Ken Hignett. They used to have bingo sessions almost every night and used to panic to get the bingo people out quickly so the room could be ready for the groups arriving. Gerry & the Pacemakers used to play. One night Cilla Black arrived to sing. I still clearly remember her arriving, so small, so young. I can't remember what songs she sang, but she was still unknown to the public.

"Back to Merseyside – Bob Wooler was a good friend of mine. We used to meet often at the late night coffee shops after our stints at the ballrooms. We were the only DJs at the time. Later on in the 1960s a guy called Derek Jeffrey came on the scene. He did a little work in the halls. I don't know what happened to him, but I'd love to know."

Jeff also had a regular spot at the Orrell Park Ballroom and also became a columnist for Mersey Beat.

He remembers: "There was a fantastic show put on by Brian Epstein at the Tower Ballroom, New Brighton. The top star was Little Richard. Bob Wooler introduced him while I presented the Beatles on stage.

"Mecca and Top Rank were the top two in venues across the country and Top Rank offered me the management of the Majestic Ballroom, Chester. I continued as a DJ at Chester, where we used to have 1,500 customers three or four times a week. There was a live band plus Pete Dee and his music, together with visiting groups from the Merseyside area. After two years at Chester, Top Rank wanted me to move around the country. I found this slightly disappointing, particularly at some of the venues such as the Majestic, Stoke On Trent. At the Majestic, Luton I met Brian Epstein for the first time when he brought Billy J. Kramer & the Dakotas."

In recent years Jeff was still in the entertainment field with two companies where he used his experience presenting dances and socials.

The most famous compere of the lot was Bob Wooler – but his impact on the local scene has overshadowed contributions from other

Mersey comperes of the time, just as the Beatles were to overshadow all the groups which were to follow for decades to come.

Bob was born Frederick James Wooler in Liverpool on 19 January 1926 and became a clerk in the local railway dock office in 1952, immediately following his National Service.

He was living in the Garston area when, in 1957, he became involved in managing a skiffle group called the Kingstrums, who came from a notorious area of Garston called 'Under the Bridge.' He once entered them in a talent contest at the Gateacre Labour Club (which was won by the Mars Bars, who later became Gerry & the Pacemakers) and recalled: "At that Labour club I remember the Kingstrums coming into direct competition with John Lennon's skiffle group, the Quarry Men. Because they came from posh places like Woolton and Aigburth, the Quarry Men were considered to be snobs 'Under the Bridge."

The Kingstrums disbanded in 1958 but the experience of working on the local rock 'n' roll scene convinced Bob that he was more suited to compering the shows put on by the local jive hives and as a compere-cum-disc jockey he worked part-time for promoters such as Wally Hill of Peak Promotions, appearing at Holyoake Hall in Smithdown Road and similar venues. He also promoted his own shows at Hambleton Hall with Vic Anton.

When the Beatles arrived back from Germany with copies of their single 'My Bonnie', Paul gave a copy to Bob, who began playing it at Hambleton Hall, and another to Virginia Sowry at Mersey Beat. The story of their recording session had already been featured on the front cover of Issue No.2.

Bob's encyclopaedic knowledge of the local scene soon made him a sought-after figure by local promoters and his advice was regularly heeded. Allan Williams offered him a full-time job as compere/host at the Top Ten club in Soho Street, but when it burned down eight days after the opening, Bob was without work, apart from his compering activities at venues such as Litherland Town Hall and Aintree Institute, but he was soon provided with a full-time employment when Ray McFall engaged him as compere at the Cavern club.

Bob had a particularly pungent wit and he also created what were to become known as 'Woolerisms', a range of phrases he bestowed on local music personalities. They included 'the Nemperor' for Brian Epstein, 'Mr Showmanship' for Rory Storm, 'The Panda Footed Prince of Prance' for Faron, leader of Faron's Flamingos, 'The Sheik of Shake; for Karl Terry, leader of the Cruisers and 'The Boswell of Beat' For me.

There was also a lot of good-natured banter between Bob and the Beatles during the Cavern introductions and John once told the Cavern audience that Bob was his long-lost father, who he hadn't seen for 15 years – and the audience believed him!

I invited Bob to write a column for Mersey Beat under the title 'The Roving I' and in Issue No. 7 he listed his top Ten Mersey groups:

"Well here it is then, my list of what I rate to be the ten most popular rock groups on Merseyside – excluding the Bluegenes, of course, they are beyond comparison. They are in a class of their own."

1) The Beatles, 2) Gerry & the Pacemakers, 3) Rory Storm & the Hurricanes, 4) The Remo 4, 5) The Strangers, 6) Johnny Sandon & the Searchers, 7) Karl Terry & the Cruisers, 8) Mark Peters & the Cyclones, 9) Ray & the Del Renas, 10) The Big Three.

Personally, I couldn't figure why he'd left out such dynamic outfits as Kingsize Taylor & the Dominoes or Howie Casey & the Seniors or why he considered groups such as the Cruisers, Cyclones and Del Renas above the Big Three.

In addition to his writing activities for Mersey Beat, Bob composed most of the copy for the advertisements placed by promoters both in Mersey Beat and the Liverpool Echo. They were concise, lively and contained many puns.

When John Lennon paid for classified advertisements in Mersey Beat he would place notices such as 'HEAR BOB WOOLER SING with the Beatles at Aintree Institute' and 'HEAR BOB BEATLE at the Woolerstute.' Apart from his compering duties, Bob advised groups on stage presentation, discussed their musical repertoires with them and often recommended numbers for them to learn. Bob's collection of American singles, which he carried around with him to the venues in a portable record case, led to a lot of bands playing the numbers which Bob had searched for and selected himself.

Having sacrificed the security of a steady job to compere shows at the ill-fated Top Ten, he finally found what he was looking for when he became compere at the Cavern in 1961, a job which lasted for six years. The audience loved his announcements: "Hello Cavern Dwellers, and welcome to the best of cellars!"

During his years at the Cavern he was to introduce the Beatles on stage more times than anyone else in the world.

The fact that the Beatles looked to him for advice was indicated when they asked him to attend their meeting with Brian Epstein on Wednesday 3 December 1961.

It was half-day closing in Liverpool that day and Epstein had requested a meeting at his office in NEMS at 4.30pm. Bob, John, George and Pete went to a pub called the Bridge to discuss Brian prior to the meeting and arrived late. Paul was 30 minutes late. Brian was slightly irritated by their tardiness and wanted to know who Bob was.

"This is me dad", said John. Bob later discussed the meeting with them. He also began to meet Epstein regularly and revealed to him that the group were, in fact, actively seeking a manager.

When Epstein began to promote shows on behalf of NEMS Enterprises in order to promote the Beatles and other groups he'd signed, he used Bob's expertise to organise, promote and run events at local venues such as the Tower Ballroom, New Brighton and the Queen's Hall, Widnes.

One of the most controversial situations regarding Wooler and the Beatles occurred at Paul McCartney's 21st birthday party on 18 June 1963.

One of Bob's traits was to make cutting remarks and he made some reference to John's recent short break with Epstein in Spain, allegedly saying: "How was the honeymoon, John?"

To a Lennon who had drunk too many beers it was like a red rag to a bull and he leapt onto Bob and battered him to the ground, giving him a black eye, bruised ribs and torn knuckles – the latter sustained by Bob when he'd tried to protect his face from John's foot as he was being kicked.

A small news item appeared in the Daily Mirror newspaper. John refused to apologise, saying: "He called me a queer so I battered his bloody ribs in." He was probably unaware at the time that Bob himself was gay.

A few months later, Bob announced their final appearance at the

Cavern. Their phenomenal success had taken him by surprise and he was lost for words, announcing them simply by saying: "It's the Beatles!"

When the Beatles moved to London, Brian employed a number of his personal friends from Liverpool, but Bob wasn't among them.

He became Ray McFall's right-hand man, managed groups such as the Carrolls and, for a short time, was married to Beryl Adams, Brian Epstein's former secretary.

With the closing of the Cavern, Bob took on various jobs as disc jockey in the north and worked for a time as a bingo caller at the former Locarno Ballroom. In the Seventies he presented an occasional promotion in Liverpool and worked on several projects with Allan Williams, primarily Beatles conventions. By the Eighties he was escorting visitors to Liverpool on special Magical Mystery Tours of the Beatles former haunts. He died on 8 February 2002.

The other major Mersey compere was Billy Butler.

Billy was born William George Butler in Salem Street, Amlwch, Anglesey on 24 January 1942. His family then moved to Liverpool and settled at 52 Grey Rock Street.

Billy was educated at Whitefield Road School until 1953, then Liverpool Collegiate until 1958. A fellow pupil was Pete Best and the school's main rival was Liverpool Institute.

He worked as plumber and dock clerk for a time, then passed an audition for TV shows in 1961 and appeared on ABC TV's Thank Your Lucky Stars in the 'Spin-a-Disc' spot. This was a part of the show in which three singles were reviewed and commented on by a panel, a sort of mini Juke Box Jury. Billy was joined by another regular, Janice Nicholls, together with various teenagers.

Although most of the episodes no longer exist, the Saturday 21 December 1963 Merseyside Special remains available. In the show Billy was joined by Bob Wooler in the 'Spin-a-Disc' section and the artists appearing were the Beatles, Gerry & the Pacemakers, Cilla Black, Tommy Quickly, Billy J. Kramer and the Breakaways.

The groups Billy joined included the Merseybeats, the Tuxedos, the Hangmen and the Cherry Pickers. He then became a Disc Jockey at the Cavern Club for five years and was also compere at the Mardi Gras, Downbeat, Victoria, Blue Angel and She clubs.

It was during 1962 that Billy sat in on gigs with the Merseybeats for six months. The other members at that time were Billy Kinsley on bass and vocals, Tony Crane on lead and vocals, Dave Elias on rhythm and Frank Sloane on drums. Billy then went on form Billy Butler & the Tuxedos.

The other members were: Alan Crowley on bass, Les Williams on lead, Ronnie Myers on drums and John O' Brien on rhythm. Bob Wooler then offered him a job as compere at the Cavern Club and he disbanded the group although they have re-formed on occasion during the years and at times have included Billy Kinsley and Kenny Parry in the line-up.

Billy also became disc jockey at the Mardi Gras club in Mount Pleasant, along with Chris Wharton and he would often get up to sing 'Long Tall Sally' or 'Whole Lotta Shakin'' with whichever band was on. The next stage of his career was in radio and he became a disc jockey at Radio Merseyside in 1971, and then joined Radio City in 1979, returned to Radio Merseyside in 1984, then back to City in 1995, then Merseyside again in 2000.

Billy also appeared in the 1979 Granada TV series Mersey Pirate along with Duggie Brown, Andrew Schofield and Frank Carson.

He has been a columnist with the Liverpool Echo and has won no less than five Scousology awards while his radio quiz show Hold Your Plums was a Sony Bronze Award winner, it was also being used as a training tool for the national curriculum. An Everton FC supporter, Billy is also a keen collector of vintage magazines, especially the Radio Times, and also comics, records and videos of retro TV shows.

In addition to his regular shows on Radio Merseyside, Billy is also active in presenting and promoting live gigs and concerts on Merseyside. He helped in the organisation of '40 Years of Music and Laughter' at the Empire Theatre, Liverpool, which took place on Monday 26 November 2007. Billy persuaded three Mersey singers to play their own Liverpool song: Ian McNabb with 'Liverpool Girl', Pete Wylie with 'Heart As Big as Liverpool' and Ian Prowse with 'Does This Train Stop On Merseyside?'

Over the years Billy has teamed up with Wally Scott for various radio shows and newspaper columns.

Mike Aherne was one of the early Liverpool disc jockeys. He was born in Liverpool on 30 September 1942 and had various jobs before he opened a club with a friend. Things were going well until the club floor collapsed! Mike worked at the Cavern Club and then joined Radio Caroline on their Northern ship, moored near the Isle of Man.

He then joined Caroline in the south until 1967 when he applied for a job with Radio One. He was only there for a short time and then moved to Australia where he appeared on a number of stations before returning to Britain in 1988. Since then he has worked on various local stations throughout the country.

The two most famous Merseyside disc jockeys were, of course, Kenny Everett and John Peel.

Kenny was born Maurice James Christopher Cole in Seaforth, Liverpool on 24 December 1944 and was educated at St Bede's Secondary Modern.

He worked in an office and in a bakery, before beginning his showbiz career with Radio Luxembourg and he adopted a stage name adapted from a film star hero of his childhood, Edward Everett Horton. He next joined the pirate ship Radio London. Kenny was the official pirate radio reporter invited to accompany the Beatles on their final tour in August 1966. He then joined BBC's Radio 1 on its launch in 1967.

On Saturday 20 May 1967 the BBC show Where It's At transmitted a pre-recorded feature by Everett on 'Sgt Pepper's Lonely Hearts Club Band', including interviews with John, Paul and Ringo. Another pre-recorded interview by Everett, in which he talked to Paul McCartney and discussed 'All You Need Is Love', was transmitted on Where It's At on Saturday 1 July 1967.

On the edition of 'Where It's At' on Saturday 25 November 1967, an 18-minute interview with John Lennon by Everett and Chris Denning was broadcast. Some of his interviews with the Beatles were issued as an Apple promotional single in Italy under the title 'Una Sensazionale Intervista dei Beatles'.

Everett edited the Beatles' fifth and final Christmas fan club record. He used his real name, Maurice Cole, on the 1969 edition.

On Saturday 27 January 1968, Everett visited John Lennon at his home in Weybridge to record an interview for The Kenny Everett Show, which was broadcast on Radio 1 on 4 February.

Everett also visited the group while they were recording at Abbey Road on Thursday 6 June 1968 and recorded an interview that was broadcast on The Kenny Everett Show on Sunday 9 June.

On Thursday 14 August 1969, Everett again dropped by the Abbey Road Studios while the Beatles were mixing some tracks and recorded an interview with John Lennon which was broadcast in two parts on his Everett Is Here radio series on Saturday 20 and Saturday 27 September.

It wasn't merely the fact that Kenny shared the same Liverpool roots as the Beatles that led to his becoming such a personal friend of the group. He also had a wacky sense of humour that appealed to them, particularly to Lennon. Kenny was also anarchic in his approach to his radio and television shows, another aspect of his talent that they liked.

His autobiography, 'The Custard Stops At Hatfield', published in October 1982, featured many anecdotes about his relationship with the Beatles.

In addition to his radio career which included stints with his own shows on Radio 1, Radio 2 and Capital Radio, he also became a television star, appearing in numerous shows including The Bob Monkhouse Show, Saturday Night Clive, Wogan and Blankety Blank, but starring in his own series which included The Kenny Everett Explosion, The Kenny Everett Video Show, The Kenny Everett Television Show and The Kenny Everett Video Cassette.

He was also the voice of an animated character 'Captain Kremmen' in the 1978 TV series of that name and he starred in the spoof horror movie Bloodbath In The House Of Death in 1984.

Kenny married Billy Fury's former girlfriend Lee Middleton in 1966, but soon after they had separated in 1989 he revealed that he was gay. Kenny died from an AIDS-related illness on Tuesday 4 April 1995. He was 51 years old.

His first single, recorded with Dave Cash when the two disc jockeys had their Kenny & Cash Show, was 'The B Side' c/w 'Knees' on Decca F12283. The number was based on Sonny & Cher's 'I Got You Babe.'

Kenny next had a minor hit on his own with 'It's So Long' c/w 'Without Her' issued on MGM 1421 on 14 June 1968. 'Nice Time' c/w 'Now For A Little Train Number' was issued on Deram DM245 on 14 March 1969. 'Happy First Birthday From Cuddley Capital' was issued on Warner Bros. SAM 20, which was a promo single celebrating Capital Radio's first birthday.

'The Captain Kremmen Story' was a flexi-disc issued on Lynetone LYN4586. 'Captain Kremmen (Retribution)' c/w 'Retribution' by Kenny with Mike Vickers was issued on DJM 10810 in 1977 and reached No.32 in the British charts. 'The Adventures of Captain Kremmen' c/w 'Conversations With Ken' was issued on Asylum Records HALC2 and was a single for Capital Radio's 'Help A London Child' appeal.

His biggest hit was 'Snot Rap' c/w 'Snot Rap Part 2' issued on RCA/KEN 1 in 1983 which reached No. 9 in the British charts following an appearance on Top Of The Pops.

John Peel, the rebel disc jockey with the eclectic tastes who was the original British radio champion of various genres including reggae, punk, house, hip hop and dance was born John Robert Parker Ravenscroft on 30 August 1939 in Heswall on the Wirral and grew up in the village of Burton.

He was to become a boarder at Shrewsbury School in Shropshire where a school report had the comment: "Perhaps it's possible that John can form some kind of nightmarish career out of his enthusiasm for unlistenable records."

Directly from the school he was called up for National Service, something the anti-establishment Peel didn't enjoy, and he was to mention: "The Army said afterwards, 'At no time has he shown any sign of adapting to the military way of life.' I took it as a compliment."

He boarded a plane at Speke Airport, Liverpool and moved to America in 1960, settling in Dallas and selling cotton insurance from the Dallas Cotton Exchange. He then took a job at the local radio station KLIF and had attracted attention because of his Merseyside accent, which he admitted he exaggerated at the time, due to the Stateside success of the Beatles, and he was to work for various radio stations before returning to Britain.

Years later, he was to tell the NME about the period: "I became a Beatles expert, but of course I hadn't been in Liverpool for years and didn't know anything about them. In those days, though, America was full of DJs who were all called James Bond who pretended to be

English and were really Canadian and who were all Ringo's cousin. I don't know why they chose Ringo. So, in the sense that I wasn't called James Bond and I really did come from England, I was almost unique."

John was to work for various radio stations before returning to Britain, playing the standard play list and Beatles records at most of them. However, when he moved to KMEN in San Bernadino, California, he was allowed to choose his own records and recalls: "I started to play records that I wanted to play. Previously it had been all chart stuff. But I had to do six hours over the weekend and I thought, if I was going to do six hours, then I'm going to play what I want to play. I started to play blues things, Doors, Love, Butterfield Blues Band and Jefferson Airplane. I worked there for 18 months and then ran foul of the law and thought I'd better leave."

This related to the local sheriff who took a dislike to the station and to Peel.

Arriving in Britain, John was now accompanied by his first wife Shirley Ann Milburn who he married in 1965, although he was unaware that she was only 15 at the time of the wedding. Shirley was also an orphan at the time she was married and the couple were divorced in 1973. Sadly, Shirley later committed suicide.

In March 1967 the pirate radio station Radio London hired him and his programme The Perfumed Garden attracted attention and it was while broadcasting there that he adopted the name John Peel on the suggestion of a secretary.

His stint on the pirate boat was only to last for six months as new laws were introduced to ban the pirates and Radio London closed down in August of that year. Fortunately, the BBC was launching its new Radio One the following month and John became one of the first disc jockeys on the station. He began broadcasting on the Top Gear programme, but there were problems as the executives regarded him as something of a loose canon, noticing his anti-establishment tendencies, but he was championed by the programme's producer Bernie Andrews.

John's contribution was The Peel Sessions, which introduced artists such as David Bowie and Pink Floyd. Then, in January 1968 John was asked to present another show, this time late at night called Night

Ride, which he began recording in March of that year. To the hierarchy of the BBC he was an anarchic figure, having John and Yoko play a tape of their unborn baby's heartbeat on the programme – and he also admitted on air that he'd once had a venereal disease.

Top Gear also continued, although Andrews had moved to Radio Two and the new producer was John Walters, whose association on the programme with John was to last for 20 years.

At one time Peel also ran his own record label Dandelion which was a progressive label he launched with his manager Clive Selwood.

Clive also headed the British side of Elektra Records at the time and took over administrative duties on the new label while Peel concentrated on the A&R side. Among the artists who recorded for the label were Gene Vincent, Bridget St. John, Medicine Head, Kevin Coyne and Clifford T Ward.

The two had set out to issue a non-profit-making label because they were keen to give a chance to artists neglected by the music industry at the time. Because of their frugal budget, they couldn't advertise extensively like other labels or afford to promote in the same way, which produced drawbacks. For all their altruism, they found that the artists they signed didn't always appreciate their efforts.

As Peel was to comment: "There is no faster way of losing friends than to set up a record label and record them. Because when the money doesn't come rolling in and you can't afford full-page ads in the music press, artists become very resentful."

Dandelion only survived for a period of three years, releasing more than two dozen albums, but only 15 singles. The records have now become collector's items. Other acts during the short life of the company included Principle Edwards Magic Theatre, Mike Hart, Stackwaddy, Ensemble, The Way We Live and Beau.

It was in 1968, while making his first television appearance on the show How It Is that he first noticed Sheila Gilhooly in the audience and she was to become his second wife on 31 August 1974.

Rod Stewart was his best man, John wore Liverpool FC's colours and 'You'll Never Walk Alone' was played as the couple walked down the aisle.

As a lifelong fan of Liverpool FC, John introduced a reference to the club in each of the names of his four children: William Robert

Anfield, Alexandra May Anfield, Thomas James Dalglish and Florence Shankly!

In addition to his revolutionary radio shows presenting new trends ranging from punk to hip hop, John also became a disc jockey on Top Of the Pops, a contrast to his eclectic radio programmes as he had to present strictly top twenty artists of the calibre of Bucks Fizz, and he decided to finish his regular appearances on the programme in 1986, although his occasional appearances stretched into the Nineties.

In the meantime, John was still discovering and presenting new acts such as The Smiths, Billy Bragg and the Jesus & Mary Chain.

John's contribution to the music industry was recognised in November 1998 when he attended Buckingham Palace where he received an OBE. This wasn't the only acknowledgement his unique musical talent was to be awarded.

For instance, he was voted 'DJ of the Year' in the music publication Melody Maker no less than eleven times. 1993 saw him receive the 'Sony Broadcaster of the Year' award and the following year the NME gave him the 'Godlike Genius award.' He also received another Gold award from Sony in 2002 and was inducted into the Radio Academy's Hall of Fame in 2003.

On 26 October 2004 when John was visiting the Inca city of Cuzco in Peru, he suddenly had a heart attack and died. He had been working on his autobiography at the time, so it was never finished by him, although it was completed by his wife and Ryan Gilbey as 'Margrave of the Marshes' in October 2005.

John's influence is still strongly felt and many tributes continue.

Merseytravel, for instance, announced on 23 October 2008, that they would be naming a train after him.

I only interviewed John once in the Sixties. I had launched the first series of features about disc jockeys in Record Mirror and arranged to meet John in an Old Compton Street coffee bar. He brought along a new discovery of his named Marc Bolan. Even then he was more interested in promoting new talent than gaining publicity for himself.

He was a giant among broadcasters and will be much missed.

Afterword

I REMEMBER as a kid, pressing my nose against the huge pane glass window of the Far East restaurant, along with a gang of other kids, to catch a glimpse of Trevor Howard and Jean Simmons, who were in Liverpool filming The Clouded Yellow.

How exciting it seemed to someone who virtually lived in the cinema, to experience the fact that a film was actually being made in the area where I lived.

Then came The Magnet, part of which was filmed on the debris in front of the Anglican Cathedral, where I used to play.

Who would have realised that over the decades Liverpool would become known as 'Hollywood on the Mersey' and more films would be set in the area than anywhere else in the country, with the exception of London.

The Arrest of Goudie, made on Merseyside in 1901, was said to be the world's first filmed crime reconstruction. There was a long gap until the next film, Penny Paradise in 1938.

In 1949 Waterfront was set in Liverpool starring Richard Burton.

This was followed by The Magnet the following year and then The Clouded Yellow.

Hollywood stars Lana Turner featured with Sean Connery in A Time And A Place and Susan Hayward was at the Pier Head filming I Thank A Fool. Freddie Fowell, later to be known as Freddie Starr, appeared as a tearaway in Violent Playground and other films of the Fifties included Beyond This Place with Van Johnson and Vera Miles. Web of Evidence and the documentary Morning In The Streets.

The Beatles never made a feature film in Liverpool, although Yellow Submarine gave a nod to the city while Gerry & the

Pacemakers did us proud with Ferry 'Cross the Mersey. The other film of the Sixties was The Reckoning.

In the Seventies we had Gumshoe, penned by Neville Smith and starring Albert Finney and the Eighties brought in several movies, although Educating Rita, said to be based in Liverpool, was actually filmed in Dublin.

The other films were No Surrender, Distant Voices Still Lives, The Fruit Machine and Shirley Valentine.

By the Nineties, Liverpool came into its own for its film locations and movies included Dancin' Thru The Dark, Blonde Fist, The Long Day Closes, The Bullion Boys, Blood On The Dole, Dark Summer, Priest, An Awfully Big Adventure, Rich Deceiver, David Copperfield and Three Businessmen.

Next we had Liam, Going Off Big Time, Shooters, Revengers Tragedy, The 51st State, Win Each Way, Dad's Dead, Digital Reaper, Millions, O Jerusalem, Across the Universe, Dead Man's Cards and the acclaimed 2008 documentary Of Time And The City.

As far as television went, Z Cars was the series that started it all – and Merseyside has been the base of many TV series and dramas and they have included The Liver Birds, A Family At War, The Onedin Line, Bread, Boys From The Blackstuff, Liverpool One, Nice Guy Eddie and Lilies. There were also the soaps – Brookside and Hollyoaks.

There were numerous documentaries – Pathe's: Liverpool –Home Of The Mersey Sound and The Beatles Come to Town and BBC's Singing City. I was involved in two of the music documentaries, The Mersey Sound and Beat City.

Alun Owen, who scripted A Hard Day's Night and TV plays such as No Trams To Lime Street, also wrote the script for Lionel Bart's stage musical Maggie May, which some critics have said was Bart's best work.

In July 1964, Alun told me: "It's a completely fictitious story all about contemporary Liverpool and a lot of the music has been based on old Liverpool and Irish folksongs.

"There is a beat club scene in the show, with a group who perform two beat numbers – they are going to augment with an orchestra."

In fact the group turned out to be the Nocturnes, the resident group at the Blue Angel and we had a big after-show party at the Blue Angel, attended by stars such as Judy Garland. Judy recorded four of the numbers from the show in her last ever studio recording session and Peter Sellers was to star in the film, although it was never made.

Since Alun's day, Liverpool has produced some of Britain's brightest television writers, including Willie Russell, Alan Bleasdale, Carla Lane, Neville Smith, Lydia LaPlante and Jimmy McGovern.

In the Nineties I spent five years developing a drama series Mersey Beat, set in Liverpool in 1961. Film & General, who had made films such as Gregory's Girl were to produce it and Johnny Byrne, the man behind All Creatures Great And Small and Heartbeat, agreed to write the original scripts and I was going to contact Liverpool writers Neville Smith, Ray Connelly, Willie Russell, Alan Bleasdale and Carla Lane to see if they could write episodes. It was based around the Mersey Beat paper and the music scene in Liverpool at the time.

Film & General approached the BBC who said they were interested in screening the series. They held on to it for three years and then suddenly said "no." Soon after they came out with a cop series and just took the name of our series.

This Morning, the morning show with Britain's largest audience was also based in Liverpool, although the presenters decided they would sooner have it in London and the programme moved there.

When John Lennon, Stuart Sutcliffe, Rod Murray and I, as the Dissenters, had the vision of making Liverpool famous, not only did we not realise the incredible success John would have or that my coining of the name Mersey Beat and the publication of the paper would become such an international brand. Had Stuart lived I'm convinced he would have become a world renowned artist...but we also could never have predicted the immense influence and success of the Mersey poets.

When Andrew Solt, director of the John Lennon film Imagine asked me to take part in the 'Mersey Beat' episode of his ten part television series History Of Rock And Roll, we were fortunate to have had advance bookings because we found that every room in every hotel in Liverpool had been fully booked because young people from all over Britain and Europe came to Liverpool at the weekends to attend dance clubs such as Cream.

In fact, Liverpool has always hosted certain clubs which have become internationally known. Following the Cavern there was Eric's and then Cream.

Eric's was the new club which opened opposite the former Cavern premises in Mathew Street on 1 October, 1976 and was run by Roger Eagle, Ken Testi and Pete Fulwell. Eagle, a jazz enthusiastic, named the club Eric's in tribute to jazz performer Eric Dolphy.

Although many punk and post punk bands performed at the venue, including the Sex Pistols, it became home of another Merseyside musical revolution, playing host to a new renaissance of acts which included Elvis Costello, Dead Or Alive, Echo & the Bunnymen, Wah!, The Teardrop Explodes, Heat and Orchestral Manoeuvres in the Dark. The club eventually closed in March 1980 after a raid by the police. In September 2008, 'Eric's The Musical' was staged at the Everyman Theatre.

Cream, like the Cavern, is known throughout the world. Darren Hughes, Andy Carroll and James Barton were the original founders of the famous club which has been running for more than a quarter of a century and has led to the development of the major festival Creamfields.

Another major Liverpool club is the Picket and the city boasts numerous other clubs such as: Angel's Paradise; Azure; Bar Fresa; Barfly; Blue Angel; Bumper; Camel Club; Carling Academy; Club Arena; Curzon Club; Dreamers; Fab Café; G Bar; Garlands; H Bar; Heebie Jeebies; Korova; Krazy House; Le Bateau; Leaf Tea Shop & Bar; Lemon Lounge; Liverpool Pier Head; The Magnet; Masquerade Bar; Mood; Nation; Noir; 02 Academy; The Olympia Laughter Lounge; Pleasure Rooms; Red Peppers; The Rude Bar; Shorrocks Hill; Society; Sugar N Spice; Thomas Valentino's; Wonder Bar; X In The City and Zanzibar Club.

These days, Liverpool has many major musical events ranging from Liverpool Music Week to the Mathew Street Festival. Although the latter is the biggest musical festival of its type in Europe, it receives scant reportage from the nationally based media.

One of Britain's biggest music festivals is the Summer Pops in Liverpool, which was launched in 2001. The festival initially took place in a Big Top Tent on the King's Dock and then moved to

Clarence Dock in 2005 while the Liverpool Echo Arena was being constructed. It then moved to Aintree Pavilion in 2007 and from 2008 returned to the King's Dock to be presented annually at the Liverpool Echo Arena.

The Summer Pops has featured many major names, including Sir Elton John, Bob Dylan, Ray Charles, Diana Ross, Tom Jones, Lionel Ritchie, the Who, James Brown, Paul Simon, Eric Clapton, Bryan Adams, Meat Loaf, Tony Bennett, Whitesnake, Def Leppard and numerous other international stars.

Another major festival is Britain's biggest dance and electronic music event – Creamfields. This huge event evolved from Liverpool's legendary dance venue Cream and had been presented on every August Bank Holiday weekend since 1998, attracting an audience of 40,000 each year.

It was originally held at Speke Airport (now John Lennon Airport), but has since moved to a new venue near Daresbury in Cheshire in 2006. In addition to its Merseyside promotion, Creamfields has become an international brand with annual events under its name in various locations around the world, including Ibeza in Spain, Belo Horizonte in Brazil, Buenos Aires in Argentina, Moscow in Russia and Istanbul in Turkey.

Liverpool Music Week is Britain's biggest indoor winter music festival. In 2008 it hosted the European MTV Awards and staged events across 20 venues throughout Liverpool city centre with 300 acts.

Liverpool's musical diversity is also to be found in several other festivals including the Chinese New Year Festival.

Also, since 1992 Liverpool has staged Britain's largest African music festival 'Africa Oye', held annually in June at Sefton Park where it attracts 40,000 people. Since 2001 Liverpool has also presented the Liverpool Arabic Arts Festival at several venues throughout the city. The 2007 event for instance included performances by El Tanbura, performing 'Phartaonic funk' and American/Yemeni rapper Hagahe AJ Masaed, playing Arabic music combined with rap.

Since 1993 Liverpool has hosted its Liverpool Irish Festival, also at various venues throughout Liverpool, presenting the Liverpool/Irish heritage in music, literature, theatre and art.

The Milapfest began in Liverpool in 1983 presenting South Asian music and arts and is generally sited at the Philharmonic Hall.

Liverpool's musical activities also play host to different musical genres.

The HIVE Festival was first launched in Liverpool by the Hive Collective in 2005. The Collective was officially launched in 2005 when they staged the world's first international festival for electronic music, an event which they have hosted annually.

The Hub festival began in 2002 and is described as "the UK's biggest free urban youth festival". It was originally staged at the Pier Head and then moved to Otterspool Promenade in 2006.

One of the longest-lasting festivals of all is the Liverpool Jazz Festival which originally began at Liverpool Stadium in 1950 and moved to the Cavern in 1960. It is presented annually at several local clubs.

Sound City also takes place at various venues around the city and is devoted to underground alternative and independent music.

The Hope Street Festival was first launched in 1997 and the second took place in 1980 and since 1996 has been staged annually.

Liverpool Now was first presented in 1990, an event in several venues which showcases new talent. It was next held in 1994 and has then become a regular event.

Other annual festivals in the city include Homotopia, a gay, lesbian, bisexual and trans-gender event which began in 2004 and the Knowsley Hall Music Festival.

If the Beatles were the only artists who emerged from Liverpool, then the city would never have been named 'The World City of Pop' by the Guinness Book of Records in 2001 or named 'The UK's Most Musical City' by the Arts Council in 2008. This is a tribute to the hundreds of amazing musicians and artists from Merseyside who have continued to create an incredible musical landscape for six decades.

There have been hundreds of chart hits by Mersey artists over the years, but here is a list of the artists who have topped the British charts:

Lita Roza – 'How Much Is That Doggie In The Window?'
Frankie Vaughan – 'The Garden of Eden'
Michael Holliday – 'The Story Of My Life'

Michael Holliday – 'Starry Eyed'
Frankie Vaughan – 'Tower of Strength'
Gerry & the Pacemakers –'How Do You Do It?'
The Beatles – 'From Me To You'
Gerry & The Pacemakers – 'I Like It'
The Searchers - 'Sweets For My Sweet'
Billy J. Kramer & the Dakotas – 'Bad To Me'
The Beatles – 'She Loves You'
Gerry & the Pacemakers – 'You'll Never Walk Alone'
The Beatles – 'I Want To Hold Your Hand'
The Searchers – 'Needles And Pins'
Cilla Black – 'Anyone Who Had A Heart'
Billy J. Kramer & the Dakotas – 'Little Children'
The Beatles – 'Can't Buy Me Love'
The Searchers – 'Don't Throw Your Love Away'
Cilla Black – 'You're My World'
The Beatles – 'A Hard Day's Night'
The Beatles – 'I Feel Fine'
The Beatles – 'Ticket To Ride'
The Beatles – 'Help!'
Ken Dodd – 'Tears'
The Beatles – 'We Can Work It Out' / 'Day Tripper'
The Beatles – 'Paperback Writer'
The Beatles – 'Yellow Submarine' / 'Eleanor Rigby'
The Beatles – 'All You Need Is Love'
The Beatles – 'Hello Goodbye'
The Beatles – 'Lady Madonna'
The Beatles – 'Hey Jude'
The Scaffold – 'Lily The Pink'
The Beatles – 'Get Back'
The Beatles – 'The Ballad of John and Yoko'
George Harrison – 'My Sweet Lord'
The Real Thing – 'You To Me Are Everything'
Wings – 'Mull of Kintyre'
John Lennon – '(Just Like) Starting Over'
John Lennon – 'Imagine'
John Lennon – 'Woman'

Paul McCartney – 'Ebony & Ivory'
Paul McCartney – 'Pipes Of Peace'
Frankie Goes To Hollywood – 'Relax'
Frankie Goes to Hollywood – 'Two Tribes'
Frankie Goes To Hollywood – 'The Power of Love'
Dead Or Alive – 'You Spin Me Round (Like A Record)'
Gerry Marsden/Christians/Holly Johnson – 'Ferry 'Cross The Mersey.'
Sonia – 'You'll Never Stop Me Loving You'
The Lightning Seeds – 'Three Lions'
The Lightning Seeds – 'Three Lions '98'
Melanie C – 'Things will Never Be the Same Again'
Melanie C – 'I Turn To You'
Atomic Kitten – 'Whole Again'
Atomic Kitten – 'Eternal Flame'
Atomic Kitten – 'The Tide Is High'